LOVE'S LABOUR'S LOST

EDITED BY

A. E. MORGAN, M.A.

PRINCIPAL AND VICE-CHANCELLOR OF McGILL UNIVERSITY
MONTREAL

AND

W. SHERARD VINES, M.A.

PROFESSOR OF ENGLISH LANGUAGE AND LITERATURE
UNIVERSITY COLLEGE, HULL

BLACKIE & SON LIMITED
LONDON AND GLASGOW

BLACKIE & SON LIMITED
66 Chandos Place, London
17 Stanhope Street, Glasgow

BLACKIE & SON (INDIA) LIMITED
103/5 Fort Street, Bombay

BLACKIE & SON (CANADA) LIMITED
Toronto

Printed in Great Britain by Blackie & Son, Ltd., Glasgow

GENERAL PREFACE

In the WARWICK SHAKESPEARE an attempt is made
to present the greater plays of the dramatist in their
literary aspect, and not merely as material for the study
of philology or grammar. Criticism purely verbal and
textual has only been included to such an extent as
may serve to help the student in his appreciation of
the essential poetry. Questions of date and literary
history have been fully dealt with in the Introductions,
but the larger space has been devoted to the inter-
pretative rather than the matter-of-fact order of scholar-
ship. Æsthetic judgments are never final, but the
Editors have attempted to suggest points of view from
which the analysis of dramatic motive and dramatic
character may be profitably undertaken. In the Notes
likewise, while it is hoped that all unfamiliar expressions
and allusions have been adequately explained, yet it has
been thought even more important to consider the
dramatic value of each scene, and the part which it
plays in relation to the whole. These general principles
are common to the whole series; in detail each Editor
is alone responsible for the plays entrusted to him.

Every volume of the series has been provided with
an Introduction, a Glossary, and an Essay upon Metre.
By the systematic arrangement of the introductory

matter, and by close attention to typographical details, every effort has been made to provide an edition that will prove convenient in use.

In the present book some lines in different portions of the text are omitted.

EDITORS' NOTE

The text of the *Globe* edition has been followed. Where we disagree with its readings there is an indication in the notes.

CONTENTS

ADDENDUM: SHAKESPEARE'S STAGE IN ITS BEARING
UPON HIS DRAMA

THE WARWICK SHAKESPEARE. General editor, Professor C. H. HERFORD, Litt.D., F.B.A.

INTRODUCTION

LIST OF PRINCIPAL ABBREVIATIONS

Abbott. *A Shakespearian Grammar.*
N.E.D. *New English Dictionary.*
Schmidt. *Shakespeare Lexicon.*
Vietor. *Shakespeare's Pronunciation* (Marburg and London, 1906).
Puttenham. *Arte of English Poesie* (Arber's Edition).
Wilson. *Art of Rhetoric* (Mair's Edition, O.U.P.).
Chambers. *William Shakespeare*, 2 vols., by E. K. Chambers (O.U.P.).
Editions of the play: Q., Q.1, the Quarto Edition of this play, 1598. F., F.1, the 1st Folio Edition of Shakespeare's works, 1623. Rowe, Theobald, Johnson, Dyce, Hart (Arden Edition). Charlton (Heath's), Brooke and Cross (Yale), *Q. & D. W.* (Cambridge Edition), by Professors Quiller-Couch and Dover Wilson. The student is asked *not* to confuse, in these notes, *Q.* of Troy Town with Q. the Quarto.

1. DATE OF COMPOSITION

The earliest printed copy that we have of this play is the Quarto of 1598 (Q. 1): *A* | PLEASANT | Conceited Comedie | CALLED | Loues labors loft. | As it vvas prefented before her Highnes | this laft Chriftmas. | Newly corrected and augmented | *By W. Shakefpere.* | Imprinted at London by *W. W.* | for *Cutbert Burby* | 1598.

It was not, then, a brand-new play, but had been " corrected and augmented ", and that, apparently, fairly soon before publication. The original draft as written before this revision has had various dates assigned it, ranging from 1588 to 1596, as *Q. & D.W.* note. Lee (*Life of Shakespeare*) placed this first draft between 1591 and 1594, and the revision in 1597; Hart, the first draft in 1590, revision in 1593–4; Acheson, 1591 and 1597 respectively; *Q. & D.W.*, Draft ' A ' in autumn, 1593, revision in 1597. (It will be noticed that Hart's date for revision and *Q. & D.W.*'s date for first draft coincide.)

Chambers puts the date of the unrevised version as late as 1595. The chief guide of all of these dates is internal evidence. The play is evidently a topical one, and there are actual and alleged references to events of the time which may help to fix a date. There are references to books and allusions to people and events. Some of the latter two especially, we should expect, would make rather for an earlier than for a later date; viz.:

Monarcho (an actual person, dead by 1580) (see note to IV. i. 96).

Armado (if this names owes anything to the Spanish Armada), 1588.

The Mask of Russians, possibly referring to a Russian ambassador who came to Elizabeth's court to find a wife for Ivan the Terrible, 1583. Chambers denies that there is any such allusion.

These items might have become a little stale by 1595, even allowing for a longer memory and greater reverence for tradition among the audience than now. Similar inferences might be made from some if not all of the literary references (not of Golding's *Ovid*, e.g., which was a life-long source to Shakespeare). Shakespeare was more openly interested in books on grammar, rhetoric, poetic, &c., then than later: e.g. Wilson's *Arte of Rhetorique*, I. i. 23 (1553, reprinted up to 1588, see Mair's Introd.); Puttenham (*Sta. Hall*, 1588), III. i. 1; Lily's Grammar (1549), V. i. 9, which last he still remembered from his schooldays, unless he had since been, as Aubrey notes, a schoolmaster in the country (see Alexander, *Shakespeare's Henry VI and Richard III*). All three books were of the sort that would appeal to the teacher.

Another early literary date is 1578, that of the performance of Sidney's dramatic piece, *The Lady of May*, before the Queen. The pedant Rombus in that play has certain resemblances to Holofernes; and Lalus, the old shepherd, anticipates Dull and Costard with the fun of verbal blunder.

Next, the visit of Marguerite de Valois to her husband Henri IV (from whom she was separated) took place in 1578. This incident may have suggested the outline of the encounter of the Princess and the King in our play. If so, how did Shakespeare get hold of it? Possibly through a literary source dealing with the events described, or through the descriptions of some traveller, as Chambers thinks: the *Mémoires* of Marguerite de Valois were not yet published. *Q. & D.W.* believe the source to have been a French comedy " plotted by some other dramatist somewhere in the ' eighties ' ".

Segar's *Book of Honor and Arms* (1590) is shown by Charlton to have provided a basis for the reference to " the first and second cause " (Armado's last speech in I. ii.).

Lastly, the effect of Lyly's brilliant fashions in style and character-conception is visible (see notes). *Euphues* (1579) and its sequel are reflected, though not fully; and there are echoes of several of his plays. *Endimion*, containing like *Love's Labour's Lost* a foolish Braggart (Sir Tophas) with his page (Epiton) and a situation parallel to *Love's Labour's Lost*, I. ii., had the date 1586 for its first performance (Bond).

It is not then outside the bounds of possibility that by 1590 Shakespeare had revived or was reviving an older play on a French theme, on more topical and English lines dictated by the events, books and circumstances referred to above. *First draft, 1590.*

During the next few years several other things had happened that aroused Shakespeare's interest. The Civil War in France between 1589 and 1594, in the course of which English aid was sent to Henry of Navarre (1589 and 1591), kept up the topical interest in a ' Navarre ' theme. But by 1590 allusions to Navarre, Biron, &c., would surely be appreciated in the theatre; although any allusion to Henry's conversion to Rome (as in IV. i. 21 ff. ' saved by merit ', &c.) must be later than July, 1593.

At home there was the mysterious business of Sir Walter Raleigh's modernist and astronomical School of Atheism, with which Marlowe's sudden death (1593) seemed not wholly unconnected; the air of enigma and circumambient darkness being increased by Chapman's *Shadow of Night* (for allusion to which in this play see IV. iii. 251, and note thereto), inspired by the practices of the coterie (printed 1594 but probably known to Shakespeare earlier). His satiric response to this School of Night was the ' little academe ' of Act I Chapman's poem, *The Shadow of Night*, was dedicated to Matthew Roydon, a member of Raleigh's band, which included Chapman himself; Marlowe, who would have been arrested for atheism had he not been killed first (1593); Stanley, Earl of Derby, Percy of Northumberland, and Sir George Carey. This clique certainly existed; though it is not conclusively proven that this is meant by the " School of Night ". Yet the arguments on behalf of the theory by *Q. & D.W.* are attractive (pp. xxxiii–iv). It solves for us the vexed problem of " the hue of dungions and the Schoole of night " (Q.). In fairness it must be noted that Cross and Brooke consider any allusion to the Raleigh coterie ' fantastic '.

In Greene's *Groatsworth of Wit* (1592) appeared the allusion to the " Young Juvenall ", which may refer to Nashe, and may be echoed in I. ii. of our play.

The Harvey-Nashe controversy yielded, in 1593, a reply to Nashe's *Pierce Peniless*, by Gabriel Harvey, called *Pierce's Supererogation*, containing the phrase "Pierce, the hoggeshead of wit ", which is quibbled on in IV. ii. 82 of this play. Nashe was advertising himself so well at this time, having made a good start as publicist in the Martin Marprelate controversy, that allusions to him in a play might well be acclaimed. Moth, the satiric ' juvenal ' who derides pedants (as Nashe did Harvey) may have been conceived as a largely topical figure about this time.

There seems to be enough matter here to suspect, with Hart, that a revision of the play took place 1593–4; it would be pleasant and convenient if we could prove this revision to have been undertaken specifically for a private performance before the Earl of *Remodelled or augmented about 1594.* Southampton at Christmas, 1593, when the theatres were closed ("Lord have mercy on us!", V. ii. 419) for the plague. The satire on the School of Night, a hit at Raleigh, the head of the party rivalled by that of Southampton and Essex, would thus obtain a special significance, as *Q. & D.W.* point out in defence of the theory that this play was not revised but written for that occasion.

Was there in any case a revision (in our case a second revision) before the appearance of newly revised and augmented Q. 1 in 1598? Was this play to be proved 'bis coctus' (IV. ii. 22), and served up once more, this time for "her Highnes" at Christmas, 1597, or 1598 old style? This is not certain. The *A further revision in 1597?* statement on the Q. 1 title page that it was performed "this last Christmas" may be the reprint from an earlier (and lost) copy, as Chambers notes. And while there are topical allusions that may involve 1595, there is nothing of the kind with a certainly later date. The 1595 happenings are:

(*a*) A 'Russian' episode in the Gray's Inn Revels (6th Jan., 1595); these entertainments also include a (probably unauthorized) performance of *The Comedy of Errors*. Was Shakespeare's already tried 'invention' of the Russian Masque pirated too?

(*b*) Robert Southwell, the poet, was executed in this year, in which his poems also appeared; among which was *St. Peter's Complaint*, containing some stanzas "supposed to echo Berowne's disquisition in IV. iii." (Chambers); but it is not known when this particular poem was written.

(*c*) The entertainment at the end of this play, and the Pyramus and Thisbe play in *A Midsummer-Night's Dream*, suggest at first sight a connexion in date (say 1595). But the *Midsummer-Night's Dream* scene may be a later improvement on the discarded earlier *Love's Labour's Lost* model.

The relevancy of a few later dates may be examined. (1) An allusion to Harington's *Metamorphosis of Ajax* (1596) might be seen in V. ii. 573; but Harington could have been in debt, on the other hand, to this very passage. (2) Chambers observes that there is nothing to determine the priority of an analogy to the ' guerdon—remuneration ' joke (III. i. 160) in J. M., *A Health to the Gentlemanly Profession of Serving Men* (before 1598, in which year ent. Sta. Reg.).

Certain inconsistencies in Q. 1 might be taken as yielding evidence in support of the theory that the play took at least two stages to reach its final form.

Evidence in the printing of Q. 1

A. Reference will be found in the notes (e.g. to Biron's speech, lines 290 ff. in IV. iii.; and parts of the dialogue, V. ii. 805 ff.) to passages where it seems as though, owing to a mistake, an early version, intended to be cancelled in favour of a later and ' improved ' revision, had not been so cancelled. There is little doubt that here were passages erroneously retained; but Chambers reminds us that these passages can be just as well interpreted as false starts at the time of original writing as changes at revision. Not that this puts revision out of court. We must consider also (B) the ' confused and inconsistent speech headings ' (discussed by *Q. & D.W.*, pp. 109 ff.).

B. In some parts of the Q. 1 Armado's speeches are headed ' *Arm*.', ' *Ar*.', ' *Arma*.'; elsewhere, as at the end, they are headed ' *Brag*.' (for ' Braggart '); as though at one period of writing Shakespeare thought of him as ' Armado ', and at another as ' the Braggart '. The Princess is sometimes called ' Queen ' in speech headings, and there is some confusion and error in the allotment of speeches to Nathaniel (later called *curat*) and Holofernes (later called *pedant*): there are other alternatives and differences in speech headings; but taken altogether they do not point conclusively to a revision, though some of them may be due to one or more revisions. Chambers reminds us, once more, that variations of nomenclature are frequent in other plays, though not so marked as in this. But, combining such differences with fanced differences in style, one might claim to discover several strata in the play: e.g. that speeches of *Arm.* in I. ii., being rather more sophisticated and allusive (they include the ' Juvenal ' and the ' first and second cause ' references), belong to a stratum distinct from those of *Ar.* in the same scene (*Ar.* carries on a very unlearned flirtation with the Maid). But this will not do as a general test; for example, Katherine is varied in Q. 1 as *Kath.*, *Lady Ka.*, *La.*, &c., in a passage where the wit is entirely homogeneous, whoever uttered it (II. i.).

C. The typography of Q. 1 shows inconsistencies (see *Q. & D.W.*, p. 115) of which only one simple instance is given here, viz. the printing of Armado's first letter (I. i.) in italics, while that of IV. i. (" By heaven ", &c.) is in roman. This suggests to *Q. & D.W.* that " the two epistles belong to different strata of the manuscript "; and that Shakespeare wrote the first letter in Italian script, which the printer copied with italics; and the second (at the time of revision) in English script, set up with roman type. It is indeed a strange discrepancy.

D. The confusion between the names ' Rosaline ' and ' Katherine ' in Q. 1 (II. i. in mod. edns.) (see note to II. i. 194) has been taken by *Q. & D.W.* to indicate a considerable revision of this scene at a time when Shakespeare decided to suppress the fun of masking and mistaken identity here and to use it, instead, in V. ii. But this suppression was not fully carried out owing to the inclusion of passages marked for cancellation; and in the text the required alterations ' Rosaline ' and ' Katherine ' were made at the wrong places. Certainly it appears that some kind of change was attempted—not very carefully—at this point.

To this circumstantial evidence on behalf of the development of *Love's Labour's Lost* from ?1590 to 1597 (inclusive) must be added considerations of style.

2. THE STYLE

Sir E. Chambers sees no evidence for two dates, and none for a very early date. He continues, " the versification is extremely adroit, and certainly not that of a beginner ". I think that a claim that Shakespeare's published work, from start to finish, shows adroit versification might be established; and that conscious adroitness would tend to be more in evidence (as in some of the sonnets, *Venus and Adonis*, and this play) early than late; and a ' beginner ' in the sense of one who publishes for the first time may be alarmingly precocious as regards technique.

Evidence from the style.

I. But what may help us is any sign of the discarding of one style for another: thus, in the dialogue of II. i. there is a good deal of rhymed anapæstic jingle; whereas in the ' masking ' part of V. ii., which Shakespeare (see immediately preceding section) may have meant to substitute for that of II. i., the more graceful and dignified iambic line is used throughout till after Costard's entry at line 485. It is, in all the circumstances, tempting to believe that this long iambic piece was a late addition.

II. We cannot help observing Costard's unparalleled lapse into dialectal speech after his entry at this point (' vara fine ', &c., see relevant notes). It is so at variance with his usual conversational style that it almost looks like a ' fossil ' fragment of an earlier dialectal type of clown.

III. Metric style has been taken by Fleay and others as a test for early or late Shakespearean work. Furnivall remarks on the high proportion of doggerel and rhyme here, as compared even with an early play like the *Comedy of Errors*. But if this play was ' corrected and augmented ' one or more times during some seven years, we cannot argue any one date from the residual metric facts; but we *may* suspect that Shakespeare designed the play as a lyrical ' revue '-like type of entertainment—which perhaps argues for an earlier date for the design rather than otherwise; and when revising it he would probably attempt to preserve the unity of that design by adhering to the rhyme-decoration scheme. Moreover, if we could agree that most of the doggerel and jingle belonged to an earlier version (as in II. i., for instance), that doggerel and jingle, which is rarer in later plays, would lead us to an early date for the first draft (or drafts) of this play (see also essay on metre in this volume).

IV. There is another example of incongruity in style of speech, already referred to; that of Armado, who in I. ii. changes suddenly from the primitively simple love-speech ("I love thee ", &c.) with Jaquenetta to a highly affected soliloquy beginning " I do affect ", &c. Why did not Shakespeare's Armado show off to and dazzle Jaquenetta with his most elegant flights as Scott's Sir Piercie Shafton did Mysie Happer? There are of course several answers; and this point need not be pressed; but see also, above, B, p. xii.

V. Perhaps this is the most cogent of Furnivall's arguments as to style if applied to the hypothetical first version: "it is more carefully polisht (than *Comedy of Errors*), it has more Stratford life in it—countryman's play, boys'-games ('more sacks to the mill', and hide and seek, 'all hid')—it dwelt more in Shakespeare's mind." The 'Stratford' part of the argument is perhaps the weaker when we remember the later 'Slender—Shallow' scenes in *Henry IV*. But the polish and the author's deep concern for style, and the 'adroitness' noted by Chambers, are important. Shakespeare designed the play when he was peculiarly conscious of his own virtuosity and sensitive to that of others: as young genius may very well be.

According to *Q. & D.W.*'s analysis, Acts I. and IV. i., excepting certain alterations already discussed, are early work. The conscious virtuosity of I. i. (to take this example) is apparent: in the complex rhyme-schemes relieved with blank verse and prose; in the contrast of Armado's epistolary style with Costard's homespun comments; and in the triumphal entry of wit, with a perfect fanfare of conceits, as in Biron's 'light seeking light' speech (line 72). Variety—the brilliant changes on numerous different 'organ-stops'—is a dazzling feature throughout the play; but in other places there may be more reason to attribute this partly to revision and augmentation; though even here we cannot be absolutely sure.

VI. The use of a good deal of loose jingling verse for dialogue, as in II. i., IV. i., IV. ii., seems like an improved use of an old device in comedy-dialogue; it looks back to the technique of Heywood and the Interludes, rather than forward.   Anapæstic jingling couplets may be found in Heywood's (?) *Johan Johan, Tyb, and Syr Johan* (about 1530); and less regular couplets (as in IV. ii.) occur in *Ralph Roister Doister* (? before 1541) and *Gammer Gurton's Needle* (1553–4).

In other plays Shakespeare deliberately takes off the old metric fashions (the Clowns' play in *A Midsummer-Night's Dream*, the " Gonzago " piece in *Hamlet*): but here he is using them seriously; the stanza form of dialogue is 'taken off' in *A Midsummer-Night's Dream* (V. i. 107, " If we offend ", &c.): but it is used seriously in parts of I. i. of *Love's Labour's Lost*, where he strives consciously to perfect existing apparatus, in the use of which he has the mastery of the young virtuoso.

VII. The Sonnets.   Furness and others have drawn attention to parallels between some of the Sonnets and passages in *L.L.L.*   The similarities of the conceits on Rosaline's dark hair in IV. 3. to those on the Dark Lady, celebrated in Sonnets CXXVII, CXXX–CXXXII, &c., are notable: e.g., Biron, IV. 3.,

> That I may swear beauty doth beauty lack
> If that she learn not of her eye to look:
> No face is fair that is not full of black,

and Sonnet CXXXII,

> Then will I swear beauty herself is black
> And all they foul that thy complexion lack.

If Rosaline were indubitably modelled on the Dark Lady, an approximately common date for both passages would be a plausible guess.   But this is not proved; and the publican's wife whom Acheson believes to have been the original of the

Dark Lady was, according to Aubrey, a very different sort of person from the Rosaline characterized here.

There are other points of similarity in other sonnets, e.g. the allusions to painting in No. LXXXIII and II. i. 13. There may even be satirical reference to Chapman, the rival poet, in Sonnet XXI and II. i. 15, as *Q. & D.W.*, following Acheson, suggest. But little more may be safely built on these foundations than a possibility that some passages in *L.L.L.* may have coincided roughly with the composition of certain sonnets. And even so we must remember (*a*) that there are analogies in this play with later work, and (*b*) that favourite conceits may be repeated by a poet (and *will* be, by a prudent one) elsewhere after a considerable interval.

SUMMARY

The circumstances in which this play came into being are, then, very conjectural; the chain of clues is little more than a chain of hints; but they seem to point (if a chain of hints may do so) to an evolution consisting of two (or even three) stages, begun some time soon after the Armada and concluded by 1598. A middle stage (?1594) is within the bounds of possibility.

3. CONTEMPORARY ALLUSIONS TO *LOVE'S LABOUR'S LOST*

(1) In Meres' *Palladis Tamia* (1598).

(2) At some length in Robert Tofte's *Alba* (1598), as follows:

> " Loues Labor Lost, I once did see a Play
> Ycleped so, so called to my paine,
> Which I to heare to my small Ioy did stay,
> Giuing attendance to my froward Dame,
> My misgiuing minde presaging to me Ill,
> Yet was I drawne to see it gainst my Will.

" This Play no Play, but Plague was vnto me,
  For there I lost the Loue I liked most:
And what to others seemde a Iest to be,
  I that in earnest found vnto my cost:
    To euery one (saue me) twas Comicall,
    Whilst Tragick like to me it did befall.

" Each Actor plaid in cunning wise his part,
  But chiefly Those entrapt in Cupid's snare:
Yet all was fained, twas not from the hart,
  They seemde to grieue, but yet they felt no care:
    Twas I that Griefe (indeed) did beare in brest,
    The others did but make a show in Iest."

(3) In a letter (dated 1604) from Sir Walter Cope to Viscount Cranbourne, with reference to a performance of the play for James I's Queen, Anne of Denmark:

" Sir, . . . I haue sent and bene all thys mornyng huntyng for players Juglers & Such kinde of Creaturs, but fynde them harde to fynde; wherefore leauing notes for them to seek me, Burbage ys come, and sayes there is no newe playe that the quene hath not seene, but they haue reuyued an olde one, cawled *Loves Labore Lost*, which for wytt & mirthe he sayes will please her exceedingly. And thys ys appointed to be playd to morrowe night at my Lord of Sowthamptons, unless yow send a wrytt to remove the corpus *cum causa* to your howse in Strande. Burbage ys my messenger ready attending your pleasure."

(4) In connexion with (3), there is a record in Audit office accounts for 1604–5 of " the acting ' By his Majesty's players ' of ' A play of Loues Labours Lost ' between New Year's Day and Twelfth Day (January 6) " [so Brooke and Cross].

4. SOURCES

There is no single plot derived from any single source. It is possible that Shakespeare obtained from another play such an incident as the meeting of Marguerite de Valois of Navarre with her husband in 1579 to " make a deal with him over the question of Aquitaine " (*Q. & D.W.*); a slender though plausible basis for our plot. His reason for choosing such a theme at all was the interest felt by the English for affairs in France between 1589 and 1595—an interest that roused Marlowe to write *The Massacre of Paris* (in ?1592-3).

Henry of Bourbon, King of Navarre (the " Burbon Knight " of *F. Q.*, V., canto xi.), became King of France in 1589, and was regarded as the champion of Protestantism against the Catholic League. Elizabeth sent him military aid in 1589 (the year in which he was victorious at Arques) and in 1591, after he won again at Ivry. His two chief supporters were named Biron and Longaville. Charlton writes that " the historical Biron was very popular in England, and had a reputation of gaiety like the dramatic Biron ". Opposed to Henry was the Duc de Maine or de Mayenne; from whose name, it is generally agreed, Shakespeare derived his Dumaine. Henry was converted to Rome in 1593— " O heresy in fair!" (IV. i. 22).

Other topical events, Chapman as the poet of Raleigh's Schoole of Night (" not utter'd by base sale of Chapmen's tongues ", II. i. 16), Nashe's controversies, Russian ' events ', &c., have been dealt with already; and some of the books, Lily's Grammar, John Lyly's works, Wilson, Puttenham, as well. The parallels in some characters of Sidney's *May Lady* and Lyly's *Endimion* to some in *Love's Labour's Lost* are certainly striking; Charlton declares, on evident grounds, that " in gross and in detail " *Love's Labour's Lost* " descends directly from John Lyly ". Another literary influence is surely Rabelais; in Bk. I. xiv, as Hart reminded readers in 1906, is a tutor called Tubal Holofernes. In Rabelais, Holofernes was a better tutor than the formal pedant Bragmardo —who is the ancestor of Sidney's Rombus in the *May Lady*; Shakespeare gave in his play the good tutor's name to the pedant.

The satire on affected latinisms in *Love's Labour's Lost* may owe something to Rabelais' Limousin student as well

as to the comic letter in Wilson's *Arte of Rhetoric* (q.v. and
see notes to I. i. 128, &c.). The Limousin, in Urquhart's
translation, says, " We transfretate the Sequan at the dilucal
and crepuscul; we deambulate by the compites and quadrives
by the Urb . . ." (II. vi.).

Lastly, the passage where Biron describes Hercules whipping a gig, &c. (IV. iii. 167 ff.) has its Rabelaisian analogue
in Rabelais II. xxx., where Epistemon describes the lowly and
absurd pursuits of the Heroes' ghosts in Hades; Nestor was
a deer-keeper; " Hector, a snap-sauce scullion . . .; Pope
Alexander, a rat-catcher ", &c., &c.

5. CRITICAL APPRECIATION

One of the first attitudes that the student would do well
to assume before passing judgment on this play is a particular one towards puns; let it be realized that for Elizabethans word-play was beautiful before it was funny.[1]
The exuberant delight in the structure and meaning of words,
that is the chief glory of Lyly and of *Love's Labour's Lost*,
is only to-day being once more sympathetically understood
and appreciated (as by Charlton),[2] practised (as by James
Joyce),[3] or discussed in theory (as by Dr. Richards).[4]

It was a time when grammar and formal systems of rhetoric
and poetic were living things, books of the gospel of new
culture of beauty renascent throughout Europe. Guides
for literary creation were eagerly sought, Priscian, Quintilian,
Cicero, Horace; so that an elegant national art might be
formed, on the best models, by means of an enriched native
language.

" In our time," wrote Vives (1523), " we need rules . . .
and all these Rules have to be wrested out of the Roman

[1] The more modern attitude of identifying the pun with acceptable
buffoonery dates probably from Horace Walpole, assumed vigour
with Lamb, and established itself among admirers and plagiarists of
Hood. In the earlier eighteenth century, word-play was accounted merely
low.
[2] See his edition of the play in Heath's Shakespeare.
[3] See *Ulysses, Work in Progress*.
[4] See *The Meaning of Meaning*.

authors." But the narrower minds worshipped the old lawgivers too abjectly; the crabbed absurdities of ink-horn terms—derided by Wilson—of latinizing ' det ' and ' dout ' with a ' b ' (see V. i. 18) resulted. The schoolboy as well as the general reader suffered from soulless pedantry, and the great humanists, whether Rabelais, or Ascham, or Shakespeare, condemned it. In *The Schoolmaster* Ascham disapproves of the old method of Latin conversation in schools, which teaches the boys bad linguistic habits. Shakespeare, bringing on Holofernes, lame in his Latin and dictatorial about that of others, and Nathaniel with his Priscian a little scratched, gives a practical illustration of this and other bad by-products of Renaissance enthusiasm. He shows us where even the sparkling Lyly and the fastidious Sidney lapsed; he parodies the overweighted antithesis of the one, the racked ' traductio ' of the other. At the same time he plainly admires both. His lavish use of word-play and conceits reflects a love for this particular form of verbal decoration which he always retained; as late as *Cymbeline* (1609–10), for example, he is still varying a well-worn conceit on coins (V. iv. 23 ff.). While he was a rival, and in some sort a parodist of the University wits, he studied, followed and improved upon their technique, fully meriting Greene's abuse of him in the *Groatsworth of Wit* (1592) as " an upstart Crow, beautified with our feathers ".[1] He not only made those feathers indubitably his own in *Love's Labour's Lost*, but grew others as a neologist and early adopter of recent borrowings, e.g. ' festinately ' (III. i. 4), ' jig off ' (III. i. 10), ' phantasime ' (IV. i. 96), ' quillets ' (IV. 3. 282), ' peregrinate ' (V. i. 13), ' excrement ' (V. i. 93); and as a scaler of dizzy and hitherto untried peaks of conversational wit. Words were still ἔπεα πτερόεντα, with an angelic life of their own, or rather, they were then reborn to that high condition. And perhaps it is not extravagant to claim that the true plot of *Love's Labour's Lost* is—*language*, the pas-

[1] I should still like to understand this remark in a sense somewhat wider than that taken by Professor P. Alexander in his *Shakespeare's Henry VI and Richard III.*

sion of adventure in that romantic terrain, named (with the
felicitous allusiveness of Florio) " A New World of Wordes ";
the sub-plot, topical comment; while the fable, the story
of what the noble and humble folk *do*, is only important as
bombast and as lining to the times that now absorb Shakespeare's genius.

From virtuosity with words and rhetorical figures for
their own sake, springs at once virtuosity with the image
over which Shakespeare, whether here or in *Venus and Adonis*,
shows himself at an early phase to win the mastery (cf., e.g.,
Boyet's speech, " Why, all his behaviours, &c.", II. i. 232 ff.).
Professor Caroline Spurgeon (*Shakespeare's Imagery and
What it Tells Us*, 1935) notes that *Love's Labour's Lost* and
As You Like It are " remarkable for having more images
than any other one of the plays, and in both plays these
form a considerable part of the entertainment ". She recog-
nizes that the images are closely bound up with the " verbal
wit "; and indeed the image, comprising both simile and
metaphor, belongs to the rhetorician's no less than the poet's
arsenal. But its lavish use here suggests that one at least
of the poet's aims was to impart concreteness to the wit
as a whole, with a strong appeal to each sense, particularly
the visual. Word-play as such might appear, even to the
educated audiences for whom it was designed, too intellec-
tual and colourless: the sensuous attractions of pageantry,
delightful both to Shakespeare himself and to generations
with whom the splendours of the Masque were evolving,
must contribute their substance.

The comparative poverty of ' fable ' led to depreciation
of the play by some nineteenth-century critics from Hazlitt
onward. Hallam complained that there was little interest in
the fable; Saintsbury (*Cambs. Hist.*, V. viii.) that Shakespeare
overloaded the plot " in every direction ". These censures
lose a great deal of their force if we regard *Love's Labour's
Lost* as an experiment in a type of play which does not depend
on a plot after the commonly accepted convention.

It is possible, again, that critics have in the past given too
much attention to the characters of our play. Should we

not regard them primarily as vehicles for the expression of wit, satire and allusion; and as characters, i.e. representations of people, only in the second place?

Walter Pater stands out among Victorian critics for penetration, and for delicately precise understanding of the poet's aim, of which he writes:[1] " the unity . . . is not so much the unity of a drama as that of a series of pictorial groups, in which the same figures reappear, in different combinations but on the same background. It is as if Shakespeare had intended to bind together, by some inventive conceit, the devices of an ancient tapestry, and give voices to its figures." And again: " this ' foppery ' of Shakespeare's day had, then, its really delightful side, a quality in no sense ' affected ', by which it satisfies a real instinct in our minds—the fancy so many of us have for an exquisite and curious skill in the use of words." He proceeds to suggest that Biron's character is conceived as a vehicle or source of this skill, " accompanied by a real insight into the laws which determine what is exquisite in language, and their root in the nature of things ".

Traditions of the Tudor stage were favourable to the subhuman or puppet-like character; the abstract persons of the Moralities and Interludes were nearly as familiar in those days as the ' Motions ' or puppet-shows, still vigorous when, in the Jacobean era, Ben Jonson achieved the next phase in abstract characterization—the Humour, with its satiric setting. Readers of *Love's Labour's Lost* may speculate on the potential aptitude of Shakespeare for this Jonsonian type of art. The Humour-puppets Armado, Holofernes, Nathaniel, Costard are personified comicalities, reflecting actions and reactions in life and literature. The matter satirized in the first three characters has been mentioned; in Costard, as in subsequent clowns (cf. especially Launcelot Gobbo of *The Merchant of Venice*), we may see the percolation of a little of this word-sensitive culture into rustic soil.

Attempts to employ the new wealth of language, and a certain pedantic argumentativeness (probably imitated from

[1] *Appreciations*, 1889 (p. 162 of 1910 ed., Macmillan).

parsons and teachers sent down with a little logic and much conceit into the country), yield a crop of false precisions or stubborn blunders. Costard insists on ' damsel ' in preference to ' wench ' (I. i. 274); he rushes in after the goose or ' l'envoy ' where Armado patently fears to tread (III. i. 99); and is quite persuaded (IV. ii. 137 ff.) that he is intellectually one too many for the wits of the court.

Whereas Spenser in *F. Q.*, V., canto ii, fulminates against democratic ideals, Shakespeare laughs (with what social implication we please) at this *mésalliance* of class-cultures. But on the other hand, the unpremeditated effects of Costard's English amount more than once to a shrewd criticism, truer than he knows. The ironic genius of Shakespeare is fully awake when Costard (IV. ii. 140) through his determination to use at all costs the newly acquired word ' obscenely ' does so in a most suitable context: and upper-class freedom of speech is at once flung impartially into the farrago of satire. There may well be an undercurrent of particular or personal satire beneath the more general; a hit—no more—at Chapman in Holofernes, another at Nashe in the conception of Moth as a clever little boy. That does not, as we recognize, prevent allusions, in a Holofernes or a Moth, to other persons or book-names. And be it noted, in passing, that the behaviour of Moth does not turn him into a butt for derision, like the clowns and fantastics; apart from his being the child Moth, the pathetical nit, there is little to laugh at; [1] and the rest of him belongs to the group of aggressive satirists, headed by Biron.

The thinnest ghost of Monarcho survives in Armado, who is also the medium of satire on more than one nodding Homer of the time. Echoes of Harvey, Lyly, and Greene are discernible in his letter of I. i. alone. We may compare such adroit changes of direction in the aim of a single character-conception with the less coherent multiple allegory in Spenser; Duessa may represent Papist Duplicity, or Mary Tudor, or merely Mary Queen of Scots, or two persons at once (*F.Q.*, B.I.). Shakespeare using com-

---

[1] And even this laughter may be aimed really at Nashe.

parable apparatus succeeds in being as enigmatic and, shall
we not agree? less rambling. It would be perfectly natural
that Shakespeare, while profiting by Lyly's excursions into
satiric and allegoric comedy (e.g. *Endimion*), should also take
a hint from, as well as warning by Spenser. His familiarity
at this time with the latter is amply demonstrated by Hart
in his prefaces to *1* and *2 Henry VI* (Arden Ed.), which
are also early plays. We may bear in mind that the first
instalment of *F. Q.* was published early in 1590.

While the fantastics and clowns are the objects of satire,
another group led by Biron and Rosaline are purveyors of
satire, and deliberately conduct the war of wits, as in IV.
i., V. ii. 490 ff., &c.; the royalty and their attendants carrying
out a sort of decorative verbal ballet in which team-work
rather than individuality is required: and admirable team-
work it is (V. ii. 1–155, II. i., &c.). Biron and Rosaline come
forward now and then for a solo; when we observe something abstract, something of a Walking Theory of Nature
about Biron (I. i. 102 ff., IV. iii. 284 ff.) or of a mouthpiece
of satire, as when he delivers an excellent ' characterism ' of
The Trencher Knight (V. ii. 316).

Rosaline, if she be the dark lady of the sonnets,[1] has
adventured into this abstract domain, where she becomes
naturalized. It would be unfair to consider either her or
Biron as a cut off the joint of everyday life; whatever their
antecedents in reality, they are now creatures of fantasy in
a wonderland of impossible pavilions, vows, rhetoric, rewards
and penalties.

This decorative wonderland is localized and to some extent
naturalized by means of an art which Shakespeare brought
to the subtlest perfection in his last (or ' sunset ') dramas
—the art of verbal scene-setting. This is achieved (as in
the late play *Cymbeline*) not so much or so well by set pieces
of description that force themselves upon us, though these
are also to be found, in *King Lear* and elsewhere, as by such

---

[1] It is debatable whether this " Whitely wanton " is the brunette of the
Sonnets: but see H. D. Gray, *The Original Version of L.L.L.*, p. 11.
Also Acheson, *Shakespeare's Sonnet Story*.

hints at local colour as gradually create the atmosphere. The curious knotted garden, the park enlivened with rustic flirtations, the sheep on the common (herded in obliquely, shadowed in a mist of jokes), or the plantain for a broken shin, prepare the way for the more descriptive ' greenwood ' matter of IV. i., which was welcome to theatre-goers of that age, if we may judge from such pieces as Greene's *Friar Bacon and Friar Bungay* (first acted 1589) or the later Robin Hood Plays,[1] as well as from Shakespeare's repeated returns to the setting, as in *M. N. D.*, *As You Like It*, or *Cymbeline*. The localization is carried further than in Lyly's *Gallathea* (?1585), for example. Furnivall, as we have seen, felt the atmosphere of Stratford environs in *Love's Labour's Lost*. But while, in *Gallathea*, the country setting is alleged to be that of Lincolnshire, it is practically that of literary-pastoral Arcadia. This is not saying, however, that the one kind of *décor* is necessarily better or worse than the other.

The fable, with its lesson, if secondary in importance, is far from negligible. For Dowden it is more than " a satirical extravaganza embodying Shakespeare's criticism upon contemporary fashions and foibles ": it is also " a protest against youthful schemes of shaping life according to notions rather than according to reality, a protest against idealizing away the facts of life ", to which we may assent, laying less emphasis on the ' youthful ', since both the idealists and realists (largely women) in the play are young. Dowden remarks that Shakespeare is not " hostile to culture; but he knows that a perfect education must include the culture, through actual experience, of the senses and of the affections ". Professor Caroline Spurgeon [2] accepts this interpretation generally, collecting (as the student may for himself) full evidence from the text to prove that " the main underlying theme of the confounding and dispelling of the fog of false idealism by the light of the experience of real life . . . presented through a series of brilliant encounters " is intensified

---

[1] *The Pastoral Comedy of Robin Hood and Little John* (1594) and *The Downfall of Robert, Earl of Huntingdon* (1598).

[2] *Op. cit.*, pp. 271 ff.

by the use of appropriate imagery—that of war and weapons, which is prominent throughout, from I. i. 8 (" Therefore, brave conquerors ", &c.) to the pole-fighting, still symbolic, though not a metaphor, in V. ii.

The main features of the plot belong to types easily found in comedy after the Renaissance and Plautine traditions: upper-class love intrigue, with disguises and misunderstandings; and a corresponding lower-class intrigue or episode (Costard—Jaquenetta), such as had already appeared at the very end of the last century in Medwall's Renaissance-flavoured comedy *Fulgens and Lucres*. The expected end of a fable with such machinery would be a happy one: but here Shakespeare refuses to fall in with convention. " In the midst of merriment and nonsense comes a sudden and grievous incursion of fact full of pain. The father of the Princess is dead " (Dowden). After this the depression lingers to the end of Act V: the lovers are set tedious tasks to gain a bliss that is but problematic—

> Cuckoo, Cuckoo; O word of fear
> Unpleasing to a married ear.

An unhappy, cynical warning note, as though Shakespeare, as a dutiful realist, were reminding his audience how much more unpalatable than fancies facts may be.

H. D. Gray (*The Original Version of Love's Labour's Lost*, 1918) believes that there was an even unhappier ending to the first draft; one in which the suitors were practically refused. But, as Chambers observes, love-comedies do not end with rejections. In demonstrating that shadow and light are nearer to each other in any given situation of our actual world than on a stage conditioned by a selective and often traditional art, Shakespeare conforms in this act with his frequent practice of building new structures on old foundations, rather than of abandoning those foundations altogether.

Grateful acknowledgments are due to Mr. Herbert Box, M.A., for his expert opinion on some of Holofernes' Latin;

to Professor Lewis Horrox and Miss Perrin for kindly placing, on occasion, reference works in Exeter University College Library at my disposal; and to Miss M. Webster, B.A., for indispensable help at and before the proof stage.

W. S. V.

LOVE'S LABOUR'S LOST

DRAMATIS PERSONÆ

FERDINAND, king of Navarre.
BIRON,
LONGAVILLE, } lords attending on the King.
DUMAIN,
BOYET, } lords attending on the Princess of France.
MERCADE,
DON ADRIANO DE ARMADO, a fantastical Spaniard.
SIR NATHANIEL, a curate.
HOLOFERNES, a schoolmaster.
DULL, a constable.
COSTARD, a clown.
MOTH, page to Armado.
A Forester.

The PRINCESS of France.
ROSALINE,
MARIA, } ladies attending on the Princess.
KATHARINE,
JAQUENETTA, a country wench.

Lords, Attendants, &c.

SCENE: *Navarre*.

LOVE'S LABOUR'S LOST

ACT I

SCENE I. *The king of Navarre's park*

Enter FERDINAND, *king of* NAVARRE, BIRON, LONGAVILLE, *and* DUMAIN

King. Let fame, that all hunt after in their lives,
Live register'd upon our brazen tombs
And then grace us in the disgrace of death;
When, spite of cormorant devouring Time,
The endeavour of this present breath may buy
That honour which shall bate his scythe's keen edge
And make us heirs of all eternity.
Therefore, brave conquerors,—for so you are,
That war against your own affections
And the huge army of the world's desires,—   10
Our late edict shall strongly stand in force:
Navarre shall be the wonder of the world;
Our court shall be a little Academe,
Still and contemplative in living art.
You three, Biron, Dumain, and Longaville,
Have sworn for three years' term to live with me
My fellow-scholars and to keep those statutes
That are recorded in this schedule here:
Your oaths are pass'd; and now subscribe your names,
That his own hand may strike his honour down   20

That violates the smallest branch herein:
If you are arm'd to do as sworn to do,
Subscribe to your deep oaths, and keep it too.

   Long. I am resolved; 't is but a three years' fast:
The mind shall banquet, though the body pine:
Fat paunches have lean pates, and dainty bits
Make rich the ribs, but bankrupt quite the wits.

   Dum. My loving lord, Dumain is mortified:
The grosser manner of these world's delights
He throws upon the gross world's baser slaves: 30
To love, to wealth, to pomp, I pine and die;
With all these living in philosophy.

   Biron. I can but say their protestation over;
So much, dear liege, I have already sworn,
That is, to live and study here three years.
But there are other strict observances;
As, not to see a woman in that term,
Which I hope well is not enrolled there;
And one day in a week to touch no food
And but one meal on every day beside,   40
The which I hope is not enrolled there;
And then, to sleep but three hours in the night,
And not be seen to wink of all the day—
When I was wont to think no harm all night
And make a dark night too of half the day—
Which I hope well is not enrolled there:
O, these are barren tasks, too hard to keep,
Not to see ladies, study, fast, not sleep!

   King. Your oath is pass'd to pass away from these.

   Biron. Let me say no, my liege, an if you please: 50
I only swore to study with your grace
And stay here in your court for three years' space.

   Long. You swore to that, Biron, and to the rest.

   Biron. By yea and nay, sir, then I swore in jest.
What is the end of study? let me know.

  King. Why, that to know, which else we should not know.

  Biron. Things hid and barr'd, you mean, from common
    sense?

  King. Ay, that is study's god-like recompense.

  Biron. Come on, then; I will swear to study so,

To know the thing I am forbid to know: 60

As thus,—to study where I well may dine,

  When I to feast expressly am forbid;

Or study where to meet some mistress fine,

  When mistresses from common sense are hid;

Or, having sworn too hard a keeping oath,

Study to break it and not break my troth.

If study's gain be thus and this be so,

Study knows that which yet it doth not know:

Swear me to this, and I will ne'er say no.

  King. These be the stops that hinder study quite   70

And train our intellects to vain delight.

  Biron. Why, all delights are vain; but that most vain,

Which with pain purchased doth inherit pain:

As, painfully to pore upon a book

  To seek the light of truth; while truth the while

Doth falsely blind the eyesight of his look:

  Light seeking light doth light of light beguile:

So, ere you find where light in darkness lies,

Your light grows dark by losing of your eyes.

Study me how to please the eye indeed   80

  By fixing it upon a fairer eye,

Who dazzling so, that eye shall be his heed

  And give him light that it was blinded by.

Study is like the heaven's glorious sun

  That will not be deep-search'd with saucy looks:

Small have continual plodders ever won

  Save base authority from others' books.

These earthly godfathers of heaven's lights

  That give a name to every fixed star

Have no more profit of their shining nights   90
  Than those that walk and wot not what they are.
Too much to know is to know nought but fame;
And every godfather can give a name.

    King. How well he 's read, to reason against reading!

    Dum. Proceeded well, to stop all good proceeding!

    Long. He weeds the corn and still lets grow the weeding.

    Biron. The spring is near when green geese are a-breed-
      ing.

    Dum. How follows that?

    Biron.   Fit in his place and time.

    Dum. In reason nothing.

    Biron.   Something then in rhyme.

    King. Biron is like an envious sneaping frost   100
        That bites the first-born infants of the spring.

    Biron. Well, say I am; why should proud summer
          boast
          Before the birds have any cause to sing?
Why should I joy in any abortive birth?
At Christmas I no more desire a rose
Than wish a snow in May's new-fangled mirth;
But like of each thing that in season grows.
So you, to study now it is too late,
Climb o'er the house to unlock the little gate.

    King. Well, sit you out: go home, Biron: adieu.   110

    Biron. No, my good lord; I have sworn to stay with you:
And though I have for barbarism spoke more
    Than for that angel knowledge you can say,
Yet confident I 'll keep what I have swore
    And bide the penance of each three years' day.
Give me the paper; let me read the same;
And to the strict'st decrees I'll write my name.

    King. How well this yielding rescues thee from shame!

    Biron. [*Reads*] ' Item, That no woman shall come within
a mile of my court:' Hath this been proclaimed?   120

Long. Four days ago.

Biron. Let 's see the penalty. [*Reads*] ' On pain of losing her tongue.' Who devised this penalty?

Long. Marry, that did I.

Biron. Sweet lord, and why?

Long. To fright them hence with that dread penalty.

Biron. A dangerous law against gentility!

[*Reads*] ' Item, If any man be seen to talk with a woman within the term of three years, he shall endure such public shame as the rest of the court can possibly devise.'   130
This article, my liege, yourself must break;

   For well you know here comes in embassy
The French king's daughter with yourself to speak—

   A maid of grace and complete majesty—
About surrender up of Aquitaine

   To her decrepit, sick and bedrid father:
Therefore this article is made in vain,

   Or vainly comes the admired princess hither.

King. What say you, lords? why, this was quite forgot.

Biron. So study evermore is overshot: 140
While it doth study to have what it would
It doth forget to do the thing it should,
And when it hath the thing it hunteth most,
'T is won as towns with fire, so won, so lost.

King. We must of force dispense with this decree;
She must lie here on mere necessity.

Biron. Necessity will make us all forsworn

   Three thousand times within this three years' space;
For every man with his affects is born,

   Not by might master'd but by special grace: 150
If I break faith, this word shall speak for me;
I am forsworn on ' mere necessity '.
So to the laws at large I write my name: [*Subscribes.*

   And he that breaks them in the least degree
Stands in attainder of eternal shame:

Suggestions are to other as to me;
But I believe, although I seem so loath,
I am the last that will last keep his oath.
But is there no quick recreation granted?
    King. Ay, that there is. Our court, you know, is haunted
    With a refined traveller of Spain;   161
A man in all the world's new fashion planted,
    That hath a mint of phrases in his brain;
One whom the music of his own vain tongue
    Doth ravish like enchanting harmony;
A man of complements, whom right and wrong
    Have chose as umpire of their mutiny:
This child of fancy that Armado hight
    For interim to our studies shall relate
In high-born words the worth of many a knight   170
    From tawny Spain lost in the world's debate.
How you delight, my lords, I know not, I;
But, I protest, I love to hear him lie
And I will use him for my minstrelsy.
    Biron. Armado is a most illustrious wight,
A man of fire-new words, fashion's own knight.
    Long. Costard the swain and he shall be our sport;
And so to study, three years is but short.

        Enter DULL *with a letter, and* COSTARD

    Dull. Which is the duke's own person?
    Biron. This, fellow: what wouldst?   180
    Dull. I myself reprehend his own person, for I am his
grace's tharborough: but I would see his own person in
flesh and blood.
    Biron. This is he.
    Dull. Signior Arme—Arme—commends you. There's
villany abroad: this letter will tell you more.
    Cost. Sir, the contempts thereof are as touching me.
    King. A letter from the magnificent Armado.

Biron. How low soever the matter, I hope in God for high words.   190

Long. A high hope for a low heaven: God grant us patience!

Biron. To hear? or forbear laughing?

Long. To hear meekly, sir, and to laugh moderately; or to forbear both.

Biron. Well, sir, be it as the style shall give us cause to climb in the merriness.

Cost. The matter is to me, sir, as concerning Jaquenetta. The manner of it is, I was taken with the manner.

Biron. In what manner?   200

Cost. In manner and form following, sir; all those three: I was seen with her in the manor-house, sitting with her upon the form, and taken following her into the park; which, put together, is in manner and form following. Now, sir, for the manner,—it is the manner of a man to speak to a woman: for the form,—in some form.

Biron. For the following, sir?

Cost. As it shall follow in my correction: and God defend the right!

King. Will you hear this letter with attention?   210

Biron. As we would hear an oracle.

Cost. Such is the simplicity of man to hearken after the flesh.

King. [*Reads*] ' Great deputy, the welkin's vicegerent and sole dominator of Navarre, my soul's earth's god, and body's fostering patron.'

Cost. Not a word of Costard yet.

King. [*Reads*] ' So it is,'—

Cost. It may be so: but if he say it is so, he is, in telling true, but so.   220

King. Peace!

Cost. Be to me and every man that dares not fight!

King. No words!

Cost. Of other men's secrets, I beseech you.

King. [*Reads*] 'So it is, besieged with sable-coloured melancholy, I did commend the black-oppressing humour to the most wholesome physic of thy health-giving air; and, as I am a gentleman, betook myself to walk. The time when. About the sixth hour; when beasts most graze, birds best peck, and men sit down to that nourishment which is called supper: so much for the time when. Now for the ground which; which, I mean, I walked upon: it is ycleped thy park. Then for the place where; where, I mean, I did encounter that obscene and most preposterous event, that draweth from my snow-white pen the ebon-coloured ink, which here thou viewest, beholdest, surveyest, or seest: but to the place where; it standeth north-north-east and by east from the west corner of thy curious-knotted garden: there did I see that low-spirited swain, that base minnow of thy mirth,'—   240

Cost. Me?

King. [*Reads*] ' that unlettered small-knowing soul,'—

Cost. Me?

King. [*Reads*] ' that shallow vassal,'—

Cost. Still me?

King. [*Reads*] ' which, as I remember, hight Costard,'—

Cost. O, me!

King. [*Reads*] ' sorted and consorted, contrary to thy established proclaimed edict and continent canon, which with,—O, with—but with this I passion to say wherewith,'—

Cost. With a wench.   251

King. [*Reads*] ' with a child of our grandmother Eve, a female; or, for thy more sweet understanding, a woman. Him I, as my ever-esteemed duty pricks me on, have sent to thee, to receive the meed of punishment, by thy sweet grace's officer, Anthony Dull; a man of good repute, carriage, bearing, and estimation.'

Dull. Me, an't shall please you; I am Anthony Dull.

King. [*Reads*] ' For Jaquenetta,—so is the weaker vessel
called which I apprehended with the aforesaid swain,—I
keep her as a vessel of thy law's fury; and shall, at the least
of thy sweet notice, bring her to trial. Thine, in all com-
pliments of devoted and heart-burning heat of duty.

DON ADRIANO DE ARMADO.'

Biron. This is not so well as I looked for, but the best
that ever I heard.

King. Ay, the best for the worst. But, sirrah, what say
you to this?

Cost. Sir, I confess the wench.

King. Did you hear the proclamation? 269

Cost. I do confess much of the hearing it, but little of
the marking of it.

King. It was proclaimed a year's imprisonment, to be
taken with a wench.

Cost. I was taken with none, sir: I was taken with a
damsel.

King. Well, it was proclaimed ' damsel '.

Cost. This was no damsel neither, sir; she was a virgin.

King. It is so varied too; for it was proclaimed ' virgin '.

Cost. If it were, I deny her virginity: I was taken with a
maid. 280

King. This maid will not serve your turn, sir.

Cost. This maid will serve my turn, sir.

King. Sir, I will pronounce your sentence: you shall fast
a week with bran and water.

Cost. I had rather pray a month with mutton and
porridge.

King. And Don Armado shall be your keeper.
My Lord Biron, see him deliver'd o'er:
And go we, lords, to put in practice that
Which each to other hath so strongly sworn. 290

[*Exeunt King, Longaville, and Dumain.*

Biron. I 'll lay my head to any good man's hat,

These oaths and laws will prove an idle scorn.
Sirrah, come on.

Cost. I suffer for the truth, sir; for true it is, I was
taken with Jaquenetta, and Jaquenetta is a true girl; and
therefore welcome the sour cup of prosperity! Affliction
may one day smile again; and till then, sit thee down,
sorrow!   [*Exeunt.*

SCENE II. *The same*

Enter ARMADO *and* MOTH

Arm. Boy, what sign is it when a man of great spirit
grows melancholy?

Moth. A great sign, sir, that he will look sad.

Arm. Why, sadness is one and the self-same thing, dear
imp.

Moth. No, no; O Lord, sir, no.

Arm. How canst thou part sadness and melancholy, my
tender juvenal?

Moth. By a familiar demonstration of the working, my
tough senior.   10

Arm. Why tough senior? why tough senior?

Moth. Why tender juvenal? why tender juvenal?

Arm. I spoke it, tender juvenal, as a congruent epitheton
appertaining to thy young days, which we may nominate
tender.

Moth. And I, tough senior, as an appertinent title to
your old time, which we may name tough.

Arm. Pretty and apt.

Moth. How mean you, sir? I pretty, and my saying
apt? or I apt, and my saying pretty?   20

Arm. Thou pretty, because little.

Moth. Little pretty, because little. Wherefore apt?

Arm. And therefore apt, because quick.

Moth. Speak you this in my praise, master?

Arm. In thy condign praise.

Moth. I will praise an eel with the same praise.

Arm. What, that an eel is ingenious?

Moth. That an eel is quick.

Arm. I do say thou art quick in answers: thou heatest my blood.   30

Moth. I am answered, sir.

Arm. I love not to be crossed.

Moth. [*Aside*] He speaks the mere contrary; crosses love not him.

Arm. I have promised to study three years with the duke.

Moth. You may do it in an hour, sir.

Arm. Impossible.

Moth. How many is one thrice told?

Arm. I am ill at reckoning; it fitteth the spirit of a tapster.

Moth. You are a gentleman and a gamester, sir.   41

Arm. I confess both: they are both the varnish of a complete man.

Moth. Then, I am sure, you know how much the gross sum of deuce-ace amounts to.

Arm. It doth amount to one more than two.

Moth. Which the base vulgar do call three.

Arm. True.

Moth. Why, sir, is this such a piece of study? Now here is three studied, ere ye 'll thrice wink: and how easy it is to put 'years' to the word 'three', and study three years in two words, the dancing horse will tell you.   52

Arm. A most fine figure!

Moth. To prove you a cipher.

Arm. I will hereupon confess I am in love: and as it is base for a soldier to love, so am I in love with a base wench. If drawing my sword against the humour of affection would deliver me from the reprobate thought of it, I would take Desire prisoner, and ransom him to any

French courtier for a new-devised courtesy. I think scorn
to sigh: methinks I should out-swear Cupid. Comfort
me, boy: what great men have been in love?   62

Moth. Hercules, master.

Arm. Most sweet Hercules! More authority, dear boy,
name more; and, sweet my child, let them be men of
good repute and carriage.

Moth. Samson, master: he was a man of good carriage,
great carriage, for he carried the town-gates on his back
like a porter: and he was in love.

Arm. O well-knit Samson! strong-jointed Samson! I do
excel thee in my rapier as much as thou didst me in carrying gates. I am in love too. Who was Samson's love, my
dear Moth?   73

Moth. A woman, master.

Arm. Of what complexion?

Moth. Of all the four, or the three, or the two, or one
of the four.

Arm. Tell me precisely of what complexion.

Moth. Of the sea-water green, sir.

Arm. Is that one of the four complexions?   80

Moth. As I have read, sir; and the best of them
too.

Arm. Green indeed is the colour of lovers; but to have
a love of that colour, methinks Samson had small reason
for it. He surely affected her for her wit.

Moth. It was so, sir; for she had a green wit.

Arm. My love is most immaculate white and red.

Moth. Most maculate thoughts, master, are masked
under such colours.

Arm. Define, define, well-educated infant.   90

Moth. My father's wit and my mother's tongue, assist
me!

Arm. Sweet invocation of a child; most pretty and
pathetical!

Moth. If she be made of white and red,
　　　Her faults will ne'er be known,
　　For blushing cheeks by faults are bred
　　　And fears by pale white shown:
　　Then if she fear, or be to blame,
　　　By this you shall not know,   100
　　For still her cheeks possess the same
　　　Which native she doth owe.
A dangerous rhyme, master, against the reason of white and
red.

Arm. Is there not a ballad, boy, of the King and the
Beggar?

Moth. The world was very guilty of such a ballad some
three ages since: but I think now 't is not to be found;
or, if it were, it would neither serve for the writing nor
the tune.   110

Arm. I will have that subject newly writ o'er, that I
may example my digression by some mighty precedent.
Boy, I do love that country girl that I took in the park
with the rational hind Costard: she deserves well.

Moth. [*Aside*] To be whipped; and yet a better love
than my master.

Arm. Sing, boy; my spirit grows heavy in love.

Moth. And that 's great marvel, loving a light wench.

Arm. I say, sing.

Moth. Forbear till this company be past.   120

Enter DULL, COSTARD, *and* JAQUENETTA

Dull. Sir, the duke's pleasure is, that you keep Costard
safe: and you must suffer him to take no delight nor no
penance; but a' must fast three days a week. For this
damsel, I must keep her at the park: she is allowed for
the day-woman. Fare you well.

Arm. I do betray myself with blushing. Maid!

Jaq. Man?

Arm. I will visit thee at the lodge.

Jaq. That's hereby.

Arm. I know where it is situate.   130

Jaq. Lord, how wise you are!

Arm. I will tell thee wonders.

Jaq. With that face?

Arm. I love thee.

Jaq. So I heard you say.

Arm. And so, farewell.

Jaq. Fair weather after you!

Dull. Come, Jacquenetta, away!

[*Exeunt Dull and Jaquenetta.*

Arm. Villain, thou shalt fast for thy offences ere thou be pardoned.   140

Cost. Well, sir, I hope, when I do it, I shall do it on a full stomach.

Arm. Thou shalt be heavily punished.

Cost. I am more bound to you than your fellows, for they are but lightly rewarded.

Arm. Take away this villain; shut him up.

Moth. Come, you transgressing slave; away!

Cost. Let me not be pent up, sir: I will fast, being loose.

Moth. No, sir; that were fast and loose: thou shalt to prison.   150

Cost. Well, if ever I do see the merry days of desolation that I have seen, some shall see.

Moth. What shall some see?

Cost. Nay, nothing, Master Moth, but what they look upon. It is not for prisoners to be too silent in their words; and therefore I will say nothing: I thank God I have as little patience as another man; and therefore I can be quiet.

[*Exeunt Moth and Costard.*

Arm. I do affect the very ground, which is base, where her shoe, which is baser, guided by her foot, which is basest, doth tread. I shall be forsworn, which is a great argument

of falsehood, if I love. And how can that be true love which
is falsely attempted? Love is a familiar; Love is a devil:
there is no evil angel but Love. Yet was Samson so tempted,
and he had an excellent strength; yet was Solomon so
seduced, and he had a very good wit. Cupid's butt-shaft
is too hard for Hercules' club; and therefore too much odds
for a Spaniard's rapier. The first and second cause will not
serve my turn; the passado he respects not, the duello he
regards not: his disgrace is to be called boy; but his glory
is to subdue men. Adieu, valour! rust, rapier! be still,
drum! for your manager is in love; yea, he loveth. Assist
me, some extemporal god of rhyme, for I am sure I shall
turn sonnet. Devise, wit; write, pen; for I am for whole
volumes in folio.   [*Exit.* 174

———

ACT II

Scene I. *The same*

Enter the Princess *of France*, Rosaline, Maria,
Katharine, Boyet, Lords, *and other* Attendants

Boyet. Now, madam, summon up your dearest spirits:
Consider who the king your father sends,
To whom he sends, and what 's his embassy:
Yourself, held precious in the world's esteem,
To parley with the sole inheritor
Of all perfections that a man may owe,
Matchless Navarre; the plea of no less weight
Than Aquitaine, a dowry for a queen.
Be now as prodigal of all dear grace
As Nature was in making graces dear   10
When she did starve the general world beside
And prodigally gave them all to you.
  Prin. Good Lord Boyet, my beauty, though but mean,
Needs not the painted flourish of your praise:
Beauty is bought by judgement of the eye,

Not utter'd by base sale of chapmen's tongues:
I am less proud to hear you tell my worth
Than you much willing to be counted wise
In spending your wit in the praise of mine.
But now to task the tasker: good Boyet,   20
You are not ignorant, all-telling fame
Doth noise abroad, Navarre hath made a vow,
Till painful study shall outwear three years,
No woman may approach his silent court:
Therefore to 's seemeth it a needful course,
Before we enter his forbidden gates,
To know his pleasure; and in that behalf,
Bold of your worthiness, we single you
As our best-moving fair solicitor.
Tell him, the daughter of the King of France,   30
On serious business, craving quick dispatch,
Importunes personal conference with his grace:
Haste, signify so much; while we attend,
Like humble-visaged suitors, his high will.
   Boyet. Proud of employment, willingly I go.
   Prin. All pride is willing pride, and yours is so.

                                 [Exit Boyet.

Who are the votaries, my loving lords,
That are vow-fellows with this virtuous duke?
   First Lord. Lord Longaville is one.
   Prin.   Know you the man?
   Mar. I know him, madam: at a marriage-feast,   40
Between Lord Perigort and the beauteous heir
Of Jaques Falconbridge, solemnized
In Normandy, saw I this Longaville:
A man of sovereign parts he is esteem'd;
Well fitted in arts, glorious in arms:
Nothing becomes him ill that he would well.
The only soil of his fair virtue's gloss,
If virtue's gloss will stain with any soil,

Is a sharp wit match'd with too blunt a will;
Whose edge hath power to cut, whose will still wills 50
It should none spare that come within his power.

Prin. Some merry mocking lord, belike; is 't so?

Mar. They say so most that most his humours know.

Prin. Such short-lived wits do wither as they grow.
Who are the rest?

Kath. The young Dumain; a well-accomplished youth,
Of all that virtue love for virtue loved:
Most power to do most harm, least knowing ill;
For he hath wit to make an ill shape good,
And shape to win grace though he had no wit. 60
I saw him at the Duke Alençon's once;
And much too little of that good I saw
Is my report to his great worthiness.

Ros. Another of these students at that time
Was there with him, if I have heard a truth.
Biron they call him; but a merrier man,
Within the limit of becoming mirth,
I never spent an hour's talk withal:
His eye begets occasion for his wit;
For every object that the one doth catch 70
The other turns to a mirth-moving jest,
Which his fair tongue, conceit's expositor,
Delivers in such apt and gracious words
That aged ears play truant at his tales
And younger hearings are quite ravished;
So sweet and voluble is his discourse.

Prin. God bless my ladies! are they all in love,
That every one her own hath garnished
With such bedecking ornaments of praise?

First Lord. Here comes Boyet.

Re-enter BOYET

Prin.   Now, what admittance, lord? 80

Boyet. Navarre had notice of your fair approach;
And he and his competitors in oath
Were all address'd to meet you, gentle lady,
Before I came.   Marry, thus much I have learnt:
He rather means to lodge you in the field,
Like one that comes here to besiege his court,
Than seek a dispensation for his oath,
To let you enter his unpeopled house.
Here comes Navarre.

Enter KING, LONGAVILLE, DUMAIN, BIRON, *and* Attendants

King. Fair princess, welcome to the court of Navarre.

Prin. ' Fair ' I give you back again; and ' welcome ' I
have not yet; the roof of this court is too high to be yours;
and welcome to the wide fields too base to be mine.   93

King. You shall be welcome, madam, to my court.

Prin. I will be welcome, then: conduct me thither.

King. Hear me, dear lady; I have sworn an oath.

Prin. Our Lady help my lord! he'll be forsworn.

King. Not for the world, fair madam, by my will.

Prin. Why, will shall break it; will and nothing else.

King. Your ladyship is ignorant what it is.   100

Prin. Were my lord so, his ignorance were wise,
Where now his knowledge must prove ignorance.
I hear your grace hath sworn out house-keeping:
'T is deadly sin to keep that oath, my lord,
And sin to break it.
But pardon me, I am too sudden-bold:
To teach a teacher ill beseemeth me.
Vouchsafe to read the purpose of my coming,
And suddenly resolve me in my suit.

King. Madam, I will, if suddenly I may.   110

Prin. You will the sooner, that I were away;
For you 'll prove perjured if you make me stay.

Biron. Did not I dance with you in Brabant once?

Ros. Did not I dance with you in Brabant once?
Biron. I know you did.
Ros. How needless was it then to ask the question!
Biron. You must not be so quick.
Ros. 'T is 'long of you that spur me with such questions.
Biron. Your wit 's too hot, it speeds too fast, 't will tire.
Ros. Not till it leave the rider in the mire.   120
Biron. What time o' day?
Ros. The hour that fools should ask.
Biron. Now fair befall your mask!
Ros. Fair fall the face it covers!
Biron. And send you many lovers!
Ros. Amen, so you be none.
Biron. Nay, then will I be gone.
King. Madam, your father here doth intimate
The payment of a hundred thousand crowns;
Being but the one half of an entire sum   130
Disbursed by my father in his wars.
But say that he or we, as neither have,
Received that sum, yet there remains unpaid
A hundred thousand more; in surety of the which,
One part of Aquitaine is bound to us,
Although not valued to the money's worth.
If then the king your father will restore
But that one half which is unsatisfied,
We will give up our right in Aquitaine,
And hold fair friendship with his majesty.   140
But that, it seems, he little purposeth,
For here he doth demand to have repaid
A hundred thousand crowns; and not demands,
On payment of a hundred thousand crowns,
To have his title live in Aquitaine;
Which we much rather had depart withal
And have the money by our father lent
Than Aquitaine so gelded as it is.

Dear princess, were not his requests so far
From reason's yielding, your fair self should make   150
A yielding 'gainst some reason in my breast
And go well satisfied to France again.

   Prin. You do the king my father too much wrong
And wrong the reputation of your name,
In so unseeming to confess receipt
Of that which hath so faithfully been paid.

   King. I do protest I never heard of it;
And if you prove it, I 'll repay it back
Or yield up Aquitaine.

   Prin.   We arrest your word.
Boyet, you can produce acquittances   160
For such a sum from special officers
Of Charles his father.

   King.   Satisfy me so.

   Boyet. So please your grace, the packet is not come
Where that and other specialties are bound:
To-morrow you shall have a sight of them.

   King. It shall suffice me: at which interview
All liberal reason I will yield unto.
Meantime receive such welcome at my hand
As honour without breach of honour may
Make tender of to thy true worthiness: 170
You may not come, fair princess, in my gates;
But here without you shall be so received
As you shall deem yourself lodged in my heart,
Though so denied fair harbour in my house.
Your own good thoughts excuse me, and farewell:
To-morrow shall we visit you again.

   Prin. Sweet health and fair desires consort your grace!

   King. Thy own wish wish I thee in every place!   [*Exit.*

   Biron. Lady, I will commend you to mine own heart.

   Ros. Pray you, do my commendations; I would be glad
to see it.   181

Biron. I would you heard it groan.

Ros. Is the fool sick?

Biron. Sick at the heart.

Ros. Alack, let it blood.

Biron. Would that do it good?

Ros. My physic says ' ay '.

Biron. Will you prick't with your eye?

Ros. No point, with my knife.

Biron. Now, God save thy life!   190

Ros. And yours from long living!

Biron. I cannot stay thanksgiving.   [*Retiring.*

Dum. Sir, I pray you, a word: what lady is that same?

Boyet. The heir of Alençon, Katharine her name.

Dum. A gallant lady. Monsieur, fare you well.   [*Exit.*

Long. I beseech you a word: what is she in the white.

Boyet. A woman sometimes, an you saw her in the light.

Long. Perchance light in the light. I desire her name.

Boyet. She hath but one for herself; to desire that were
     a shame.

Long. Pray you, sir, whose daughter?   200

Boyet. Her mother's, I have heard.

Long. God's blessing on your beard!

Boyet. Good sir, be not offended.
She is an heir of Falconbridge.

Long. Nay, my choler is ended.
She is a most sweet lady.

Boyet. Not unlike, sir, that may be.   [*Exit Long.*

Biron. What's her name in the cap?

Boyet. Rosaline, by good hap.

Biron. Is she wedded or no?   210

Boyet. To her will, sir, or so.

Biron. You are welcome, sir: adieu.

Boyet. Farewell to me, sir, and welcome to you.
                                                [*Exit Biron.*

Mar. That last is Biron, the merry mad-cap lord:

Not a word with him but a jest.

    Boyet.   And every jest but a word.

    Prin. It was well done of you to take him at his word.

    Boyet. I was as willing to grapple as he was to board.

    Mar. Two hot sheeps, marry.

    Boyet.   And wherefore not ships?

No sheep, sweet lamb, unless we feed on your lips.   219

    Mar. You sheep, and I pasture: shall that finish the jest?

    Boyet. So you grant pasture for me. [*Offering to kiss her.*

    Mar.   Not so, gentle beast:

My lips are no common, though several they be.

    Boyet. Belonging to whom?

    Mar.   To my fortunes and me.

    Prin. Good wits will be jangling; but, gentles, agree:

This civil war of wits were much better used

On Navarre and his book-men; for here 't is abused.

    Boyet. If my observation, which very seldom lies,

By the heart's still rhetoric disclosed with eyes,

Deceive me not now, Navarre is infected.

    Prin. With what?   230

    Boyet. With that which we lovers entitle affected.

    Prin. Your reason?

    Boyet. Why, all his behaviours did make their retire

To the court of his eye, peeping thorough desire:

His heart, like an agate, with your print impress'd,

Proud with his form, in his eye pride express'd:

His tongue, all impatient to speak and not see,

Did stumble with haste in his eyesight to be;

All senses to that sense did make their repair,

To feel only looking on fairest of fair: 240

Methought all his senses were lock'd in his eye,

As jewels in crystal for some prince to buy;

Who, tendering their own worth from where they were

    glass'd,

Did point you to buy them, along as you pass'd:

His face's own margent did quote such amazes
That all eyes saw his eyes enchanted with gazes.
I 'll give you Aquitaine and all that is his,
An you give him for my sake but one loving kiss.

 Prin. Come to our pavilion: Boyet is disposed. 249
 Boyet. But to speak that in words which his eye hath
  disclosed.
I only have made a mouth of his eye,
By adding a tongue which I know will not lie.

 Ros. Thou are an old love-monger and speakest skilfully.
 Mar. He is Cupid's grandfather and learns news of him.
 Ros. Then was Venus like her mother, for her father is
  but grim.
 Boyet. Do you hear, my mad wenches?
 Mar.   No.
 Boyet.   What then, do you see?
 Ros. Ay, our way to be gone.
 Boyet.   You are too hard for me.

               [Exeunt.

ACT III

Scene I. *The same*

Enter Armado *and* Moth

 Arm. Warble, child; make passionate my sense of hearing.
 Moth. Concolinel.   *[Singing.*
 Arm. Sweet air! Go, tenderness of years; take this key,
give enlargement to the swain, bring him festinately hither:
I must employ him in a letter to my love.
 Moth. Master, will you win your love with a French
brawl?
 Arm. How meanest thou? brawling in French? 9
 Moth. No, my complete master: but to jig off a tune
at the tongue's end, canary to it with your feet, humour

it with turning up your eyelids, sigh a note and sing a note, sometime through the throat, as if you swallowed love with singing love, sometime through the nose, as if you snuffed up love by smelling love; with your hat penthouse-like o'er the shop of your eyes; with your arms crossed on your thin-belly doublet like a rabbit on a spit; or your hands in your pocket like a man after the old painting; and keep not too long in one tune, but a snip and away. These are complements, these are humours; these betray nice wenches, that would be betrayed without these; and make them men of note—do you note me?— that most are affected to these.　　　23

Arm. How hast thou purchased this experience?

Moth. By my penny of observation.

Arm. But O,—but O,—

Moth. 'The hobby-horse is forgot.'

Arm. Callest thou my love ' hobby-horse '?

Moth. No, master; the hobby-horse is but a colt, and your love perhaps a hackney. But have you forgot your love?　　　31

Arm. Almost I had.

Moth. Negligent student! learn her by heart.

Arm. By heart and in heart, boy.

Moth. And out of heart, master: all those three I will prove.

Arm. What wilt thou prove?

Moth. A man, if I live; and this, by, in, and without, upon the instant: by heart you love her, because your heart cannot come by her; in heart you love her, because your heart is in love with her; and out of heart you love her, being out of heart that you cannot enjoy her.　　　42

Arm. I am all these three.

Moth. And three times as much more, and yet nothing at all.

Arm. Fetch hither the swain: he must carry me a letter.

Moth. A message well sympathized; a horse to be ambassador for an ass.

Arm. Ha, ha! what sayest thou?

Moth. Marry, sir, you must send the ass upon the horse,
for he is very slow-gaited. But I go.   51

Arm. The way is but short: away!

Moth. As swift as lead, sir.

Arm. The meaning, pretty ingenious?
Is not lead a metal heavy, dull, and slow?

Moth. Minimè, honest master; or rather, master, no.

Arm. I say lead is slow.

Moth.   You are too swift, sir, to say so:
Is that lead slow which is fired from a gun?

Arm. Sweet smoke of rhetoric!
He reputes me a cannon; and the bullet, that's he: 60
I shoot thee at the swain.

Moth.   Thump then and I flee.   [*Exit.*

Arm. A most acute juvenal; volable and free of grace!
By thy favour, sweet welkin, I must sigh in thy face:
Most rude melancholy, valour gives thee place.
My herald is return'd.

Re-enter MOTH *with* COSTARD

Moth. A wonder, master! here's a costard broken in a
    shin.

Arm. Some enigma, some riddle: come, thy l'envoy;
    begin.

Cost. No egma, no riddle, no l'envoy; no salve in
the mail, sir: O, sir, plantain, a plain plantain! no l'envoy,
no l'envoy; no salve, sir, but a plantain!   70

Arm. By virtue, thou enforcest laughter; thy silly
thought my spleen; the heaving of my lungs provokes
me to ridiculous smiling. O, pardon me, my stars! Doth
the inconsiderate take salve for l'envoy, and the word
l'envoy for a salve?

Moth. Do the wise think them other? is not l'envoy a salve?

Arm. No, page: it is an epilogue or discourse, to make plain

Some obscure precedence that hath tofore been sain.

I will example it:

    The fox, the ape and the humble-bee,   80
    Were still at odds, being but three.

There's the moral. Now the l'envoy.

Moth. I will add the l'envoy. Say the moral again.

Arm.   The fox, the ape, the humble-bee,
    Were still at odds, being but three.

Moth. Until the goose came out of door,
    And stay'd the odds by adding four.

Now will I begin your moral, and do you follow with my l'envoy.

    The fox, the ape and the humble-bee,   90
    Were still at odds, being but three.

Arm. Until the goose came out of door,
    Staying the odds by adding four.

Moth. A good l'envoy, ending in the goose: would you desire more?

Cost. The boy hath sold him a bargain, a goose, that's flat.

Sir, your pennyworth is good, an your goose be fat.

To sell a bargain well is as cunning as fast and loose:

Let me see; a fat l'envoy; ay, that's a fat goose.

Arm. Come hither, come hither. How did this argument
  begin?   100

Moth. By saying that a costard was broken in a shin.

Then call'd you for the l'envoy.

Cost. True, and I for a plantain: thus came your argument in;

Then the boy's fat l'envoy, the goose that you bought;

And he ended the market.

Arm. But tell me; how was there a costard broken in a shin?

Moth. I will tell you sensibly.

Cost. Thou hast no feeling of it, Moth: I will speak that
l'envoy: 110
I Costard, running out, that was safely within,
Fell over the threshold, and broke my shin.

Arm. We will talk no more of this matter.

Cost. Till there be more matter in the shin.

Arm. Sirrah Costard, I will enfranchise thee.

Cost. O, marry me to one Frances: I smell some l'envoy,
some goose, in this.

Arm. By my sweet soul, I mean setting thee at liberty,
enfreedoming thy person: thou wert immured, restrained,
captivated, bound.   120

Cost. True, true; and now you will be my purgation and
let me loose.

Arm. I give thee thy liberty, set thee from durance; and,
in lieu thereof, impose on thee nothing but this: bear this
significant [*giving a letter*] to the country maid Jaquenetta:
there is remuneration: for the best ward of mine honour is
rewarding my dependents. Moth, follow.   [*Exit.*

Moth. Like the sequel, I. Signior Costard, adieu.   128

Cost. My sweet ounce of man's flesh! my incony Jew!
                                                  [*Exit Moth.*
Now will I look to his remuneration. Remuneration! O,
that 's the Latin word for three farthings: three farthings
—remuneration.—' What 's the price of this inkle?'—' One
penny.'—' No, I 'll give you a remuneration:' why, it carries
it. Remuneration! why, it is a fairer name than French
crown. I will never buy and sell out of this word.

Enter BIRON

Biron. O, my good knave Costard! exceedingly well met.

Cost. Pray you, sir, how much carnation ribbon may a
man buy for a remuneration?

Biron. What is a remuneration?   139

Cost. Marry, sir, halfpenny farthing.   140
Biron. Why, then, three-farthing worth of silk.
Cost. I thank your worship: God be wi' you!
Biron. Stay, slave; I must employ thee:
As thou wilt win my favour, good my knave,
Do one thing for me that I shall entreat.
Cost. When would you have it done, sir?
Biron. This afternoon.
Cost. Well, I will do it, sir: fare you well.
Biron. Thou knowest not what it is.
Cost. I shall know, sir, when I have done it.   150
Biron. Why, villain, thou must know first.
Cost. I will come to your worship to-morrow morning.
Biron. It must be done this afternoon. Hark, slave, it is
        but this:
The princess comes to hunt here in the park,
And in her train there is a gentle lady;
When tongues speak sweetly, then they name her name,
And Rosaline they call her: ask for her;
And to her white hand see thou do commend
This seal'd-up counsel. There 's thy guerdon; go.   159
        [*Giving him a shilling.*

Cost. Gardon, O sweet gardon! better than remuneration,
a 'leven-pence farthing better: most sweet gardon! I will
do it, sir, in print. Gardon! Remuneration!   [*Exit.*
Biron. And I, forsooth, in love! I, that have been love's
        whip;
A very beadle to a humorous sigh;
A critic, nay, a night-watch constable;
A domineering pedant o'er the boy;
Than whom no mortal so magnificent!
This wimpled, whining, purblind, wayward boy;
This senior-junior, giant-dwarf, Dan Cupid;
Regent of love-rhymes, lord of folded arms,   170
The anointed sovereign of sighs and groans,

Liege of all loiterers and malcontents,
Sole imperator and great general
Of trotting 'paritors:—O my little heart!—
And I to be a corporal of his field,
And wear his colours like a tumbler's hoop!
What, I! I love! I sue! I seek a wife!
A woman, that is like a German clock,
Still a-repairing, ever out of frame,
And never going aright, being a watch,   180
But being watch'd that it may still go right!
Nay, to be perjured, which is worst of all;
And, among three, to love the worst of all;
A wightly wanton with a velvet brow,
With two pitch-balls stuck in her face for eyes;
Ay, and, by heaven, one that will do the deed
Though Argus were her eunuch and her guard:
And I to sigh for her! to watch for her!
To pray for her! Go to; it is a plague
That Cupid will impose for my neglect   190
Of his almighty dreadful little might.
Well, I will love, write, sigh, pray, sue and groan:
Some men must love my lady and some Joan.   [*Exit.*

ACT IV

SCENE I. *The same*

Enter the PRINCESS *and her train, a* Forester, BOYET,
ROSALINE, MARIA, *and* KATHARINE

Prin. Was that the king, that spurr'd his horse so hard
Against the steep uprising of the hill?
Boyet. I know not; but I think it was not he.
Prin. Whoe'er a' was, a' show'd a mounting mind.
Well, lords, to-day we shall have our dispatch:
On Saturday we will return to France.

Then, forester, my friend, where is the bush
That we must stand and play the murderer in?

    For. Hereby, upon the edge of yonder coppice;
A stand where you may make the fairest shoot.   10

    Prin. I thank my beauty, I am fair that shoot,
And thereupon thou speak'st the fairest shoot.

    For. Pardon me, madam, for I meant not so.

    Prin. What, what? first praise me and again say no?
O short-lived pride!   Not fair? alack for woe!

    For. Yes, madam, fair.

    Prin.   Nay, never paint me now:
Where fair is not, praise cannot mend the brow.
Here, good my glass, take this for telling true:
Fair payment for foul words is more than due.

    For. Nothing but fair is that which you inherit.   20

    Prin. See, see, my beauty will be saved by merit!
O heresy in fair, fit for these days!
A giving hand, though foul, shall have fair praise.
But come, the bow: now mercy goes to kill,
And shooting well is then accounted ill.
Thus will I save my credit in the shoot:
Not wounding, pity would not let me do 't:
If wounding, then it was to show my skill,
That more for praise than purpose meant to kill.
And out of question so it is sometimes,   30
Glory grows guilty of detested crimes,
When, for fame's sake, for praise, an outward part,
We bend to that the working of the heart;
As I for praise alone now seek to spill
The poor deer's blood, that my heart means no ill.

    Boyet. Do not curst wives hold that self-sovereignty
Only for praise sake, when they strive to be
Lords o'er their lords?

    Prin. Only for praise: and praise we may afford
To any lady that subdues a lord.   40

Boyet. Here comes a member of the commonwealth.

Enter COSTARD

Cost. God dig-you-den all! Pray you, which is the head lady?

Prin. Thou shalt know her, fellow, by the rest that have no heads.

Cost. Which is the greatest lady, the highest?

Prin. The thickest and the tallest.

Cost. The thickest and the tallest! it is so; truth is truth.
An your waist, mistress, were as slender as my wit, 49
One o' these maids' girdles for your waist should be fit.
Are not you the chief woman? you are the thickest here.

Prin. What 's your will, sir? what 's your will?

Cost. I have a letter from Monsieur Biron to one Lady
Rosaline.

Prin. O, thy letter, thy letter! he 's a good friend of mine:
Stand aside, good bearer. Boyet, you can carve;
Break up this capon.

Boyet.　　　　　　I am bound to serve.
This letter is mistook, it importeth none here;
It is writ to Jaquenetta.

Prin.　　　　　　We will read it, I swear.
Break the neck of the wax, and every one give ear. 59

Boyet. [*Reads*] ' By heaven, that thou art fair, is most infallible; true, that thou art beauteous; truth itself, that thou art lovely. More fairer than fair, beautiful than beauteous, truer than truth itself, have commiseration on thy heroical vassal! The magnanimous and most illustrate king Cophetua set eye upon the pernicious and indubitate beggar Zenelophon; and he it was that might rightly say, Veni, vidi, vici; which to annothanize in the vulgar, —O base and obscure vulgar!—videlicet, He came, saw, and overcame: he came, one; saw, two; overcame, three. Who came? the king: why did he come? to see: why

did he see? to overcome: to whom came he? to the
beggar: what saw he? the beggar: who overcame he?
the beggar. The conclusion is victory: on whose side?
the king's. The captive is enriched: on whose side? the
beggar's. The catastrophe is a nuptial: on whose side?
the king's: no, on both in one, or one in both. I am the
king; for so stands the comparison: thou the beggar;
for so witnesseth thy lowliness. Shall I command thy love?
I may: shall I enforce thy love? I could: shall I entreat
thy love? I will. What shalt thou exchange for rags?
robes; for tittles? titles; for thyself? me. Thus, expecting
thy reply, I profane my lips on thy foot, my eyes on thy
picture, and my heart on thy every part. Thine, in the
dearest design of industry,   84
                    DON ADRIANO DE ARMADO.'
Thus dost thou hear the Nemean lion roar
    'Gainst thee, thou lamb, that standest as his prey.
Submissive fall his princely feet before,
    And he from forage will incline to play:
But if thou strive, poor soul, what art thou then?
Food for his rage, repasture for his den.   90
    Prin. What plume of feathers is he that indited this
        letter?
What vane? what weathercock? did you ever hear better?
    Boyet. I am much deceived but I remember the style.
    Prin. Else your memory is bad, going o'er it erewhile.
    Boyet. This Armado is a Spaniard, that keeps here in
        court;
A phantasime, a Monarcho, and one that makes sport
To the prince and his bookmates.
    Prin.   Thou fellow, a word:
Who gave thee this letter?
    Cost.   I told you; my lord.
    Prin. To whom shouldst thou give it?
    Cost. From my lord to my lady.   100

Prin. From which lord to which lady?

Cost. From my lord Biron, a good master of mine,
To a lady of France that he call'd Rosaline.

Prin. Thou hast mistaken his letter. Come, lords, away.
[*To Ros.*] Here, sweet, put up this: 't will be thine another
    day.   [*Exeunt Princess and train.*

Boyet. Who is the suitor? who is the suitor?

Ros.   Shall I teach you to know?

Boyet. Ay, my continent of beauty.

Ros.   Why, she that bears the bow.
Finely put off!

Boyet. My lady goes to kill horns; but, if thou marry,
Hang me by the neck, if horns that year miscarry.   110
Finely put on!

Ros. Well, then, I am the shooter.

Boyet.   And who is your deer?

Ros. If we chose by the horns, yourself come not near.
Finely put on, indeed!

Mar. You still wrangle with her, Boyet, and she strikes
    at the brow.

Boyet. But she herself is hit lower: have I hit her now?

Ros. Shall I come upon thee with an old saying, that
was a man when King Pepin of France was a little boy,
as touching the hit it?   119

Boyet. So I may answer thee with one as old, that was
a woman when Queen Guinover of Britain was a little
wench, as touching the hit it.

Ros.   Thou canst not hit it, hit it, hit it,
        Thou canst not hit it, my good man.

Boyet.   An I cannot, cannot, cannot,
        An I cannot, another can.
                   [*Exeunt Ros. and Kath.*

Cost. By my troth, most pleasant: how both did fit it!

Mar. A mark marvellous well shot, for they both did
    hit it.

Boyet. A mark! O, mark but that mark! A mark, says
    my lady!   129
Let the mark have a prick in 't, to mete at, if it may be.
    Mar. Wide o' the bow hand! i' faith, your hand is out.
    Cost. Indeed, a' must shoot nearer, or he 'll ne'er hit the
    clout.
    Boyet. An if my hand be out, then belike your hand is in.
    Cost. Then will she get the upshoot by cleaving the pin.
She 's too hard for you, sir: challenge her to bowl.
    Boyet. I fear too much rubbing. Good night, my good
    owl.   [*Exeunt Boyet and Maria.*
    Cost. By my soul, a swain! a most simple clown!
Lord, Lord, how the ladies and I have put him down!
O' my troth, most sweet jests! most incony vulgar wit!
When it comes so smoothly off, so obscenely, as it were, so
    fit.   140
Armado o' th' one side,—O, a most dainty man!
To see him walk before a lady and to bear her fan!
To see him kiss his hand! and how most sweetly a' will
    swear!
And his page o' t' other side, that handful of wit!
Ah, heavens, it is a most pathetical nit!
Sola, Sola!   [*Shout within.*
                            [*Exit Costard, running.*

SCENE II. *The same*

Enter HOLOFERNES, SIR NATHANIEL, *and* DULL

Nath. Very reverend sport, truly; and done in the
testimony of a good conscience.

Hol. The deer was, as you know, sanguis, in blood; ripe
as the pomewater, who now hangeth like a jewel in the
ear of caelo, the sky, the welkin, the heaven; and anon
falleth like a crab on the face of terra, the soil, the land, the
earth.

Nath. Truly, Master Holofernes, the epithets are sweetly varied, like a scholar at the least: but, sir, I assure ye, it was a buck of the first head.   10

Hol. Sir Nathaniel, *haud credo.*

Dull. 'T was not a *haud credo*: 't was a pricket.

Hol. Most barbarous intimation! yet a kind of insinuation, as it were, *in via,* in way, of explication; *facere,* as it were, replication, or rather, *ostentare,* to show, as it were, his inclination, after his undressed, unpolished, uneducated, unpruned, untrained, or rather, unlettered, or ratherest, unconfirmed fashion, to insert again my *haud credo* for a deer.   19

Dull. I said the deer was not a *haud credo*; 't was a pricket.

Hol. Twice-sod simplicity, *bis coctus*!

O thou monster Ignorance, how deformed dost thou look!

Nath. Sir, he hath never fed of the dainties that are bred
    in a book;

he hath not eat paper, as it were; he hath not drunk ink:
his intellect is not replenished; he is only an animal, only
sensible in the duller parts:

And such barren plants are set before us, that we thankful
    should be,

Which we of taste and feeling are, for those parts that do
    fructify in us more than he.

For as it would ill become me to be vain, indiscreet, or a
    fool,

So were there a patch set on learning, to see him in a school:
But *omne bene*, say I ; being of an old father's mind,   31
Many can brook the weather that love not the wind.

Dull. You two are book-men: can you tell me by your
    wit

What was a month old at Cain's birth, that 's not five weeks
    old as yet?

Hol. Dictynna, goodman Dull; Dictynna, goodman Dull.

Dull. What is Dictynna?

Nath. A title to Phœbe, to Luna, to the moon.

Hol. The moon was a month old when Adam was no
   more,
And raught not to five weeks when he came to five-score.
The allusion holds in the exchange.   40

Dull. 'T is true indeed; the collusion holds in the exchange.

Hol. God comfort thy capacity! I say, the allusion holds
in the exchange.

Dull. And I say, the pollusion holds in the exchange;
for the moon is never but a month old: and I say beside
that, 't was a pricket that the princess killed.

Hol. Sir Nathaniel, will you hear an extemporal epitaph
on the death of the deer? And, to humour the ignorant,
call I the deer the princess killed a pricket.

Nath. Perge, good Master Holofernes, perge; so it shall
please you to abrogate scurrility.   51

Hol. I will something affect the letter, for it argues facility.
The preyful princess pierced and prick'd a pretty pleasing
      pricket;
   Some say a sore; but not a sore, till now made sore with
      shooting.
The dogs did yell; put L to sore, then sorel jumps from
      thicket;
   Or pricket sore, or else sorel; the people fall a-hooting.
If sore be sore, then L to sore makes fifty sores one sorel.
Of one sore I an hundred make by adding but one more L.

Nath. A rare talent!

Dull. [*Aside*] If a talent be a claw, look how he claws him
with a talent.   61

Hol. This is a gift that I have, simple, simple; a foolish
extravagant spirit, full of forms, figures, shapes, objects,
ideas, apprehensions, motions, revolutions: these are begot
in the ventricle of memory, nourished in the womb of pia
mater, and delivered upon the mellowing of occasion. But

the gift is good in those in whom it is acute, and I am
thankful for it.   68

Nath. Sir, I praise the Lord for you: and so may my
parishioners; for their sons are well tutored by you, and
their daughters profit very greatly under you: you are a
good member of the commonwealth.

Hol. Mehercle, if their sons be ingenuous, they shall
want no instruction; if their daughters be capable, I will
put it to them: but vir sapit qui pauca loquitur; a soul
feminine saluteth us.

Enter JAQUENETTA *and* COSTARD

Jaq. God give you good morrow, master Parson.

Hol. Master Parson, quasi pers-on. An if one should
be pierced, which is the one?   79

Cost. Marry, master schoolmaster, he that is likest to a
hogshead.

Hol. Piercing a hogshead! a good lustre of conceit in a
turf of earth; fire enough for a flint, pearl enough for a
swine: 't is pretty; it is well.

Jaq. Good master Parson, be so good as read me this
letter: it was given me by Costard, and sent me from Don
Armado: I beseech you, read it.

Hol. Fauste, precor gelida quando pecus omne sub
umbra Ruminat,—and so forth. Ah, good old Mantuan!
I may speak of thee as the traveller doth of Venice;   90

> Venetia, Venetia,
> Chi non ti vede non ti pretia.

Old Mantuan, old Mantuan! who understandeth thee not,
loves thee not. Ut, re, sol, la, mi, fa. Under pardon, sir,
what are the contents? or rather, as Horace says in his
—What, my soul, verses?

Nath. Ay, sir, and very learned.

Hol. Let me hear a staff, a stanze, a verse; lege, domine.

Nath. [*Reads*]
If love make me forsworn, how shall I swear to love?
    Ah, never faith could hold, if not to beauty vow'd!   100
Though to myself forsworn, to thee I 'll faithful prove;
    Those thoughts to me were oaks, to thee like osiers bow'd.
Study his bias leaves and makes his book thine eyes,
    Where all those pleasures live that art would comprehend:
If knowledge be the mark, to know thee shall suffice;
    Well learned is that tongue that well can thee commend,
All ignorant that soul that sees thee without wonder;
    Which is to me some praise that I thy parts admire:
Thy eye Jove's lightning bears, thy voice his dreadful
      thunder,
    Which, not to anger bent, is music and sweet fire.   110
Celestial as thou art, O, pardon love this wrong,
That sings heaven's praise with such an earthly tongue.

Hol. You find not the apostraphas, and so miss the
accent: let me supervise the canzonet. Here are only
numbers ratified; but, for the elegancy, facility, and
golden cadence of poesy, caret. Ovidius Naso was the man:
and why, indeed, Naso, but for smelling out the odor-
iferous flowers of fancy, the jerks of invention? Imitari
is nothing: so doth the hound his master, the ape his
keeper, the tired horse his rider. But, damosella virgin,
was this directed to you?   121

Jaq. Ay, sir, from one Monsieur Biron, one of the
strange queen's lords.

Hol. I will overglance the superscript: ' To the snow-
white hand of the most beauteous Lady Rosaline.' I will
look again on the intellect of the letter, for the nomination
of the party writing to the person written unto: ' Your
ladyship's in all desired employment, BIRON.' Sir Nathaniel,
this Biron is one of the votaries with the king; and here
he hath framed a letter to a sequent of the stranger queen's,
which accidentally, or by the way of progression, hath

miscarried. Trip and go, my sweet; deliver this paper into the royal hand of the king: it may concern much. Stay not thy complement; I forgive thy duty: adieu.   134

Jaq. Good Costard, go with me. Sir, God save your life!

Cost. Have with thee, my girl.   [*Exeunt Cost. and Jaq.*

Nath. Sir, you have done this in the fear of God, very religiously; and, as a certain father saith,—

Hol. Sir, tell not me of the father; I do fear colourable colours. But to return to the verses: did they please you, Sir Nathaniel?   141

Nath. Marvellous well for the pen.

Hol. I do dine to-day at the father's of a certain pupil of mine; where, if, before repast, it shall please you to gratify the table with a grace, I will, on my privilege I have with the parents of the foresaid child or pupil, undertake your ben venuto; where I will prove those verses to be very unlearned, neither savouring of poetry, wit, nor invention: I beseech your society.

Nath. And thank you too; for society, saith the text, is the happiness of life.   151

Hol. And, certes, the text most infallibly concludes it. [*To Dull*] Sir, I do invite you too; you shall not say me nay: pauca verba. Away! the gentles are at their game, and we will to our recreation.   [*Exeunt.*

Scene III. *The same*

Enter BIRON, *with a paper*

Biron. The king he is hunting the deer; I am coursing myself: they have pitched a toil; I am toiling in a pitch, —pitch that defiles: defile! a foul word. Well, set thee down, sorrow! for so they say the fool said, and so say I, and I the fool: well proved, wit! By the Lord, this love is as mad as Ajax: it kills sheep; it kills me, I a sheep: well proved again o' my side! I will not love: if I do, hang me; i' faith, I will not. O, but her eye,—by this light, but for her eye, I would not love her; yes, for her two eyes. Well, I do nothing in the world but lie, and lie in my throat. By heaven, I do love: and it hath taught me to rhyme and to be melancholy; and here is part of my rhyme, and here my melancholy. Well, she hath one o' my sonnets already: the clown bore it, the fool sent it, and the lady hath it: sweet clown, sweeter fool, sweetest lady! By the world, I would not care a pin, if the other three were in. Here comes one with a paper: God give him grace to groan!   [*Stands aside.*

Enter the KING, *with a paper*

King. Ay me!   19
Biron. [*Aside*] Shot, by heaven! Proceed, sweet Cupid: thou hast thumped him with thy bird-bolt under the left pap. In faith, secrets!
King [*Reads*].
So sweet a kiss the golden sun gives not
  To those fresh morning drops upon the rose,
As thy eye-beams, when their fresh rays have smote
  The night of dew that on my cheeks down flows;
Nor shines the silver moon one half so bright
  Through the transparent bosom of the deep,
As doth thy face through tears of mine give light;
  Thou shinest in every tear that I do weep: 30
No drop but as a coach doth carry thee;
  So ridest thou triumphing in my woe.
Do but behold the tears that swell in me,
  And they thy glory through my grief will show:
But do not love thyself; then thou wilt keep
My tears for glasses, and still make me weep.
O queen of queens! how far dost thou excel,
No thought can think, nor tongue of mortal tell.
How shall she know my griefs? I 'll drop the paper:

Sweet leaves, shade folly. Who is he comes here?   40
[*Steps aside.*

What, Longaville! and reading! listen, ear.

Biron. Now, in thy likeness, one more fool appear!

Enter LONGAVILLE, *with a paper*

Long. Ay me, I am forsworn!

Biron. Why, he comes in like a perjure, wearing papers.

King. In love, I hope: sweet fellowship in shame!

Biron. One drunkard loves another of the name.

Long. Am I the first that have been perjured so?

Biron. I could put thee in comfort. Not by two that I
   know:

Thou makest the triumviry, the corner-cap of society,

The shape of Love's Tyburn that hangs up simplicity.   50

Long. I fear these stubborn lines lack power to move.

O sweet Maria, empress of my love!

These numbers will I tear, and write in prose.

Biron. O, rhymes are guards on wanton Cupid's hose:

Disfigure not his slop.

Long.   This same shall go.   [*Reads.*

Did not the heavenly rhetoric of thine eye,

   'Gainst whom the world cannot hold argument,

Persuade my heart to this false perjury?

   Vows for thee broke deserve not punishment.

A woman I forswore; but I will prove,   60

   Thou being a goddess, I forswore not thee:

My vow was earthly, thou a heavenly love;

   Thy grace being gain'd cures all disgrace in me.

Vows are but breath, and breath a vapour is:

   Then thou, fair sun, which on my earth dost shine,

Exhalest this vapour-vow; in thee it is:

   If broken then, it is no fault of mine:

If by me broke, what fool is not so wise

To lose an oath to win a paradise?

Biron. This is the liver-vein, which makes flesh a deity,
A green goose a goddess: pure, pure idolatry.   71
God amend us, God amend! we are much out o' the way.
  Long. By whom shall I send this?—Company! stay.

[Steps aside.

  Biron. All hid, all hid; an old infant play.
Like a demigod here sit I in the sky,
And wretched fools' secrets heedfully o'er-eye.
More sacks to the mill! O heavens, I have my wish!

Enter Dumain, with a paper

Dumain transform'd! four woodcocks in a dish!
  Dum. O most divine Kate!
  Biron. O most profane coxcomb!   80
  Dum. By heaven, the wonder in a mortal eye!
  Biron. By earth, she is not, corporal, there you lie.
  Dum. Her amber hair for foul hath amber quoted.
  Biron. An amber-colour'd raven was well noted.
  Dum. As upright as the cedar.
  Biron.   Stoop, I say;
Her shoulder is with child.
  Dum.   As fair as day.
  Biron. Ay, as some days; but then no sun must shine.
  Dum. O that I had my wish!
  Long.   And I had mine!
  King. And I mine too, good Lord!
  Biron. Amen, so I had mine: is not that a good word?
  Dum. I would forget her; but a fever she   91
Reigns in my blood and will remember'd be.
  Biron. A fever in your blood! why, then incision
Would let her out in saucers: sweet misprision!
  Dum. Once more I 'll read the ode that I have writ.
  Biron. Once more I 'll mark how love can vary wit.
  Dum. [*Reads*]
          On a day—alack the day!—

> Love, whose month is ever May,
> Spied a blossom passing fair
> Playing in the wanton air: 100
> Through the velvet leaves the wind,
> All unseen, can passage find;
> That the lover, sick to death,
> Wish himself the heaven's breath.
> Air, quoth he, thy cheeks may blow;
> Air, would I might triumph so!
> But, alack, my hand is sworn
> Ne'er to pluck thee from thy thorn;
> Vow, alack, for youth unmeet,
> Youth so apt to pluck a sweet!   110
> Do not call it sin in me,
> That I am forsworn for thee;
> Thou for whom Jove would swear
> Juno but an Ethiope were;
> And deny himself for Jove,
> Turning mortal for thy love.

This will I send and something else more plain,
That shall express my true love's fasting pain.
O, would the king, Biron, and Longaville,
Were lovers too!   Ill, to example ill,   120
Would from my forehead wipe a perjured note;
For none offend where all alike do dote.

   Long. [*Advancing*] Dumain, thy love is far from charity,
That in love's grief desirest society:
You may look pale, but I should blush, I know,
To be o'erheard and taken napping so.

   King. [*Advancing*] Come, sir, you blush; as his your case
     is such;
You chide at him, offending twice as much;
You do not love Maria; Longaville
Did never sonnet for her sake compile,   130
Nor never lay his wreathed arms athwart

His loving bosom to keep down his heart.
I have been closely shrouded in this bush
And mark'd you both and for you both did blush:
I heard your guilty rhymes, observed your fashion,
Saw sighs reek from you, noted well your passion:
Ay me! says one; O Jove! the other cries;
One, her hairs were gold, crystal the other's eyes;
[*To Long.*] You would for paradise break faith and troth;
[*To Dum.*] And Jove, for your love, would infringe an
        oath.   140
What will Biron say when that he shall hear
Faith so infringed, which such zeal did swear?
How will he scorn! how will he spend his wit!
How will he triumph, leap and laugh at it!
For all the wealth that ever I did see,
I would not have him know so much by me.
    Biron. Now step I forth to whip hypocrisy. [*Advancing.*
Ah, good my liege, I pray thee, pardon me!
Good heart, what grace hast thou, thus to reprove
These worms for loving, that art most in love?   150
Your eyes do make no coaches; in your tears
There is no certain princess that appears;
You 'll not be perjured, 't is a hateful thing;
Tush, none but minstrels like of sonneting!
But are you not ashamed? nay, are you not,
All three of you, to be thus much o'ershot?
You found his mote; the king your mote did see;
But I a beam do find in each of three.
O, what a scene of foolery have I seen,
Of sighs, of groans, of sorrow and of teen!   160
O me, with what strict patience have I sat,
To see a king transformed to a gnat!
To see great Hercules whipping a gig,
And profound Solomon to tune a jig,
And Nestor play at push-pin with the boys,

And critic Timon laugh at idle toys!
Where lies thy grief, O, tell me, good Dumain?
And, gentle Longaville, where lies thy pain?
And where my liege's? all about the breast:
A caudle, ho!
    King.   Too bitter is thy jest.   170
Are we betray'd thus to thy over-view?
    Biron. Not you to me, but I betray'd by you:
I, that am honest; I, that hold it sin
To break the vow I am engaged in;
I am betray'd, by keeping company
With men like men of inconstancy.
When shall you see me write a thing in rhyme?
Or groan for love? or spend a minute's time
In pruning me?   When shall you hear that I
Will praise a hand, a foot, a face, an eye,   180
A gait, a state, a brow, a breast, a waist,
A leg, a limb?
    King.   Soft! whither away so fast?
A true man or a thief that gallops so?
    Biron. I post from love: good lover, let me go.

Enter JAQUENETTA *and* COSTARD

    Jaq. God bless the king!
    King.   What present hast thou there?
    Cost. Some certain treason.
    King.   What makes treason here?
    Cost. Nay, it makes nothing, sir.
    King.   If it mar nothing neither,
The treason and you go in peace away together.
    Jaq. I beseech your grace, let this letter be read:
Our parson misdoubts it; 't was treason, he said.   190
    King. Biron, read it over.   [*Giving him the paper.*
Where hadst thou it?
    Jaq. Of Costard.

King. Where hadst thou it?

Cost. Of Dun Adramadio, Dun Adramadio.

[*Biron tears the letter*.

King. How now! what is in you? why dost thou tear it?

Biron. A toy, my liege, a toy: your grace needs not fear it.

Long. It did move him to passion, and therefore let's
hear it.

Dum. It is Biron's writing, and here is his name.

[*Gathering up the pieces*.

Biron. [*To Costard*] Ah, you whoreson loggerhead! you
were born to do me shame.   200

Guilty, my lord, guilty! I confess, I confess.

King. What?

Biron. That you three fools lack'd me fool to make up
the mess:

He, he, and you, and you, my liege, and I,

Are pick-purses in love, and we deserve to die.

O, dismiss this audience, and I shall tell you more.

Dum. Now the number is even.

Biron.   True, true; we are four.

Will these turtles be gone?

King.   Hence, sirs; away!

Cost. Walk aside the true folk, and let the traitors stay.

[*Exeunt Costard and Jaquenetta*.

Biron. Sweet lords, sweet lovers, O, let us embrace! 210

As true we are as flesh and blood can be:

The sea will ebb and flow, heaven show his face;

Young blood doth not obey an old decree:

We cannot cross the cause why we were born;

Therefore of all hands must we be forsworn.

King. What, did these rent lines show some love of thine?

Biron. Did they, quoth you? Who sees the heavenly
Rosaline,

That, like a rude and savage man of Ind,

At the first opening of the gorgeous east,

Bows not his vassal head and strooken blind   220
  Kisses the base ground with obedient breast?
What peremptory eagle-sighted eye
  Dares look upon the heaven of her brow,
That is not blinded by her majesty?
  King. What zeal, what fury hath inspired thee now?
My love, her mistress, is a gracious moon;
  She an attending star, scarce seen a light.
  Biron. My eyes are then no eyes, nor I Biron:
  O, but for my love, day would turn to night!
Of all complexions the cull'd sovereignty   230
  Do meet, as at a fair, in her fair cheek,
Where several worthies make one dignity,
  Where nothing wants that want itself doth seek.
Lend me the flourish of all gentle tongues,—
  Fie, painted rhetoric!   O, she needs it not:
To things of sale a seller's praise belongs,
  She passes praise; then praise too short doth blot.
A wither'd hermit, five-score winters worn,
  Might shake off fifty, looking in her eye:
Beauty doth varnish age, as if new-born,   240
  And gives the crutch the cradle's infancy:
O, 't is the sun that maketh all things shine.
  King. By heaven, thy love is black as ebony.
  Biron. Is ebony like her?   O wood divine!
A wife of such wood were felicity.
O, who can give an oath? where is a book?
  That I may swear beauty doth beauty lack,
If that she learn not of her eye to look;
  No face is fair that is not full so black.
  King. O paradox!   Black is the badge of hell,   250
  The hue of dungeons and the suit of night;
And beauty's crest becomes the heavens well.
  Biron. Devils soonest tempt, resembling spirits of light.
O, if in black my lady's brows be deck'd,

It mourns that painting and usurping hair
Should ravish doters with a false aspect;
   And therefore is she born to make black fair.
Her favour turns the fashion of the days,
   For native blood is counted painting now;
And therefore red, that would avoid dispraise,   260
   Paints itself black, to imitate her brow.

Dum. To look like her are chimney-sweepers black.

Long. And since her time are colliers counted bright.

King. And Ethiopes of their sweet complexion crack.

Dum. Dark needs no candles now, for dark is light.

Biron. Your mistresses dare never come in rain,
For fear their colours should be wash'd away.

King. 'T were good, yours did; for, sir, to tell you plain,
I 'll find a fairer face not wash'd to-day.

Biron. I 'll prove her fair, or talk till doomsday here. 270

King. No devil will fright thee then so much as she.

Dum. I never knew man hold vile stuff so dear.

Long. Look, here 's thy love: my foot and her face see.

Biron. O, if the streets were paved with thine eyes,
Her feet were much too dainty for such tread!

King. But what of this? are we not all in love?

Biron. Nothing so sure; and thereby all forsworn.

King. Then leave this chat; and, good Biron, now prove
Our loving lawful, and our faith not torn.

Dum. Ay, marry, there; some flattery for this evil.   280

Long. O, some authority how to proceed;
Some tricks, some quillets, how to cheat the devil.

Dum. Some salve for perjury.

Biron.   'T is more than need.
Have at you, then, affection's men at arms.
Consider what you first did swear unto,
To fast, to study, and to see no woman;
Flat treason 'gainst the kingly state of youth.
Say, can you fast? your stomachs are too young;

And abstinence engenders maladies.
And where that you have vow'd to study, lords,   290
In that each of you have forsworn his book,
Can you still dream and pore and thereon look?
For when would you, my lord, or you, or you,
Have found the ground of study's excellence
Without the beauty of a woman's face?
[From women's eyes this doctrine I derive;
They are the ground, the books, the academes
From whence doth spring the true Promethean fire.]
Why, universal plodding poisons up
The nimble spirits in the arteries,   300
As motion and long-during action tires
The sinewy vigour of the traveller.
Now, for not looking on a woman's face,
You have in that forsworn the use of eyes
And study too, the causer of your vow;
For where is any author in the world,
Teaches such beauty as a woman's eye?
Learning is but an adjunct to ourself
And where we are our learning likewise is:
Then when ourselves we see in ladies' eyes,   310
Do we not likewise see our learning there?
O, we have made a vow to study, lords,
And in that vow we have forsworn our books.
For when would you, my liege, or you, or you,
In leaden contemplation have found out
Such fiery numbers as the prompting eyes
Of beauty's tutors have enrich'd you with?
Other slow arts entirely keep the brain;
And therefore, finding barren practisers,
Scarce show a harvest of their heavy toil: 320
But love, first learned in a lady's eyes,
Lives not alone immured in the brain;
But, with the motion of all elements,

Courses as swift as thought in every power,
And gives to every power a double power,
Above their functions and their offices.
It adds a precious seeing to the eye;
A lover's eyes will gaze an eagle blind;
A lover's ear will hear the lowest sound,
When the suspicious head of theft is stopp'd:　　　330
Love's feeling is more soft and sensible
Than are the tender horns of cockled snails;
Love's tongue proves dainty Bacchus gross in taste:
For valour, is not Love a Hercules,
Still climbing trees in the Hesperides?
Subtle as Sphinx; as sweet and musical
As bright Apollo's lute, strung with his hair;
And when Love speaks, the voice of all the gods
Make heaven drowsy with the harmony.
Never durst poet touch a pen to write　　　340
Until his ink were temper'd with Love's sighs;
O, then his lines would ravish savage ears
And plant in tyrants mild humility.
From women's eyes this doctrine I derive:
They sparkle still the right Promethean fire;
They are the books, the arts, the academes,
That show, contain and nourish all the world:
Else none at all in aught proves excellent.
Then fools you were these women to forswear,
Or keeping what is sworn, you will prove fools.　　　350
For wisdom's sake, a word that all men love,
Or for love's sake, a word that loves all men,
Or for men's sake, the authors of these women,
Or women's sake, by whom we men are men,
Let us once lose our oaths to find ourselves,
Or else we lose ourselves to keep our oaths.
It is religion to be thus forsworn,
For charity itself fulfils the law,

And who can sever love from charity?

    King. Saint Cupid, then! and, soldiers, to the field! 360

    Biron. Advance your standards, and upon them, lords;
Peli-mell, down with them! but be first advised,
In conflict that you get the sun of them.

    Long. Now to plain-dealing; lay these glozes by:
Shall we resolve to woo these girls of France?

    King. And win them too: therefore let us devise
Some entertainment for them in their tents.

    Biron. First, from the park let us conduct them thither;
Then homeward every man attach the hand
Of his fair mistress: in the afternoon   370
We will with some strange pastime solace them,
Such as the shortness of the time can shape;
For revels, dances, masks and merry hours
Forerun fair Love, strewing her way with flowers.

    King. Away, away! no time shall be omitted
That will betime, and may by us be fitted.

    Biron. Allons! allons! Sow'd cockle reap'd no corn;
And justice always whirls in equal measure:
Light wenches may prove plagues to men forsworn;
If so, our copper buys no better treasure. [*Exeunt.* 380

ACT V

SCENE I. *The same*

Enter HOLOFERNES, SIR NATHANIEL, *and* DULL

    Hol. Satis quod sufficit.

    Nath. I praise God for you, sir: your reasons at dinner
have been sharp and sententious: pleasant without scurrility,
witty without affection, audacious without impudency,
learned without opinion, and strange without heresy. I
did converse this quondam day with a companion of the

king's, who is intituled, nominated, or called, Don Adriano
de Armado.

Hol. Novi hominem tanquam te: his humour is lofty,
his discourse peremptory, his tongue filed, his eye ambitious,
his gait majestical, and his general behaviour vain, ridiculous, and thrasonical. He is too picked, too spruce, too
affected, too odd, as it were, too peregrinate, as I may call it.

Nath. A most singular and choice epithet.   14

                      [Draws out his table-book.

Hol. He draweth out the thread of his verbosity finer
than the staple of his argument. I abhor such fanatical
phantasimes, such insociable and point-devise companions; such rackers of orthography, as to speak dout,
fine, when he should say doubt; det, when he should pronounce debt,—d, e, b, t, not d, e, t: he clepeth a calf,
cauf; half, hauf; neighbour vocatur nebour; neigh abbre-
viated ne. This is abhominable,—which he would call
abbominable: it insinuateth me of insanie: anne intelligis,
domine? to make frantic, lunatic.   24

Nath. Laus Deo, bene intelligo.

Hol. Bon, bon, fort bon! Priscian a little scratched, 't will
serve.

Nath. Videsne quis venit?

Hol. Video, et gaudeo.

           Enter ARMADO, MOTH, *and* COSTARD

Arm. Chirrah!   *[To Moth.* 30

Hol. Quare chirrah, not sirrah?

Arm. Men of peace, well encountered.

Hol. Most military sir, salutation.

Moth. [*Aside to Costard*] They have been at a great feast
of languages, and stolen the scraps.

Cost. O, they have lived long on the alms-basket of
words. I marvel thy master hath not eaten thee for a
word; for thou art not so long by the head as honorifi-

cabilitudinitatibus: thou art easier swallowed than a flap-
dragon.   40

Moth. Peace! the peal begins.

Arm. [*To Hol.*] Monsieur, are you not lettered?

Moth. Yes, yes; he teaches boys the horn-book. What
is a, b, spelt backward, with the horn on his head?

Hol. Ba, pueritia, with a horn added.

Moth. Ba, most silly sheep with a horn. You hear his
learning.

Hol. Quis, quis, thou consonant?

Moth. The third of the five vowels, if you repeat them;
or the fifth, if I.   50

Hol. I will repeat them,—a, e, i,—

Moth. The sheep: the other two concludes it,—o, u.

Arm. Now, by the salt wave of the Mediterraneum, a
sweet touch, a quick venue of wit! snip, snap, quick and
home! it rejoiceth my intellect: true wit!

Moth. Offered by a child to an old man; which is wit-old.

Hol. What is the figure? what is the figure?

Moth. Horns.

Hol. Thou disputest like an infant: go, whip thy gig.   59

Moth. Lend me your horn to make one, and I will
whip about your infamy circum circa,—a gig of a cuckold's
horn.

Cost. An I had but one penny in the world, thou shouldst
have it to buy gingerbread: hold, there is the very remuneration I had of thy master, thou halfpenny purse of wit,
thou pigeon-egg of discretion. O, an the heavens were so
pleased that thou wert but my bastard, what a joyful
father wouldst thou make me! Go to: thou hast it ad dunghill, at the fingers' ends, as they say.

Hol. O, I smell false Latin; dunghill for unguem.   70

Arm. Arts-man, preambulate, we will be singuled from
the barbarous. Do you not educate youth at the charge-
house on the top of the mountain?

Hol. Or mons, the hill.

Arm. At your sweet pleasure, for the mountain.

Hol. I do, sans question.

Arm. Sir, it is the king's most sweet pleasure and affection to congratulate the princess at her pavilion in the posteriors of this day, which the rude multitude call the afternoon.   80

Hol. The posterior of the day, most generous sir, is liable, congruent and measurable for the afternoon: the word is well culled, chose, sweet and apt, I do assure you, sir, I do assure.

Arm. Sir, the king is a noble gentleman, and my familiar, I do assure ye, very good friend: for what is inward between us, let it pass. I do beseech thee, remember thy courtesy; I beseech thee, apparel thy head: and among other important and most serious designs, and of great import indeed, too, but let that pass: for I must tell thee, it will please his grace, by the world, sometime to lean upon my poor shoulder, and with his royal finger, thus, dally with my excrement, with my mustachio; but, sweet heart, let that pass. By the world, I recount no fable: some certain special honours it pleaseth his greatness to impart to Armado, a soldier, a man of travel, that hath seen the world; but let that pass. The very all of all is,—but, sweet heart, I do implore secrecy,—that the king would have me present the princess, sweet chuck, with some delightful ostentation, or show, or pageant, or antique, or firework. Now, understanding that the curate and your sweet self are good at such eruptions and sudden breaking out of mirth, as it were, I have acquainted you withal, to the end to crave your assistance.   104

Hol. Sir, you shall present before her the Nine Worthies. Sir, as concerning some entertainment of time, some show in the posterior of this day, to be rendered by our assistants, at the king's command, and this most gallant,

illustrate, and learned gentleman, before the princess; I
say none so fit as to present the Nine Worthies.   110

Nath. Where will you find men worthy enough to present
them?

Hol. Joshua, yourself; myself and this gallant gentleman, Judas Maccabæus; this swain, because of his great
limb or joint, shall pass Pompey the Great; the page,
Hercules,—

Arm. Pardon, sir; error: he is not quantity enough for
that Worthy's thumb: he is not so big as the end of his
club.   119

Hol. Shall I have audience? he shall present Hercules
in minority: his enter and exit shall be strangling a snake;
and I will have an apology for that purpose.

Moth. An excellent device! so, if any of the audience
hiss, you may cry ' Well done, Hercules! now thou crushest
the snake!' that is the way to make an offence gracious,
though few have the grace to do it.

Arm. For the rest of the Worthies?—

Hol. I will play three myself.

Moth. Thrice-worthy gentleman!

Arm. Shall I tell you a thing?   130

Hol. We attend.

Arm. We will have, if this fadge not, an antique. I
beseech you, follow.

Hol. Via, goodman Dull! thou hast spoken no word all
this while.

Dull. Nor understood none neither, sir.

Hol. Allons! we will employ thee.

Dull. I 'll make one in a dance, or so; or I will play
On the tabor to the Worthies, and let them dance the hay.

Hol. Most dull, honest Dull! To our sport, away!   140
                                                    [*Exeunt.*

Scene II. *The same*

Enter the Princess, Katharine, Rosaline, *and* Maria

Prin. Sweet hearts, we shall be rich ere we depart,
If fairings come thus plentifully in:
A lady wall'd about with diamonds!
Look you what I have from the loving king.

Ros. Madame, came nothing else along with that?

Prin. Nothing but this! yes, as much love in rhyme
As would be cramm'd up in a sheet of paper,
Writ o' both sides the leaf, margent and all,
That he was fain to seal on Cupid's name.

Ros. That was the way to make his godhead wax,   10
For he hath been five thousand years a boy.

Kath. Ay, and a shrewd unhappy gallows too.

Ros. You 'll ne'er be friends with him; a' kill'd your
        sister.

Kath. He made her melancholy, sad, and heavy;
And so she died: had she been light, like you,
Of such a merry, nimble, stirring spirit,
She might ha' been a grandam ere she died:
And so may you; for a light heart lives long.

Ros. What 's your dark meaning, mouse, of this light
        word?

Kath. A light condition in a beauty dark.   20

Ros. We need more light to find your meaning out.

Kath. You 'll mar the light by taking it in snuff;
Therefore I 'll darkly end the argument.

Ros. Look, what you do, you do it still i' the dark.

Kath. So do not you, for you are a light wench.

Ros. Indeed I weigh not you, and therefore light.

Kath. You weigh me not? O, that 's you care not for me.

Ros. Great reason; for ' past cure is still past care '.

Prin. Well bandied both; a set of wit well play'd.
But, Rosaline, you have a favour too: 30
Who sent it? and what is it?
   Ros.   I would you knew:
An if my face were but as fair as yours,
My favour were as great; be witness this.
Nay, I have verses too, I thank Biron:
The numbers true; and, were the numbering too,
I were the fairest goddess on the ground:
I am compared to twenty thousand fairs.
O, he hath drawn my picture in his letter!
   Prin. Any thing like?
   Ros. Much in the letters; nothing in the praise.   40
   Prin. Beauteous as ink; a good conclusion.
   Kath. Fair as a text B in a copy-book.
   Ros. 'Ware pencils, ho! let me not die your debtor,
My red dominical, my golden letter:
O that your face were not so full of O's!
   Kath. A pox of that jest! and I beshrew all shrows.
   Prin. But, Katharine, what was sent to you from fair
    Dumain?
   Kath. Madam, this glove.
   Prin.   Did he not send you twain?
   Kath. Yes, madam, and moreover
Some thousand verses of a faithful lover,   50
A huge translation of hypocrisy,
Vilely compiled, profound simplicity.
   Mar. This and these pearls to me sent Longaville:
The letter is too long by half a mile.
   Prin. I think no less. Dost thou not wish in heart
The chain were longer and the letter short?
   Mar. Ay, or I would these hands might never part.
   Prin. We are wise girls to mock our lovers so.
   Ros. They are worse fools to purchase mocking so.
That same Biron I 'll torture ere I go: 60

O that I knew he were but in by the week!
How I would make him fawn and beg and seek
And wait the season and observe the times
And spend his prodigal wits in bootless rhymes
And shape his service wholly to my hests
And make him proud to make me proud that jests!
So perttaunt-like would I o'ersway his state
That he should be my fool and I his fate.

   Prin. None are so surely caught, when they are catch'd,
As wit turn'd fool: folly, in wisdom hatch'd,   70
Hath wisdom's warrant and the help of school
And wit's own grace to grace a learned fool.

   Ros. The blood of youth burns not with such excess
As gravity's revolt to wantonness.

   Mar. Folly in fools bears not so strong a note
As foolery in the wise, when wit doth dote;
Since all the power thereof it doth apply
To prove, by wit, worth in simplicity.

   Prin. Here comes Boyet, and mirth is in his face.   79

Enter BOYET

   Boyet. O, I am stabb'd with laughter! Where 's her
grace?

   Prin. Thy news, Boyet?

   Boyet.   Prepare, madam, prepare!
Arm, wenches, arm! encounters mounted are
Against your peace: Love doth approach disguised,
Armed in arguments; you 'll be surprised:
Muster your wits; stand in your own defence;
Or hide your heads like cowards, and fly hence.

   Prin. Saint Denis to Saint Cupid! What are they
That charge their breath against us? say, scout, say.

   Boyet. Under the cool shade of a sycamore
I thought to close mine eyes some half an hour;   90
When, lo! to interrupt my purposed rest,

Toward that shade I might behold addrest
The king and his companions: warily
I stole into a neighbour thicket by,
And overheard what you shall overhear;
That, by and by, disguised they will be here.
Their herald is a pretty knavish page,
That well by heart hath conn'd his embassage:
Action and accent did they teach him there;
' Thus must thou speak,' and ' thus thy body bear:'   100
And ever and anon they made a doubt
Presence majestical would put him out;
' For,' quoth the king, ' an angel shalt thou see;
Yet fear not thou, but speak audaciously.'
The boy replied, ' An angel is not evil;
I should have fear'd her had she been a devil.'
With that, all laugh'd and clapp'd him on the shoulder,
Making the bold wag by their praises bolder:
One rubb'd his elbow thus, and fleer'd and swore
A better speech was never spoke before;   110
Another, with his finger and his thumb,
Cried, ' Via! we will do 't, come what will come;'
The third he caper'd, and cried, ' All goes well;'
The fourth turn'd on the toe, and down he fell.
With that, they all did tumble on the ground,
With such a zealous laughter, so profound,
That in this spleen ridiculous appears,
To check their folly, passion's solemn tears.
   Prin. But what, but what, come they to visit us?
   Boyet. They do, they do; and are apparell'd thus,   120
Like Muscovites or Russians, as I guess.
Their purpose is to parle, to court and dance;
And every one his love-feat will advance
Unto his several mistress, which they 'll know
By favours several which they did bestow.
   Prin. And will they so? the gallants shall be task'd;

For, ladies, we will every one be mask'd;
And not a man of them shall have the grace,
Despite of suit, to see a lady's face.
Hold, Rosaline, this favour thou shalt wear,   130
And then the king will court thee for his dear;
Hold, take thou this, my sweet, and give me thine,
So shall Biron take me for Rosaline.
And change you favours too; so shall your loves
Woo contrary, deceived by these removes.
   Ros. Come on, then; wear the favours most in sight.
   Kath. But in this changing what is your intent?
   Prin. The effect of my intent is to cross theirs:
They do it but in mocking merriment;
And mock for mock is only my intent.   140
Their several counsels they unbosom shall
To loves mistook, and so be mock'd withal
Upon the next occasion that we meet,
With visages display'd, to talk and greet.
   Ros. But shall we dance, if they desire us to 't?
   Prin. No, to the death, we will not move a foot;
Nor to their penn'd speech render we no grace,
But while 't is spoke each turn away her face.
   Boyet. Why, that contempt will kill the speaker's
      heart,
And quite divorce his memory from his part.   150
   Prin. Therefore I do it; and I make no doubt
The rest will ne'er come in, if he be out.
There 's no such sport as sport by sport o'erthrown,
To make theirs ours and ours none but our own:
So shall we stay, mocking intended game,
And they, well mock'd, depart away with shame.
                   [Trumpets sound within.
   Boyet. The trumpet sounds: be mask'd; the maskers
      come.   *[The Ladies mask.*

Enter Blackamoors with music; MOTH; *the* KING,
BIRON, LONGAVILLE, *and* DUMAIN, *in Russian
habits, and masked*

Moth. All hail, the richest beauties on the earth!—
Boyet. Beauties no richer than rich taffeta.
Moth. A holy parcel of the fairest dames   160
                              [*The Ladies turn their backs to him.*
That ever turn'd their—backs—to mortal views!
  Biron. [*Aside to Moth*] Their eyes, villain, their eyes.
  Moth. That ever turn'd their eyes to mortal views!—
Out—
  Boyet. True; out indeed.
  Moth. Out of your favours, heavenly spirits, vouchsafe
Not to behold—
  Biron. [*Aside to Moth*] Once to behold, rogue.
  Moth. Once to behold with your sun-beamed eyes,
——with your sun-beamed eyes—   170
  Boyet. They will not answer to that epithet;
You were best call it ' daughter-beamed eyes '.
  Moth. They do not mark me, and that brings me out.
  Biron. Is this your perfectness? be gone, you rogue!
                                    [*Exit Moth.*
  Ros. What would these strangers? know their minds,
      Boyet:
If they do speak our language, 't is our will
That some plain man recount their purposes:
Know what they would.
  Boyet. What would you with the princess?
  Biron. Nothing but peace and gentle visitation.   180
  Ros. What would they, say they?
  Boyet. Nothing but peace and gentle visitation.
  Ros. Why, that they have; and bid them so be gone.
  Boyet. She says, you have it, and you may be gone.
  King. Say to her, we have measured many miles
To tread a measure with her on this grass.

Boyet. They say, that they have measured many a mile
To tread a measure with you on this grass.

Ros. It is not so.   Ask them how many inches
Is in one mile: if they have measured many,   190
The measure then of one is easily told.

Boyet. If to come hither you have measured miles,
And many miles, the princess bids you tell
How many inches doth fill up one mile.

Biron. Tell her, we measure them by weary steps.

Boyet. She hears herself.

Ros.   How many weary steps,
Of many weary miles you have o'ergone,
Are number'd in the travel of one mile?

Biron. We number nothing that we spend for you:
Our duty is so rich, so infinite,   200
That we may do it still without accompt.
Vouchsafe to show the sunshine of your face,
That we, like savages, may worship it

Ros. My face is but a moon, and clouded too.

King. Blessed are clouds, to do as such clouds do!
Vouchsafe, bright moon, and these thy stars, to shine,
Those clouds removed, upon our watery eyne.

Ros. O vain petitioner! beg a greater matter;
Thou now request'st but moonshine in the water.

King. Then, in our measure do but vouchsafe one change.
Thou bid'st me beg: this begging is not strange.   211

Ros. Play, music, then!   Nay, you must do it soon.

[*Music plays.*

Not yet! no dance! Thus change I like the moon.

King. Will you not dance? How come you thus estranged?

Ros. You took the moon at full, but now she's changed.

King. Yet still she is the moon, and I the man.
The music plays; vouchsafe some motion to it.

Ros. Our ears vouchsafe it.

King.   But your legs should do it.

Ros. Since you are strangers and come here by chance,
We 'll not be nice: take hands. We will not dance. 220
    King. Why take we hands, then?
    Ros.   Only to part friends:
Curtsy, sweet hearts; and so the measure ends.
    King. More measure of this measure; be not nice.
    Ros. We can afford no more at such a price.
    King. Prize you yourselves: what buys your company?
    Ros. Your absence only.
    King.   That can never be.
    Ros. Then cannot we be bought: and so, adieu;
Twice to your visor, and half once to you.
    King. If you deny to dance, let 's hold more chat.
    Ros. In private, then.
    King.   I am best pleased with that. 230
                       [They converse apart.
    Biron. White-handed mistress, one sweet word with thee.
    Prin. Honey, and milk, and sugar; there is three.
    Biron. Nay then, two treys, and if you grow so nice,
Metheglin, wort, and malmsey: well run, dice!
There 's half-a-dozen sweets.
    Prin.   Seventh sweet, adieu:
Since you can cog, I 'll play no more with you.
    Biron. One word in secret.
    Prin.   Let it not be sweet.
    Biron. Thou grievest my gall.
    Prin.   Gall! bitter.
    Biron.   Therefore meet.
                       [They converse apart.
    Dum. Will you vouchsafe with me to change a word?
    Mar. Name it.
    Dum.   Fair lady,—
    Mar.   Say you so? Fair lord,—
Take that for your fair lady.
    Dum.   Please it you, 241

As much in private, and I 'll bid adieu.

                                             [They converse apart.

  Kath. What, was your vizard made without a tongue?

  Long. I know the reason, lady, why you ask.

  Kath. O for your reason! quickly, sir; I long.

  Long. You have a double tongue within your mask,
And would afford my speechless vizard half.

  Kath. Veal, quoth the Dutchman. Is not ' veal ' a calf?

  Long. A calf, fair lady!

  Kath.   No, a fair lord calf.

  Long. Let 's part the word.

  Kath.   No, I 'll not be your half:
Take all, and wean it; it may prove an ox.   251

  Long. Look, how you butt yourself in these sharp mocks!
Will you give horns, chaste lady? do not so.

  Kath. Then die a calf, before your horns do grow.

  Long. One word in private with you, ere I die.

  Kath. Bleat softly then; the butcher hears you cry.

                                        [They converse apart.

  Boyet. The tongues of mocking wenches are as keen
As is the razor's edge invisible,
Cutting a smaller hair than may be seen,
Above the sense of sense; so sensible   260
Seemeth their conference; their conceits have wings
Fleeter than arrows, bullets, wind, thought, swifter things.

  Ros. Not one word more, my maids; break off, break off.

  Biron. By heaven, all dry-beaten with pure scoff!

  King. Farewell, mad wenches; you have simple wits.

  Prin. Twenty adieus, my frozen Muscovits.

                 [Exeunt King, Lords, and Blackamoors.
Are these the breed of wits so wonder'd at?

  Boyet. Tapers they are, with your sweet breaths puff'd
    out.

  Ros. Well-liking wits they have; gross, gross; fat, fat.

  Prin. O poverty in wit, kingly-poor flout!   270

Will they not, think you, hang themselves to-night?
  Or ever, but in vizards, show their faces?
This pert Biron was out of countenance quite.
  Ros. O, they were all in lamentable cases!
The king was weeping-ripe for a good word.
  Prin. Biron did swear himself out of all suit.
  Mar. Dumain was at my service, and his sword:
No point, quoth I; my servant straight was mute.
  Kath. Lord Longaville said, I came o'er his heart;
And trow you what he call'd me?
  Prin.   Qualm, perhaps.   280
  Kath. Yes, in good faith.
  Prin.   Go, sickness as thou art!
  Ros. Well, better wits have worn plain statute-caps.
But will you hear? the king is my love sworn.
  Prin. And quick Biron hath plighted faith to me.
  Kath. And Longaville was for my service born.
  Mar. Dumain is mine, as sure as bark on tree.
  Boyet. Madam, and pretty mistresses, give ear:
Immediately they will again be here
In their own shapes; for it can never be
They will digest this harsh indignity.   290
  Prin. Will they return?
  Boyet.   They will, they will, God knows,
And leap for joy, though they are lame with blows:
Therefore change favours; and, when they repair,
Blow like sweet roses in this summer air.
  Prin. How blow? how blow? speak to be understood.
  Boyet. Fair ladies mask'd are roses in their bud;
Dismask'd, their damask sweet commixture shown,
Are angels vailing clouds, or roses blown.
  Prin. Avaunt, perplexity! What shall we do,
If they return in their own shapes to woo?   300
  Ros. Good madam, if by me you 'll be advised,
Let 's mock them still, as well known as disguised:

Let us complain to them what fools were here,
Disguised like Muscovites, in shapeless gear;
And wonder what they were and to what end
Their shallow shows and prologue vilely-penn'd
And their rough carriage so ridiculous,
Should be presented at our tent to us.
   Boyet. Ladies, withdraw: the gallants are at hand.
   Prin. Whip to our tents, as roes run o'er land.   310
      [*Exeunt Princess, Rosaline, Katharine, and Maria.*

   Re-enter the KING, BIRON, LONGAVILLE, *and*
      DUMAIN, *in their proper habits*

   King. Fair sir, God save you! Where 's the princess?
   Boyet. Gone to her tent. Please it your majesty
Command me any service to her thither?
   King. That she vouchsafe me audience for one word.
   Boyet. I will; and so will she, I know, my lord.   [*Exit.*
   Biron. This fellow pecks up wit as pigeons pease,
And utters it again when God doth please:
He is wit's pedler, and retails his wares
At wakes and wassails, meetings, markets, fairs;
And we that sell by gross, the Lord doth know,   320
Have not the grace to grace it with such show.
This gallant pins the wenches on his sleeve;
Had he been Adam, he had tempted Eve;
A' can carve too, and lisp: why, this is he
That kiss'd his hand away in courtesy;
This is the ape of form, monsieur the nice,
That, when he plays at tables, chides the dice
In honourable terms: nay, he can sing
A mean most meanly; and in ushering
Mend him who can: the ladies call him sweet;   330
The stairs, as he treads on them, kiss his feet:
This is the flower that smiles on every one,
To show his teeth as white as whale's bone;

And consciences, that will not die in debt,
Pay him the due of honey-tongued Boyet.
   King. A blister on his sweet tongue, with my heart,
That put Armado's page out of his part!
   Biron. See where it comes! Behaviour, what wert thou
Till this madman show'd thee? and what art thou now?

       Re-enter the PRINCESS, *ushered by* BOYET;
         ROSALINE, MARIA, *and* KATHARINE

   King. All hail, sweet madam, and fair time of day!   340
   Prin. ' Fair ' in ' all hail ' is foul, as I conceive.
   King. Construe my speeches better, if you may.
   Prin. Then wish me better; I will give you leave.
   King. We came to visit you, and purpose now
To lead you to our court; vouchsafe it then.
   Prin. This field shall hold me; and so hold your vow;
Nor God, nor I, delights in perjured men.
   King. Rebuke me not for that which you provoke:
The virtue of your eye must break my oath.   349
   Prin. You nickname virtue: vice you should have spoke;
For virtue's office never breaks men's troth.
Now by my maiden honour, yet as pure
  As the unsullied lily, I protest,
A world of torments though I should endure,
  I would not yield to be your house's guest;
So much I hate a breaking cause to be
Of heavenly oaths, vow'd with integrity.
   King. O, you have lived in desolation here,
Unseen, unvisited, much to our shame.
   Prin. Not so, my lord; it is not so, I swear;   360
We have had pastimes here and pleasant game:
A mess of Russians left us but of late.
   King. How, madam! Russians!
   Prin.   Ay, in truth, my lord;
Trim gallants, full of courtship and of state.

Ros. Madam, speak true. It is not so, my lord:
My lady, to the manner of the days,
In courtesy gives undeserving praise.
We four indeed confronted were with four
In Russian habit: here they stay'd an hour,
And talk'd apace; and in that hour, my lord,   370
They did not bless us with one happy word.
I dare not call them fools; but this I think,
When they are thirsty, fools would fain have drink.

Biron. This jest is dry to me. Fair gentle sweet,
Your wit makes wise things foolish: when we greet,
With eyes best seeing, heaven's fiery eye,
By light we lose light: your capacity
Is of that nature that to your huge store
Wise things seem foolish and rich things but poor.

Ros. This proves you wise and rich, for in my eye,—
Biron. I am a fool, and full of poverty.   381
Ros. But that you take what doth to you belong,
It were a fault to snatch words from my tongue.
Biron. O, I am yours, and all that I possess!
Ros. All the fool mine?
Biron.   I cannot give you less.
Ros. Which of the vizards was it that you wore?
Biron. Where? when? what vizard? why demand you
      this?
Ros. There, then, that vizard; that superfluous case
That hid the worse and show'd the better face.
King. We are descried; they 'll mock us now downright.
Dum. Let us confess and turn it to a jest.   391
Prin. Amazed, my lord? why looks your highness sad?
Ros. Help, hold his brows! he 'll swoon! Why look you
      pale?
Sea-sick, I think, coming from Muscovy.
Biron. Thus pour the stars down plagues for perjury.
Can any face of brass hold longer out?

Here stand I: lady, dart thy skill at me;
  Bruise me with scorn, confound me with a flout;
Thrust thy sharp wit quite through my ignorance;
  Cut me to pieces with thy keen conceit;   400
And I will wish thee never more to dance,
  Nor never more in Russian habit wait.
O, never will I trust to speeches penn'd,
  Nor to the motion of a schoolboy's tongue,
Nor never come in vizard to my friend,
  Nor woo in rhyme, like a blind harper's song!
Taffeta phrases, silken terms precise,
  Three-piled hyperboles, spruce affectation,
Figures pedantical; these summer-flies
  Have blown me full of maggot ostentation: 410
I do forswear them; and I here protest,
  By this white glove,—how white the hand, God knows!—
Henceforth my wooing mind shall be express'd
  In russet yeas and honest kersey noes:
And, to begin, wench,—so God help me, la!—
My love to thee is sound, sans crack or flaw.
  Ros. Sans sans, I pray you.
  Biron.   Yet I have a trick
Of the old rage: bear with me, I am sick;
I 'll leave it by degrees.   Soft, let us see:
Write, ' Lord have mercy on us ' on those three;   420
They are infected; in their hearts it lies;
They have the plague, and caught it of your eyes;
These lords are visited; you are not free,
For the Lord's tokens on you do I see.
  Prin. No, they are free that gave these tokens to us.
  Biron. Our states are forfeit: seek not to undo us.
  Ros. It is not so; for how can this be true,
That you stand forfeit, being those that sue?
  Biron. Peace! for I will not have to do with you.
  Ros. Nor shall not, if I do as I intend.   430

Biron. Speak for yourselves; my wit is at an end.

King. Teach us, sweet madam, for our rude transgression
Some fair excuse.

Prin.   The fairest is confession.
Were not you here but even now disguised?

King. Madam, I was.

Prin.   And were you well advised?

King. I was, fair madam.

Prin.   When you then were here,
What did you whisper in your lady's ear?

King. That more than all the world I did respect her.

Prin. When she shall challenge this, you will reject her.

King. Upon mine honour, no.

Prin.   Peace, peace! forbear:
Your oath once broke, you force not to forswear.   441

King. Despise me, when I break this oath of mine.

Prin. I will: and therefore keep it.   Rosaline,
What did the Russian whisper in your ear?

Ros. Madam, he swore that he did hold me dear
As precious eyesight, and did value me
Above this world; adding thereto moreover
That he would wed me, or else die my lover.

Prin. God give thee joy of him! the noble lord
Most honourably doth uphold his word.   450

King. What mean you, madam? by my life, my troth,
I never swore this lady such an oath.

Ros. By heaven, you did; and to confirm it plain,
You gave me this: but take it, sir, again.

King. My faith and this the princess I did give:
I knew her by this jewel on her sleeve.

Prin. Pardon me, sir, this jewel did she wear;
And Lord Biron, I thank him, is my dear.
What, will you have me, or your pearl again?

Biron. Neither of either; I remit both twain.   460
I see the trick on 't; here was a consent,

Knowing aforehand of our merriment,
To dash it like à Christmas comedy:
Some carry-tale, some please-man, some slight zany,
Some mumble-news, some trencher-knight, some Dick,
That smiles his cheek in years and knows the trick
To make my lady laugh when she 's disposed,
Told our intents before; which once disclosed,
The ladies did change favours: and then we,
Following the signs, woo'd but the sign of she.   470
Now, to our perjury to add more terror,
We are again forsworn, in will and error.
Much upon this it is: and might not you   [*To Boyet.*
Forestall our sport, to make us thus untrue?
Do not you know my lady's foot by the squier,
     And laugh upon the apple of her eye?
And stand between her back, sir, and the fire,
     Holding a trencher, jesting merrily?
You put our page out: go, you are allow'd;
Die when you will, a smock shall be your shroud.   480
You leer upon me, do you? there 's an eye
Wounds like a leaden sword.
     Boyet.   Full merrily
Hath this brave manage, this career, been run.
     Biron. Lo, he is tilting straight! Peace! I have done.

Enter COSTARD

Welcome, pure wit! thou partest a fair fray.
     Cost. O Lord, sir, they would know
Whether the three Worthies shall come in or no.
     Biron. What, are there but three?
     Cost.   No, sir; but it is vara fine,
For every one pursents three.
     Biron.   And three times thrice is nine.
     Cost. Not so, sir; under correction, sir; I hope it is not
     so.   490

You cannot beg us, sir, I can assure you, sir; we know
    what we know:
I hope, sir, three times thrice, sir,—

    Biron. Is not nine.

    Cost, Under correction, sir, we know whereuntil it doth
amount.

    Biron. By Jove, I always took three threes for nine.

    Cost. O Lord, sir, it were pity you should get your living
    by reckoning, sir.

    Biron. How much is it?   499

    Cost. O Lord, sir, the parties themselves, the actors, sir,
will show whereuntil it doth amount: for mine own part,
I am, as they say, but to parfect one man in one poor man,
Pompion the Great, sir.

    Biron. Art thou one of the Worthies?

    Cost. It pleased them to think me worthy of Pompion
the Great: for mine own part, I know not the degree of
the Worthy, but I am to stand for him.

    Biron. Go, bid them prepare.

    Cost. We will turn it finely off, sir; we will take some
    care.   [*Exit*. 509

    King. Biron, they will shame us: let them not approach.

    Biron. We are shame-proof, my lord: and 't is some
    policy
To have one show worse than the king's and his com-
    pany.

    King. I say they shall not come.

    Prin. Nay, my good lord, let me o'errule you now:
That sport best pleases that doth least know how:
Where zeal strives to content, and the contents
Dies in the zeal of that which it presents:
Their form confounded makes most form in mirth,
When great things labouring perish in their birth.

    Biron. A right description of our sport, my lord.   520

Enter ARMADO

Arm. Anointed, I implore so much expense of thy royal sweet breath as will utter a brace of words.

[*Converses apart with the King, and delivers him a paper.*

Prin. Doth this man serve God?

Biron. Why ask you?

Prin. He speaks not like a man of God's making.

Arm. That is all one, my fair, sweet, honey monarch; for, I protest, the schoolmaster is exceeding fantastical; too too vain, too too vain: but we will put it, as they say, to fortuna de la guerra. I wish you the peace of mind, most royal couplement! [*Exit.* 530

King. Here is like to be a good presence of Worthies. He presents Hector of Troy; the swain, Pompey the Great; the parish curate, Alexander; Armado's page, Hercules; the pedant, Judas Maccabæus:
And if these four Worthies in their first show thrive,
These four will change habits, and present the other five.

Biron. There is five in the first show.

King. You are deceived; 't is not so.

Biron. The pedant, the braggart, the hedge-priest, the fool and the boy:— 540
Abate throw at novum, and the whole world again
Cannot pick out five such, take each one in his vein.

King. The ship is under sail, and here she comes amain.

Enter COSTARD, *for Pompey*

Cost. I Pompey am,—

Boyet. You lie, you are not he.

Cost. I Pompey am,—

Boyet. With libbard's head on knee.

Biron. Well said, old mocker: I must needs be friends with thee.

Cost. I Pompey am, Pompey surnamed the Big,—

Dum. The Great.

Cost. It is, ' Great ', sir:—

Pompey surnamed the Great;

That oft in field, with targe and shield, did make my foe
    to sweat: 550

And travelling along this coast, I here am come by chance,

And lay my arms before the legs of this sweet lass of
    France.

If your ladyship would say, ' Thanks, Pompey,' I had done.

Prin. Great thanks, great Pompey.

Cost. 'T is not so much worth; but I hope I was perfect:
I made a little fault in ' Great '.

Biron. My hat to a halfpenny, Pompey proves the best
Worthy.

      Enter Sir Nathaniel, *for Alexander*

Nath. When in the world I lived, I was the world's
    commander;

By east, west, north, and south, I spread my conquering
    might: 560

My scutcheon plain declares that I am Alisander,—

Boyet. Your nose says, no, you are not; for it stands too
    right.

Biron. Your nose smells ' no ' in this, most tender-smell-
    ing knight.

Prin. The conqueror is dismay'd.   Proceed, good
    Alexander.

Nath. When in the world I lived, I was the world's
    commander,—

Boyet. Most true, 't is right; you were so, Alisander.

Biron. Pompey the Great,—

Cost. Your servant, and Costar   568

Biron. Take away the conqueror, take away Alisander.

Cost. [*To Sir Nath.*] O, sir, you have overthrown
Alisander the conqueror!   You will be scraped out of the
painted cloth for this: your lion, that holds his poll-axe

sitting on a close-stool, will be given to Ajax: he will
be the ninth Worthy. A conqueror, and afeard to speak!
run away for shame, Alisander. [*Nath. retires.*] There,
an 't shall please you; a foolish mild man; an honest man,
look you, and soon dashed. He is a marvellous good
neighbour, faith, and a very good bowler: but, for Alisander,
—alas, you see how 't is,—a little o'erparted. But there are
Worthies a-coming will speak their mind in some other
sort.   581

  Prin. Stand aside, good Pompey.

       Enter HOLOFERNES, *for Judas*; *and* MOTH,
                for Hercules

  Hol. Great Hercules is presented by this imp,
    Whose club kill'd Cerberus, that three-headed canis;
And when he was a babe, a child, a shrimp,
    Thus did he strangle serpents in his manus.
Quoniam he seemeth in minority,
Ergo I come with this apology.
Keep some state in thy exit, and vanish.   [*Moth retires.*
    Judas I am,—   590
  Dum. A Judas!
  Hol. Not Iscariot, sir.
    Judas I am, ycliped Maccabæus.
  Dum. Judas Maccabæus clipt is plain Judas.
  Biron. A kissing traitor. How art thou proved Judas?
  Hol. Judas I am,—
  Dum. The more shame for you, Judas.
  Hol. What mean you, sir?
  Boyet. To make Judas hang himself.
  Hol. Begin, sir; you are my elder.   600
  Biron. Well followed: Judas was hanged on an elder.
  Hol. I will not be put out of countenance.
  Biron. Because thou hast no face.
  Hol. What is this?

Boyet. A cittern-head.

Dum. The head of a bodkin.

Biron. A Death's face in a ring.

Long. The face of an old Roman coin, scarce seen.

Boyet. The pommel of Cæsar's falchion.

Dum. The carved-bone face on a flask.   610

Biron. Saint George's half-cheek in a brooch.

Dum. Ay, and in a brooch of lead.

Biron. Ay, and worn in the cap of a tooth-drawer.
And now forward; for we have put thee in countenance.

Hol. You have put me out of countenance.

Biron. False; we have given thee faces.

Hol. But you have out-faced them all.

Biron. An thou wert a lion, we would do so.

Boyet. Therefore, as he is an ass, let him go.
And so adieu, sweet Jude! nay, why dost thou stay?   620

Dum. For the latter end of his name.

Biron. For the ass to the Jude; give it him:—Jud-as,
away!

Hol. This is not generous, not gentle, not humble.

Boyet. A light for Monsieur Judas! it grows dark, he
may stumble.   [*Hol. retires.*

Prin. Alas, poor Maccabæus, how hath he been baited!

Enter ARMADO, *for Hector*

Biron. Hide thy head, Achilles: here comes Hector in
arms.

Dum. Though my mocks come home by me, I will now
be merry.

King. Hector was but a Troyan in respect of this.   630

Boyet. But is this Hector?

King. I think Hector was not so clean-timbered.

Long. His leg is too big for Hector's.

Dum. More calf, certain.

Boyet. No; he is best indued in the small.

Biron. This cannot be Hector.

Dum. He 's a god or a painter; for he makes faces.

Arm. The armipotent Mars, of lances the almighty,
Gave Hector a gift,—

Dum. A gilt nutmeg. 640

Biron. A lemon.

Long. Stuck with cloves.

Dum. No, cloven.

Arm. Peace!—
The armipotent Mars, of lances the almighty,
    Gave Hector a gift, the heir of Ilion;
A man so breathed, that certain he would fight; yea
    From morn till night, out of his pavilion.
I am that flower,—

Dum.   That mint.

Long.   That columbine.

Arm. Sweet Lord Longaville, rein thy tongue. 650

Long. I must rather give it the rein, for it runs against
Hector.

Dum. Ay, and Hector's a greyhound.

Arm. The sweet war-man is dead and rotten; sweet
chucks, beat not the bones of the buried: when he breathed,
he was a man. But I will forward with my device. [*To the
Princess*] Sweet royalty, bestow on me the sense of hearing.

Prin. Speak, brave Hector: we are much delighted.

Arm. I do adore thy sweet grace's slipper.

Boyet. [*Aside to Dum.*] Loves her by the foot. 660

Arm. This Hector far surmounted Hannibal,—

Cost. The party is gone, fellow Hector, she is gone.

Arm. What meanest thou?

Cost. Faith, unless you play the honest Troyan, the poor
wench is cast away.

Arm. Dost thou infamonize me among potentates? thou
shalt die.

Cost. Then shall Hector be whipped for Jaquenetta that

is quick by him and hanged for Pompey that is dead by
him.   670

Dum. Most rare Pompey!

Boyet. Renowned Pompey!

Biron. Greater than great, great, great, great Pompey!
Pompey the Huge!

Dum. Hector trembles.

Biron. Pompey is moved. More Ates, more Ates! stir
them on! stir them on!

Dum. Hector will challenge him.

Biron. Ay, if a' have no more man's blood in 's belly
than will sup a flea.   680

Arm. By the north pole, I do challenge thee.

Cost. I will not fight with a pole, like a northern man:
I 'll slash; I 'll do it by the sword. I bepray you, let me
borrow my arms again.

Dum. Room for the incensed Worthies!

Cost. I 'll do it in my shirt.

Dum. Most resolute Pompey!

Moth. Master, let me take you a button-hole lower. Do
you not see Pompey is uncasing for the combat? What
mean you? You will lose your reputation.   690

Arm. Gentlemen and soldiers, pardon me; I will not
combat in my shirt.

Dum. You may not deny it: Pompey hath made the
challenge.

Arm. Sweet bloods, I both may and will.

Biron. What reason have you for 't?

Arm. The naked truth of it is, I have no shirt; I go woolward for penance.

Boyet. True, and it was enjoined him in Rome for want
of linen: since when, I 'll be sworn, he wore none but a
dishclout of Jaquenetta's, and that a' wears next his heart
for a favour.   702

Enter MERCADE

Mer. God save you, madam!

Prin. Welcome, Mercade;
But that thou interrupt'st our merriment.

Mer. I am sorry, madam; for the news I bring
Is heavy in my tongue. The king your father—

Prin. Dead, for my life!

Mer. Even so; my tale is told.

Biron. Worthies, away! the scene begins to cloud.   710

Arm. For mine own part, I breathe free breath. I have
seen the day of wrong through the little hole of discretion,
and I will right myself like a soldier.   [*Exeunt Worthies.*

King. How fares your majesty?

Prin. Boyet, prepare; I will away to-night.

King. Madam, not so; I do beseech you, stay.

Prin. Prepare, I say. I thank you, gracious lords,
For all your fair endeavours; and entreat,
Out of a new-sad soul, that you vouchsafe
In your rich wisdom to excuse or hide   720
The liberal opposition of our spirits,
If over-boldly we have borne ourselves
In the converse of breath: your gentleness
Was guilty of it. Farewell, worthy lord!
A heavy heart bears not a nimble tongue:
Excuse me so, coming too short of thanks
For my great suit so easily obtain'd.

King. The extreme parts of time extremely forms
All causes to the purpose of his speed,
And often at his very loose decides   730
That which long process could not arbitrate:
And though the mourning brow of progeny
Forbid the smiling courtesy of love
The holy suit which fain it would convince,
Yet, since love's argument was first on foot,
Let not the cloud of sorrow justle it

From what it purposed; since, to wail friends lost
Is not by much so wholesome-profitable
As to rejoice at friends but newly found.

    Prin. I understand you not: my griefs are double.   740

    Biron. Honest plain words best pierce the ear of grief;
And by these badges understand the king.
For your fair sakes have we neglected time,
Play'd foul play with our oaths: your beauty, ladies,
Hath much deform'd us, fashioning our humours
Even to the opposed end of our intents:
And what in us hath seem'd ridiculous,—
As love is full of unbefitting strains,
All wanton as a child, skipping and vain,
Form'd by the eye and therefore, like the eye,   750
Full of strange shapes, of habits and of forms,
Varying in subjects as the eye doth roll
To every varied object in his glance:
Which parti-coated presence of loose love
Put on by us, if, in your heavenly eyes,
Have misbecomed our oaths and gravities,
Those heavenly eyes, that look into these faults,
Suggested us to make. Therefore, ladies,
Our love being yours, the error that love makes
Is likewise yours: we to ourselves prove false,   760
By being once false for ever to be true
To those that make us both,—fair ladies, you:
And even that falsehood, in itself a sin,
Thus purifies itself and turns to grace.

    Prin. We have received your letters full of love;
Your favours, the ambassadors of love:
And, in our maiden council, rated them
At courtship, pleasant jest and courtesy,
As bombast and as lining to the time:
But more devout than this in our respects   770
Have we not been; and therefore met your loves

In their own fashion, like a merriment.

Dum. Our letters, madam, show'd much more than jest.

Long. So did our looks.

Ros.   We did not quote them so.

King. Now, at the latest minute of the hour,
Grant us your loves.

Prin.   A time, methinks, too short
To make a world-without-end bargain in.
No, no, my lord, your grace is perjured much,
Full of dear guiltiness; and therefore this:
If for my love, as there is no such cause,   780
You will do aught, this shall you do for me:
Your oath I will not trust; but go with speed
To some forlorn and naked hermitage,
Remote from all the pleasures of the world;
There stay until the twelve celestial signs
Have brought about the annual reckoning.
If this austere insociable life
Change not your offer made in heat of blood;
If frosts and fasts, hard lodging and thin weeds
Nip not the gaudy blossoms of your love,   790
But that it bear this trial and last love;
Then, at the expiration of the year,
Come challenge me, challenge me by these deserts,
And, by this virgin palm now kissing thine,
I will be thine; and till that instant shut
My woeful self up in a mourning house,
Raining the tears of lamentation
For the remembrance of my father's death.
If this thou do deny, let our hands part,
Neither intitled in the other's heart.   800

King. If this, or more than this, I would deny,
To flatter up these powers of mine with rest,
The sudden hand of death close up mine eye!
Hence ever then my heart is in thy breast.

[*Biron.* And what to me, my love? and what to me?
　Ros. You must be purged too, your sins are rack'd,
You are attaint with faults and perjury:
Therefore if you my favour mean to get,
A twelvemonth shall you spend, and never rest,
But seek the weary beds of people sick.]　　　810
　Dum. But what to me, my love? but what to me?
A wife?
　Kath. A beard, fair health, and honesty;
With three-fold love I wish you all these three.
　Dum. O, shall I say, I thank you, gentle wife?
　Kath. Not so, my lord; a twelvemonth and a day
I 'll mark no words that smooth-faced wooers say:
Come when the king doth to my lady come;
Then, if I have much love, I 'll give you some.
　Dum. I 'll serve thee true and faithfully till then.
　Kath. Yet swear not, lest ye be forsworn again.　　　820
　Long. What says Maria?
　Mar.　　　　　　　　At the twelvemonth's end
I 'll change my black gown for a faithful friend.
　Long. I 'll stay with patience; but the time is long.
　Mar. The liker you; few taller are so young.
　Biron. Studies my lady? mistress, look on me;
Behold the window of my heart, mine eye,
What humble suit attends thy answer there:
Impose some service on me for thy love.
　Ros. Oft have I heard of you, my Lord Biron,
Before I saw you; and the world's large tongue　　　830
Proclaims you for a man replete with mocks,
Full of comparisons and wounding flouts,
Which you on all estates will execute
That lie within the mercy of your wit.
To weed this wormwood from your fruitful brain,
And therewithal to win me, if you please,
Without the which I am not to be won,

You shall this twelvemonth term from day to day
Visit the speechless sick and still converse
With groaning wretches; and your task shall be,   840
With all the fierce endeavour of your wit
To enforce the pained impotent to smile.

   Biron. To move wild laughter in the throat of death?
It cannot be; it is impossible:
Mirth cannot move a soul in agony.

   Ros. Why, that 's the way to choke a gibing spirit,
Whose influence is begot of that loose grace
Which shallow laughing hearers give to fools:
A jest's prosperity lies in the ear
Of him that hears it, never in the tongue   850
Of him that makes it: then, if sickly ears,
Deaf'd with the clamours of their own dear groans,
Will hear your idle scorns, continue then,
And I will have you and that fault withal;
But if they will not, throw away that spirit,
And I shall find you empty of that fault,
Right joyful of your reformation.

   Biron. A twelvemonth! well; befall what will befall,
I 'll jest a twelvemonth in an hospital.

   Prin. [*To the King*] Ay, sweet my lord; and so I take my
     leave.   860

   King. No, madam; we will bring you on your way.

   Biron. Our wooing doth not end like an old play;
Jack hath not Jill: these ladies' courtesy
Might well have made our sport a comedy.

   King. Come, sir, it wants a twelvemonth and a day,
And then 't will end.

   Biron.   That 's too long for a play.

Re-enter ARMADO

   Arm. Sweet majesty, vouchsafe me,—

   Prin. Was not that Hector?   868

Dum. The worthy knight of Troy.

Arm. I will kiss thy royal finger, and take leave. I am a votary; I have vowed to Jaquenetta to hold the plough for her sweet love three years. But, most esteemed greatness, will you hear the dialogue that the two learned men have compiled in praise of the owl and the cuckoo? it should have followed in the end of our show.   875

King. Call them forth quickly; we will do so.

Arm. Holla! approach.

Re-enter HOLOFERNES, NATHANIEL, MOTH,
      COSTARD, *and others*

This side is Hiems, Winter, this Ver, the Spring; the one maintained by the owl, the other by the cuckoo. Ver, begin.

THE SONG

SPRING

When daisies pied and violets blue   880
      And lady-smocks all silver-white
And cuckoo-buds of yellow hue
      Do paint the meadows with delight,
The cuckoo then, on every tree,
Mocks married men; for thus sings he,
            Cuckoo;
Cuckoo, cuckoo: O word of fear,
Unpleasing to a married ear!

When shepherds pipe on oaten straws
      And merry larks are ploughmen's clocks,   890
When turtles tread, and rooks, and daws,
      And maidens bleach their summer smocks,
The cuckoo then, on every tree,
Mocks married men: for thus sings he,
            Cuckoo;
Cuckoo, cuckoo; O word of fear,
Unpleasing to a married ear!

Winter

When icicles hang by the wall
　And Dick the shepherd blows his nail
And Tom bears logs into the hall   900
　And milk comes frozen home in pail,
When blood is nipp'd and ways be foul,
Then nightly sings the staring owl,
　　　　Tu-whit;
Tu-who, a merry note,
While greasy Joan doth keel the pot.

When all aloud the wind doth blow
　And coughing drowns the parson's saw
And birds sit brooding in the snow
　And Marian's nose looks red and raw,   910
When roasted crabs hiss in the bowl,
Then nightly sings the staring owl,
　　　　Tu-whit;
Tu-who, a merry note,
While greasy Joan doth keel the pot.

Arm. The words of Mercury are harsh after the songs
of Apollo. You that way: we this way.   [*Exeunt.*

NOTES

Dramatis Personæ

Ferdinand, King of Navarre. *Q. & D. W.* point out that the name Ferdinand does not appear once in the dialogue.

Act I—Scene 1

There are no act or scene divisions in Q.; and only act divisions in F.

3. **disgrace,** disfigurement. With the half punning antithesis " grace "—" disgrace " begins, if we ignore the less mannered antithesis of " lives "—" tombs " above, the verbal and rhetorical play which is so important in this comedy.

5. **breath,** life.

6. **bate.** See Glossary.

13, 14. **a little . . . art.** For the significance of the little academe, see Introduction, p. x. We may see with Furness an antithesis *still* and *contemplative*; and a further reference in " living art " to the " ars vivendi " of Stoic philosophy as expressed in the writings of Cicero and Seneca (cf. *Q. & D. W.*, p. 133).

13. **Academe** (achademe Q.). The form is found elsewhere in the seventeenth century, i.e. Peacham, *Emblems*, 1642: Milton, *P.R.*, IV. 244, " See there the olive grove of Academe ", 1671 (N.E.D.).

20. **his own . . . down,** i.e. his own handwriting shall accuse him of a dishonourable act.

21. **branch,** minor detail.

28. **mortified,** dead to the world's pleasures. Cf. N.T., Romans, viii. 13.

32. **these.** Furness believes " these " to refer to love, wealth, &c. But he quotes "A. C." 's supposition of Variorum Ed. 1821 that Dumain's companions are referred to. Biron's " their " in the

89

following line might be taken to support this latter view. But the idea that in philosophy a higher love (or wealth, or pomp) than mere earthly love, &c., may be found is not improbable. Cf. the contrast drawn between the earthly and the heavenly in the *Hymne of Heavenly Love* of Spenser, that Platonic poet.

43. **wink,** shut the eyes. **of . . . day,** of = during. Abbott, § 176.

44. **no harm,** i.e. think it no harm to sleep.

57. **common sense,** the capacity of most people; not quite perhaps with the same meaning as in l. 64, where = common knowledge.

59. **Come on,** (Q. com'on) punning with " common ".

71. **train,** allure, entice. Cf. *Com. Errors*, iii. 2. 45:
> train me not with thy note, to drown me.

73. **inherit,** here = gain, obtain (Schmidt).

76. **falsely,** treacherously (Johnson).

77. **Light . . . beguile,** i.e. The eyes seeking for truth in books, deprive themselves of light (i.e. become dim). So Furness: but there is probably also an antithesis between the idea of the brightness of truth in books and the brightness of a woman's face (see l. 82); the former is a delusive light, but the latter one a most promising beacon.

80. **me,** (Abbott, § 220) " me " probably means " for me ", " by my advice ", i.e. " I would have you study thus." Less probably " study " may be an active verb, of which the passive is found in *Macbeth*, i. 4. 9.

82, 83. **Who . . . blinded by.** And when the man's eye is thus dazzled at first, the woman's eye shall next become the object that attracts it (= that it *heeds*); and so the beauty that at first blinded it shall restore light to it.

dazzling, intransitive use. Charlton quotes *3 Henry VI*, ii. 1. 25.
> Dazzle mine eyes, or do I see three suns?

heed, the object of its heed or care; though Dr. Johnson suggested " direction, lodestar ".

86. **Small** = little; adjective used for noun, as frequently in Shakespeare (Abbott, § 5). Cf. " by small and small ", *Richard II*, iii. 2. 198, and in the present play " fair ".

88. **godfathers,** i.e. astronomers. Is there a reference here to the astronomical practice of the School of Night (*Q. & D. W.*, pp. xxxi–ii)? And see Introduction, p. x.

97. **green geese,** these were fattened on green spring grass and sold at Green Goose Fair on Whitmonday. There is some

ground for rejecting the belief that " green geese " here =
" simpleton " (as Furness). Biron is pleading for the natural
course of things. Let each season, he argues, come in its natural
course, with its appropriate delight; and so spring will give us
the fun of the fair, including fun with the girls. Cf. also iv. 3. 71,
" a green goose a goddess ", where Biron is certainly referring to
a girl. (The note in *Q. & D. W.*, p. 203, if jocular, seems to
agree with this view.)

98. **his** = its. (See *Antony and Cleopatra* in this edn., Glossary,
p. 224.)

100. **sneaping.** See Glossary.

101. **infants . . . spring,** buds. Cf. *Hamlet*, i. 3. 39:
    The canker galls the infants of the spring.

102. **Why should . . .** &c. Biron retorts that he will certainly
play the part of a frost to the new-born and *unnatural* project
of the academe (see note to " green geese " ante).

106. **new-fangled,** here, probably dressed up anew, i.e. for
the new season.

mirth: S. Walker's conjecture for the Q.F. reading "shows"
(open-air shows such as might be seen at Spring fairs or on May
Day; or, simply, display of leafage, &c.). This conjecture,
or Theobald's "earth", provides a rhyme to l. 104; but this is
scarcely an adequate reason for the change.

107. **But like of** = but I like. Cf. *Much Ado*, v. 4. 59:
    I am your husband if you like of me (Abbott, § 177).

108. **to study,** gerundive construction = " in studying ", or
apodosis, " if you study ".

109. Reading follows Q. F. reads "That were to climb o'er
the house to unlock the gate ".

110. **sit you out,** sit out of the (card) game; keep out of it.
" Sit " is F.1 reading. Q.'s and other F.'s read " fit ".

112. **barbarism,** on behalf of the uncultured or unlearned
life. There may also be satirical reference to Barbarism, the
" foulest vice " of rhetoric as described by Puttenham in his
Arte of English Poesie (1589), Book III, Chap. xxii.

114. **swore.** F.1 reading, which *Q. & D. W.* prefer. The
rhyme scheme of the stanza demands "swore". Q., F.1 read
"sworn".

127. **gentility,** politeness—possibly that of letting the woman
have the last word.

136, 138. **father . . . hither,** probably a fairly good rhyme,
though not noted by Vietor; he does however refer (*a*) to the
rhyme "hither-weather" (p. 21), suggesting that the first vowel

sound in "hither" was "e" (?ɛ); and (b) on p. 52 there is some evidence that the first vowel-sound in "father" might have been "æ": possibly the two sounds were even nearer than that.

140. **overshot,** i.e. eclipsed by other considerations.

146. **lie ... on** = stay ... from.

149. **affects,** natural desires.

150. **special grace,** a religious phrase. C. Wordsworth refers to the Catechism (cit. Furness) "to serve him without his special grace". Shakespeare uses "grace" in the religious sense.

152. **mere.** See Glossary.

155. **Stands in ... of,** "is condemned or sentenced to" (Hart).

156. **Suggestions,** temptations, as frequently. Cf. *King John,* iii. 1. 292, "these giddy, loose suggestions".

159. **quick** = lively.

161. **With** = by.

162. **planted,** invested (with), furnished with.

164. **One whom.** "One who" F.1; "who" for "whom" is frequent in Shakespeare.

166. **complements.** See Glossary.

167. **mutiny,** quarrels.

168. **hight.** See Glossary.

169. **interim,** "something done during an interval, respite" (*Q. & D. W.*).

171. **tawny,** brown, sunburnt. Hart notes that this epithet is used several times by Greene.

debate, war, contention. "A Spenserian word (*F.Q.* ii. 8. 54, 'the whole debate')" (*Q. & D. W.*). Was Armado to recite Spanish Romances? If so, he does not carry out this proposal in the play, as it stands. One is tempted to suspect a loose end left through haste in revision.

174. **minstrelsy,** possibly minstrel (abstract for concrete); or simply for minstrelsy, i.e. the singing of romances.

176. **fire-new,** i.e. fresh from the mint. Occurs several times in Shakespeare, who coined the term. Cf. *Lear,* v. 3. 132, "Despite thy victor sword and fire-new fortune".

181. **reprehend,** for represent. Much of the comic effect of Shakespeare's clowns (of whom Dogberry is perhaps the most famous) depends on the use of the wrong word, or the mis-pronunciation of a word (cf. "egma", iii. 1. 68).

182. **tharborough.** See Glossary.

187. **contempts,** for "contents".

191. **a high . . . heaven.** The meaning is " so high a hope as yours is directed to a disproportionately low object ". He would expect a prayer to God to be aimed at the *highest* Heaven. This *antitheton* (Puttenham, b. III, p. 219, Arber) reminds us of many such in Lyly, cf. e.g. that in *Euphues and his England* (p. 90, *Works*, Vol. II, ed. Bond), where " high " and " low " are similarly contrasted.

193. **laughing,** so Capell and others. Qq., Ff. read " hearing ", which Hart defends, quoting Ezekiel, ii. 5 (q.v.).

196. **style, climb,** a pun on " stile ".

197. **merriness.** See Glossary.

199. **taken with the manner,** (mainour = mod. F. *man-œuvre*) taken in the act. This term is noted (Pollock and Mait-land, *Hist. of Eng. Law*, Chap. viii, 2, p. 495) as extant in the thirteenth century.

201. **In manner and form following.** Hart quotes (inter alia) Lyly, *Mydas*, v. ii. (1592), " you shall have the beard, in manner and form following ".

Further puns on " manner " (manor) and " form " (" form " also = a bench) occur in this speech. Charlton, in an illuminating note (p. 118), observes how the Elizabethan sense of power over words is here satisfied by repeating these words singly " to stretch to the fullest extent, with or without violence, their connotation, by using the word as different parts of speech, or by punning on entirely different meanings of the same word, or on the general and particular, common and unusual, radical and derivative, technical and literal uses of it ".

214. **welkin.** See Glossary.

220. **but so,** no little value, a poor sort of creature.

226. **humour.** According to the old medicine melancholy was one of the four humours, of which the other three were the choleric, the phlegmatic, and the sanguine. These four fluids were connected with or arose from the four elements, earth, air, fire and water (see note to *Antony and Cleopatra* in this edition, iii. 3. 40), and they gave rise to the four temperaments or com-plexions, corresponding to them.

228. **the time when . . . &c.** Cf. Wilson, *Arte of Rhetorique* (Mair, p. 21–2), " Examining of the circumstances " of the story of David and Goliath. " iii. Where was it done? About the vale of *Terebinthus*. vii. What time did he it? This deede was done, when Saull first reigned . . ." &c. Shakespeare is evidently mocking textbook methods.

234. **obscene,** here, probably = " common " or " vulgar " (so Charlton).

preposterous. See Glossary. Hart compares with Nashe's *Pasquil's Returne*, " a preposterous Humour noted in the Ecclesiasticall Histories ".

235, 236. **snow-white . . . ebon-coloured,** another " antitheton ". Cf. Lyly, *Sapho and Phao* (1583 ?), II. iv. 125 (Bond's Edition), " white silver draweth blacke lines ".

ebon-coloured. This is the earliest example of a compound adjective with " ebon " noted in *N.E.D.* The next earliest is Greene, *Poems* (1592), where " ebon-black " occurs (in *Hexametra Alexis*). This poem appeared in Greene's *Mourning Garment* (1590); and Greene, who is poetically fond of ebony, may have got in his compound first.

236. **viewest, beholdest.** Barton (*Links between Shakespeare and the Law*) sees a parody of legal tautology.

238. **north-north-east and by east.** Was Shakespeare recalling this passage in Lyly's *Gallathea* (possibly acted as late as 1588), I. iv, p. 88, Vol. II, *Works*, Bond:

> *Dicke.* Well begin with your points, for a lacke onlie points in this world.
> *Mariner.* North. North and by East. North North East. North-east and by North. North-east. North-east and by East . . . &c.?

239. **curious-knotted garden,** i.e. with flower beds carefully and ingeniously laid out in figures. Cf. Bacon, *Essays. Of Gardens.*

240. **minnow.** *Q. & D. W.* would read " minion " with Dr. Johnson; and consider that " to call the large-limbed Costard a ' minnow ' seems pointlessly stupid . . ." But that may be the very point—that Costard may be physically large, but morally a contemptible " minnow ", meriting derision.

244. **vassal.** See Glossary.

248. **sorted,** associated.

249. **continent canon,** restraining law; but Charlton renders law enjoining continence "; and, as he hints, there may be a quibble on the two meanings.

250. **passion,** am deeply moved, grieve. Cf. *Venus and Adonis*, 1059, " Dumbly she passions ", and (*Q. & D. W.*) Spenser, *F.Q.*, II. ix. 41.

255. **meed.** See Glossary.

257. **carriage:** deportment, as in i. 2. 66. Cf. *Much Ado*, i. 3. 31: " fashion a carriage to rob love from any ".

259. **weaker vessel,** i.e. woman; the phrase is found in 1 Peter, iii. 7, but Shakespeare may have picked it up from his contemporaries Lyly and Greene. Hart collects two instances from Lyly (*Euphues, Sapho and Phao*) and one from Greene's *Mamillia.*

265, 267. **the best . . . worst.** There may be two " intentions " of wit here: (*a*) his best effort at style results in the most appalling English; (*b*) his best style is used for the worst matter. Hart cites Lyly, *Campaspe* (1581), V. i, p. 350 (Bond), where Diogenes says, in criticism of Perim's dancing, "the better, the worser". The tone of the whole letter suggests a deliberate illustration of one of the rhetorical vices which Puttenham (Bk. III, p. 266, Arber) calls " *Bomphologia* or Pompious speech ".

278. **so varied,** i.e. these variants also occur in the text of the law.

292. **idle scorn,** will be ineffective and scorned.

296. **prosperity! Affliction.** See note to l. 181 above.

Scene 2

Scene 2, Capell (see note to scene 1 above).

5. **imp.** See Glossary.

8. **juvenal,** youth (Lat. *juvenalis*, youthful). This is the earliest instance recorded by *N.E.D.* There may be also a punning allusion to Nashe, compared as a satiric writer, with the Roman Satirist Juvenal (A.D. 60–140). The pun is actually made by Greene, in his *Groatsworth of Wit* (1592), where he writes of the "young Iuvenall, that byting Saytrist".

9. **familiar,** easily understood (Schmidt), as in *Troilus and Cressida*, iii. 3. 113: "I do not strain at the position—it is familiar."

of the working, i.e. of the different ways in which these passions manifest themselves.

10. **senior.** Malone and others. F.1, *signeur.* Q., *signeor.*

13. **congruent,** suitable.

epitheton (= epithet). This early form is found in Puttenham, and also (cf. Hart) in Greene's *Planetomachia*.

18. **Pretty and apt,** possibly Armado merely meant by this, "pretty apt". Q. & D. W. favour this explanation, as Halliwell, who quotes Jonson, *Poetaster*, 5. 1, where Crispinus replies to the usual greeting, " Pretty and well, I thank you ". Moth, however, humorously misunderstands the phrase.

22. **Little pretty,** "pretty" could then mean other things than " daintily beautiful "; it might imply stoutness and valour, as when applied to soldiers. Moth may be taking it up in this latter sense: "I have very little of the fine warrior about me— I am too small for that." "praty men " in this sense is found *c.* 1400 (*N.E.D.*).

25. **condign.** See Glossary.

28. **an eel is quick,** " quick " is used this time to mean full of life; the difficulty of killing eels is well known, and was almost proverbial in the Elizabethan story as told by the fool in *Lear*, ii. 4. 122: " cry to it, nuncle, as the cockney did to the eels when she put 'em in the paste alive." The cockney was referred to as a type of stupidity. If Armado knew the story, the allusion would certainly heat his blood.

33. **crosses,** i.e. coins with a cross stamped on them. Moth means that Armado " had a hole in his pocket ". *Q. & D. W.* refer also to iii. 1. 126 ff, where Armado can afford no more remuneration than three farthings.

40. **of a tapster,** and so, unspeakably vulgar. A tapster was low, easily fooled (*1 Henry IV*, ii. 4) and ignorant (*ibid.*, and *Troilus and Cressida*, i. 2. 123).

45. **deuce-ace.** See Glossary.

52. **the dancing horse.** This was Banks' performing horse, called Morocco, to which there were many references in the literature of that and the next decades. Furness quotes, *inter alia*, Ben Jonson's Epigram (cxxxiii) mentioning " old Banks the jugler. . . . . Grave tutor to the learned horse." In another quotation (from Don Zara del Fogo, 1656) we are told that the horse could dance and sing. Mr. Banks was (in Jonson's phrase) burned beyond the sea for one witch ".

53. **figure,** i.e. rhetorical figure or ornament, such as were classified and described by a Wilson or a Puttenham.

57. **humour.** See note to i. 226.

58. **affection** (= passion) was a humour emanating from the liver.

60. **French courtier . . . courtesy,** i.e. exchange it for one of the latest French gestures or acts of politeness.

61. **out-swear,** possibly forswear, renounce.

65. **sweet my child.** The possessive adjectives, when unemphatic, are sometimes transposed. Cf. " Sweet my mother," *Romeo and Juliet*, iii. 5. 200 (Abbott, § 13).

68. **carriage,** with a pun on (*a*) the meaning as in i. 1. 257 and (*b*) on Samson's " carrying " escapade.

75. **complexion,** the old medical term for temperaments corresponding to the four Humours (see note to i. 1. 226). Tryon, *Way to Health,* 1683 (cit. *N.E.D.*): " A mans Complexion, of which there are commonly reckon'd four kinds, viz. the Cholerick, the Phlegmatick, the Sanguine and the Melancholy." Hence Moth's remark " of all the four ", &c. The word came to be used more loosely of the appearance of the skin, and even of the colour of the object; so the Prince of Morocco, in *Merchant of Venice*, ii. 1. 1:

> Mislike me not for my complexion.

79. **sea-water green,** see preceding note. Charlton dismisses the phrase as " pure playful invention "; but one must remember that the traditions of the alchemists remained alive well into the next century; and I suspect that Moth's fun is allusive.

Thos. Vaughan (*Anthroposophia Theomagica, Works,* edited Waite) wrote of water in the seventeenth century: " the water hath several complexions, according to the several parts of the creature." In *Lumen de Lumine* Vaughan quotes Raymond Lully of the " celestial water " or " First Matter ", which " *has the colour of a green lizard* ". This " mother of metals " has a complexion of its own, which is however derived from those of two elements, earth and water (v. Waite, p. 272). This was apparently part of the existing alchemic tradition; and Shakespeare might well have heard or read of it—" the best of them too "—and might use it for a little alchemic fun at someone's expense.

83. **Green . . . lovers.** Popularly, green typified " hope and happiness " (Charlton). Hart observes that earlier it had denoted inconstancy.

86. **a green wit.** Several editors see a pun on " wit " and the green withes (pron. " wits ") that bound Samson.

90. **Define,** be precise, explain.

95. **If she be made, &c.** The point of this verse is that if the lady's complexion be made up with cosmetics, she will not betray herself by a blush or by pallor; for her cheeks will *always* possess through artifice those colours which, indeed, are naturally those of a woman; but the natural red and white are not *always* unchanged. The " still " (=*always*) points, surely, to the artificial " make-up ".

102. **owe** = own.

105. **the King and the Beggar,** alluding to the ballad of King Cophetua and the beggar maid (in *Percy's Reliques*), see iv. I. 65, and note. Furness notes that Falstaff mentions King Cophetua in *2 Henry IV*, v. 3. 106, " Let King Cophetua know the truth thereof ".

109, 110. **it would . . . tune,** possibly for the words and tune of a ballad suitable for you. Does he hint that the needy Armado is anything but a king?

112. **example,** find an excuse in the shape of an example.

digression, departure, i.e. disobedience of the law forbidding communication with women.

114. **rational hind:** the two meanings of the word play seem to be (*a*) reasoning or arguing rustic—Costard is fond of argument (i. 2. 270 ff.); (*b*) a *rational* hind (stag) as distinguished from the ordinary deer one meets in a park.

122. **nor no penance,** nor no = single negative.

122. **penance,** a blunder, perhaps, for " pleasance " (Hart).

124. **allowed . . . daywoman,** engaged as dairymaid. Day, see Glossary.

allowed, admitted, see v. 2. 479 of this play.

129. **That's hereby,** a *double entendu* seems to be intended; possibly (*a*) " that's quite near " and (*b*) " that's as it may be ".

133. **With that face?,** " a piece of slang equivalent to ' you don't mean it ' " (Hart). She may also mean to retort " none of your wonders can possibly be as astounding as your face " (see *Q. & D. W.*, p. 139).

141. **on a full stomach,** with a good heart (Hart, who notes that " full-stomacht " is used by Greene and Nashe).

144, 145. **fellows . . . rewarded,** *fellows* = servants; Costard is sneering at the small wages which Armado pays.

149. **fast and loose.** A cheating game, played with a belt, which was deceptively arranged so as to persuade the " dupe " that he could fasten it to the table with a skewer; but when he thought he had done so, it was found to be *loose* and was easily removed. See note to *Antony and Cleopatra* in this edition, iv. 12. 28.

151. **days of desolation,** a misapplied phrase from, possibly, Zephaniah, i. 15: " a day of wasteness and desolation ". Costard, improving perhaps on Sidney's Lalus (see Introduction), prepares the way for Dogberry and other Shakespearian clowns in his pretentious search for the right word and his choice of the wrong; a type of humour especially grateful, no doubt, to a word-conscious age. He means some such word as " jubilation ".

155. **words.** Johnson wishes to read " wards ". Charlton suspects the quibble " words—wards ".

158. **affect,** love.

base . . . baser . . . basest, this is a mild example of the Figure called by Puttenham " *Traductio*, or the Tranlacer " (p. 213), which consists in ringing the changes on the various forms of any given word.

160. **forsworn,** break my oath, cf. " digression ", l. 112 above.

argument, proof, cf. Latin.

162. **familiar,** an attendant devil or imp such as witches were supposed to keep; often assuming the forms of small animals (see Ewen, *Witchcraft and Demonianism*, passim).

165. **butt-shaft,** " the strong unbarbed arrow used by citizens in shooting at the butt " (Gifford), cf. *Romeo and Juliet*, ii. 4. 15.

167. **Spaniard's rapier,** " the light Spanish sword for the thrust " (Hart, note in *Merry Wives*, ii. 1. 227), where he quotes Cotgrave: " Espa Espagnole—A Rapier or Tuck ").

first and second cause. *Q. & D. W.* (139) refer to Charlton's discovery that this phrase (referring to the technique of quarrels antecedent to a duel) can be traced to *The Book of Honor and Armes* (1590) attributed to Sir Wm. Segar, where the causes of quarrel are reduced to two: (1) accusation of a crime meriting death, and (2) honour, which should be preferred before life.

168. **passado.** See Glossary.

duello, the established code of duellists. (This passage is the earliest containing the word recorded by *N.E.D.*)

171. **manager,** wielder, manipulator; a handler.

172. **extemporal,** i.e. some god of improvisation in rhyme. *N.E.D.* notes the word twice (2nd " ext.-ly ") in Harvey's letter book, 1577. (See Camden Soc.'s edition.)

173. **turn sonnet,** turn sonnetteer. The "thing done" for the agent, as elsewhere in Shakespeare. *Q. & D. W.* quote *Much Ado*, ii. 3. 19, " turned orthography ".

Act II—Scene 1

1. **dearest spirits,** inmost or most earnest courage (Schmidt) or perhaps " mental activity " in this context.

2. **who,** for whom. See Abbott, § 274.

5. **inheritor,** possessor, owner, as in *Hamlet*, v. 1. 121:

> and must the inheritor himself have no more?

6. **owe** = own, as frequently.

7. **plea,** the thing demanded in a plea, or by a plaintiff or petitioner; almost as in *The Merchant of Venice*, iv. 1. 198:

> though justice be thy plea.

9, 10. **dear . . . dear,** the meaning-play is (*a*) amiable, (*b*) precious and unique.

14. **flourish,** " gloss, ostentatious embellishment" (Schmidt). Cf. *Richard III*, i. 3. 241. " Poor painted queen, vain flourish of my fortune!"

16. **chapmen.** See Glossary. Is there a dig at George Chapman, the rival poet? See Introduction.

20. **task the tasker,** see note on *base*. Boyet was a " tasker " because he set the princess the task of " parleying " with the King.

28. **bold of,** confident in. For a similar use of " of ", cf. *Henry VIII*, iv. 2. 43: " of his own body he was ill " (= " in his own body ").

29. **best-moving fair solicitor,** best persuading, accomplished advocate. So Schmidt: Furness takes " fair " to mean " just ".

41. **Lord Perigort, &c.** At first sight this looks like an allusion to an historical event; but only the names are derived from history, and were probably found by Shakespeare during his reading of the English Chronicles for *Henry VI*, as Cross and Brooke suggest. Perigort may = Perigord, a district near Bordeaux, mentioned by Holinshed; and " Fauconbridge " occurs in Grafton in a passage probably used by Shakespeare in connexion with *3 Henry VI*; see i. 1. 239, and note thereto in the Arden edition. And see also Shakespeare's *King John*, passim.

46. **would well,** wishes to do well (Capell).

49. **match'd,** combined or joined with (Johnson).

blunt, dull in regard to the feelings of others, in that it is willing to spare none (Furness).

58. **least knowing ill.** This looks, at first sight, like a contradiction. Halliwell's rendering is " (he) is nevertheless ignorant of evil "; but cf. v. 2. 744 of this play:

> your beauty, ladies,
> Hath much deform'd us, fashioning our humours,"

where " fashioning " = " since it hath fashioned ". The same construction yields good sense here and, I think, enhances the " snap " of the antithesis; he has *most* power to harm because he has *least* experience in discrimination of what is ill. He is young and witty, but his wit has not yet the discipline of tact won by experience.

62. **much . . . saw,** this is the " report " mentioned in the following line.

65. **if,** this is Q. reading. F. reads " as ".

69. **begets occasion,** creates opportunity. Biron was observant, as satirists must be.

72. **conceit,** thought.

74. **play truant,** i.e. give up their present occupation. Cf. the well-known passage in Sidney's *Apologie for Poetrie*: " a tale which holdeth children from play, and old men from the chimney corner " (printed 1595).

78. **her own** = her own " fancy man ".

80. **what admittance,** what leave of entry (have you obtained for us?).

82. **competitors,** associates, as in *Antony and Cleopatra*, v. 1. 42:

> thou, my brother, my competitor.

83. **address'd,** ready; frequent in this sense in Shakespeare (v. Schmidt).

88. **unpeopled,** the F. reading. Q.1 reads "unpeeled", which is unacceptable.

92, 93. **the roof . . . mine.** Note the strained antithesis of this deliberately courtly speech. Lyly's *Euphues* abounds in antitheses, which are one of the characteristics of his style.

98. **Not . . . will,** i.e. not willingly.

99. **it; will . . .** So Capell and others for "it will" of Q.F. There seems to be no strong reason for disturbing "it will", which means "its will"; "it" as a possessive occurs several times in Shakespeare, notably *Lear*, i. 4. 236, of the hedge sparrow that "had it head bit off by it young". For aggravated examples of Shakespeare's favourite "will" quibble, see *Sonnets*, 135, 136.

103. **sworn out,** banished by means of an oath; and thus, given up hospitality.

104. **'Tis deadly sin,** perhaps because so gross a breach of the laws of hospitality would amount to a sin—an eighth deadly sin, in fact. The point of these lines is explained by Halliwell (cit. Furness): "the Princess merely means to say that the King has placed himself in a dilemma. It is a sin to keep the oath; while of course a sin would be committed in breaking this or any oath; in either case, he will commit a sin."

109. **suddenly . . . suit,** and immediately settle the business which is the subject of my quest.

resolve, "almost = to answer" (German, *Bescheid geben*), Schmidt.

117. **quick,** quick at taking me up, sharp. But Rosaline wilfully misconstrues it as "rapid, headlong".

123. **fair . . . mask,** for the mocking intent of this complimentary "fair befall", cf. l. 202 of this scene: "God's blessing on your beard!" For the phrase "fair befall" (= "good luck to"), cf. *Richard III*, i. 3. 282, "now fair befal thee and thy noble house", and *ibid.*, iii. 5. 47.

128. Note the abrupt change in manner and matter with the introduction of "the intractable matter of a money account" (Hunter) into the middle of a scene of light *badinage*. *Q. & D. W.* (p. 129) suggest that this speech may be based upon historical matter: "the visit of Catherine de Medici and her daughter, Marguerite de Valois, Queen of Navarre, to the court of the latter's husband . . . in 1579 . . . in order to make a deal with him over the question of Aquitaine." These editors further suggest that Shakespeare might possibly have been working over an old play dealing with these incidents. Some remnants of the style of that old play, remaining in this speech, might help to account for the change of manner.

intimate, propose.

129. **The payment,** according to Theobald, this payment was to be to himself. He was demanding back this moiety; whereas, the King argues, he should have been paying the other moiety as well as this one, so that Aquitaine, which was mortgaged for this sum, might be taken out of pawn and restored to him. But he " not demands " this; and the King is vexed at being left with the not very valuable land instead of hard cash.

145. **To . . . live,** to have once more a valid right (to Aquitaine).

146. **depart withal,** part with, give up.

148. **gelded,** deprived of value, depreciated.

150. **From reason's yielding,** from being such as may be reasonably conceded.

151. **A yielding . . . reason,** i.e. the emotional yielding caused by admiration, and so opposed to the dictates of reason.

155. **unseeming.** (Abbott, § 442.)

159. **arrest,** take as security. The phrase " arrest your word " seems to be rare (see *N.E.D.*). Hart notes an earlier instance in Sidney's *Arcadia.*

163. **packet,** mail.

164. **specialties,** special terms or articles of the contract (Schmidt).

bound, tied up, packed up.

170. **Make tender of,** offer.

174. **fair.** The Q. reading. F. reads " farther ".

180. **do my commendations,** i.e. " go through the motions " of commending me to your heart, here and now.

185. **let it blood,** referring to the then common medical practice of bleeding a patient (phlebotomy).

187. **physic,** the medical faculty (as in Gascoigne, *Steele Glas*, 984) or even, " the doctor ". See note on " medicine " as possible abstract for concrete, *Antony and Cleopatra*, i. 5. 36–7, in this edition.

189. **No point** = not at all. Cf. the French negative *point*. Malone refers to this entry in Florio's *Worlde of Wordes*, 1598: " Punto . . . never a whit, no jot, no point as the frenchmen say." There is a pun here on negative " point ", and the point of a knife.

191. **and yours,** " and save yours "; taking up Biron's " save " deliberately in a rather different sense.

192. **stay thanksgiving.** Why? There seems to be no point to this remark unless, as *Q. & D. W.* suggest, there is a play on " living—leaving " in Rosaline's previous line. " Leaving " would then mean " leave-taking ", and Biron would retort thus:

" I can't stay for any ceremonious leave-taking." As for the pronunciation, see Vietor, *Shakespeare's Pronunciation*, 1906, pp. 11–13 for similar rhymes, e.g. " teeth: with " (v. 2a, 1. 269); and also the " sheeps-ships " pun in this scene below. Wyld (*A Short History of English*, p. 172) mentions Gill's (1621) transliteration of " leave " as " live ".

194. **Katharine.** Capell's conjecture for " Rosalin " of Q. F. Capell argued that Boyet is assisting the disguise of the masked ladies by further confusing the suitor. The lady whom Dumaine sees is actually Rosaline making her exit: Boyet declares she is Katharine. Q. & D. W. (pp. 117 ff.), further developing Charlton's theory, believe that Shakespeare, when revising, abandoned the disguise motif here, since he was making better use of it in v. 2: but that in the marking of the considerable changes on the text for this purpose, confusions arose; one of which was the putting in of the word " Rosaline " at the wrong place. It should have been placed in line 209 where Q. read " Katharin " (Rosaline is restored in our text). And see Introduction.

198. **light in the light,** i.e. wanton when examined closely (as in the full light of day). For similar word-play, cf. i. 1. 77 of this play, and *Antony and Cleopatra* (in this edition), note to i. 4. 23.

202. **beard.** To refer lightly to anyone's beard was in those days to taunt or even to insult.

204. **heir of Falconbridge,** i.e. Maria.

heir, here used of females instead of males. Also, it may be used in the looser sense of " offspring ", " child " (*Merry Wives*, v. 5. 43).

211. **To her will.** Shakespeare makes it plain, in his characterization of Rosaline, that she is " wedded to her will ". Furness refers to Massey (*Secret Drama of Shakespeare's Sonnets*), who sees in Rosaline some of the wilfulness of Lady Penelope Rich.

or so, " or something of the kind " (Q. & D. W.).

212. **You are welcome,** probably means " in that case you are welcome to the lady ".

213. **Farewell . . . you,** possibly, " it is literally ' fare *well* ' for me when I'm rid of you; and your going is welcome ".

218. **sheeps.** Maria cannot resist this favourite pun which the pronunciation of the time allowed. Hart refers to *The Two Gentlemen of Verona*, i. 1. 73 and *Comedy of Errors*, iv. 1. 94 for repetitions of the pun. By a " hot ship " is meant a " fire-ship "; a cant term for a wanton woman. For similarity in pronunciation see note (above) to l. 193.

219. **feed on your lips:** several editors, following Malone, cit. *Venus and Adonis*, 232–3: " Feed where thou wilt, on mountain or in dale; Graze on my lips."

222. **common . . . several.** In the parlance of the time fields were so called, viz. (*a*) the common fields shared by a village, and (*b*) the enclosed fields or " severals " belonging to individuals. *Several* also meant " separate " (from each other), as her lips were: which explains the pun.

225. **civil war of wits.** *Q. & D. W.* consider this to be the " only passage in the play which can be interpreted as a direct reference to the French wars 1589–94 ".

228. **By the heart's . . . eyes,** i.e. (if I am not deceived into noting wrongly) the silent eloquence of the heart which is expressed in the eyes.

231. **affected,** in love. To affect = to love is frequent in Shakespeare; cf. this play, i. 2. 85.

233. **Why, all, &c.** The whole of this speech is an elaboration of his previous remark (l. 228) about " the heart's still rhetoric disclosed with eyes "; and he goes on to describe, in fanciful detail, how the other senses tried to express themselves through the eyes; so intense and expressive did he find Navarre's gaze to be.

234. **To the court.** The " conceit " seems to be that his behaviours (activities of speaking, and the other senses) retire to the stronghold of his eye, whence to launch their attack (so *Q. & D. W.*). They peep through desire, as through the castle window: i.e. the eloquence of all the senses contributes to the expression of desire in the eye. (See note to l. 233.)

235. **agate,** the stone of a signet ring on which figures, &c., were cut.

237. **impatient . . . see,** " impatient *at having* only the natural function of speech, and not that of vision " (so Dyce).

240. **To feel . . . looking,** to have only the experience of looking.

241, 242, 243. **locked . . . in crystal . . . glass'd.** It is surely clear from these three lines that the jewels were enclosed in a glass receptacle; otherwise the simile of the jewels in crystal would not apply to the " senses *locked* in his eye ". Hart's note, recording gifts of gems *made of crystal* to Queen Elizabeth, does not seem to permit of this point being taken.

243. **glass'd** may be taken to mean " enclosed in a glass vessel or casket ".

tendering, offering, exhibiting.

244. **point you** (F., " point out "), direct you.

245. **margent,** explanatory notes, references, parallels, &c., were then printed in the margins of books, as may be seen in North's *Plutarch.* Cf. *Romeo and Juliet,* i. 3. 85:

> And what obscured in this fair volume lies
> Find written in the margent of his eyes.

249. **disposed,** disposed to mirth, as in v. 2. 467 of this play.

254. **Cupid's . . . news of him,** there seem to be two intimations here: (*a*) that Boyet is " no longer young ", (*b*) that he is being " taught " by his mythical grandson " to suck eggs "; a hint at the impudence of Cupid.

255. **Venus.** Cupid's mother would thus be Boyet's daughter! The Boyet of these lines might be imagined as an elderly person, rather hard of feature, and very different from the Boyet of v. 2, the " flower that smiles " with white teeth, the honey-tongued Boyet whose only wrinkles are those of laughter. Such an apparent inconsistency might point to careless revision (see Introduction); but it might also be argued that in the present passage the girls are merely teasing Boyet by exaggerating the fact that he is not elderly, but older than they are. Thirty-five seems old to twenty.

Act III—Scene 1

1. **make passionate:** the phrase, as Hart points out, occurs in Puttenham's *Arte of English Poesie*, Chap. X, where he writes (*of Proportion by situation*): " which maner of Situation, even without respect of the rime, doth . . . *make* it either . . . more merry, or mournfull, and many wayes *passionate* to the eare and heart of the hearer. The sense in both passages is that of " susceptible, easily moved to strong feeling ".

3. **Concolinel.** See Glossary.

5. **enlargement,** liberty.

festinately, quickly. A latinate word that has now fallen out of use (Lat. *festinare*, to hurry). Shakespeare; taking a hint from Wilson (*Arte of Rhetorique*, Book III, " Plainnesse, what it is "), may be deriding inkhorn terms in his play, along with other affectations; but he uses the word seriously when he puts it into the mouth of Cornwall (*King Lear*, iii. 7. 10), who is no figure of fun.

7. **a French brawl** (brawl. See Glossary). Why should Moth mention a dance here? Possibly because Armado was moved to dance to " Concolinel "; song tunes were then frequently dance tunes. If the song was a French song as Marshall suggests (cit. Furness), the point would be stronger.

11. **canary,** dance in the manner of " the Canaries ", a Spanish dance, the idea of which is said to have been derived from the aborigines of the Canary Islands (*N.E.D.*). Mrs. Quickly (*Merry Wives of Windsor*) in ii. 2. 62 knows the word better than " quandaries ", for which she employs it; suggesting that it was a popular dance.

11. **humour it,** comply with its peculiar nature in your action: accommodate (your gesture) to it. See also "humour", I. i. 226, of this play.

15. **penthouse-like,** like an overhanging projection to protect a window or door from the weather. v. Parker, *Concise Glossary of Architecture* (1905), p. 192. The hat so worn would suggest a gloomy frame of mind.

17. **crossed,** the attitude of the man who is melancholy through love or other causes. Both the position of the hat (v. note above to l. 15) and of the arms seem to be mentioned in this epigram on Ford:

> Deep in a dump alone John Ford was gat
> With folded arms and melancholy hat.

thin-belly doublet, a doublet not stuffed out with bombast (cotton stuffing) which gave an effect of "stoutness". Stubbes (*Anatomie of Abuse, cit.* Furness) laments the fashion of stuffing the doublet so as to "disproportion the body of man".

18. **old painting.** Steevens declares that the most indolent of the ancient masters concealed the hands in portraits they were painting, so as to avoid having to draw them. Furness points out that only *one* picture was mentioned in the text, and hints that Steevens' allegation is rather sweeping.

19. **snip and away,** a variant of the then more common "a snatch and away". Hart quotes Gabriel Harvey, *Foure Letters* (1592): "A snatch and away, with Neoptolemus, and the common sort of students."

20. **complements.** See Glossary.

humours. This word, brought into fashion from the medical terms of the day, was as loosely used by the public as catch-words generally are. For its proper meaning, see note to i. I. 226. Here it seems to mean little more than "peculiarities", "special modes of deportment".

22. **do you note me?.** Qq. and Ff. read ". . . men of note: do you conjecture men that most are affected to these?" "me" is Hanmer's conjecture (1744). But it is still possible to take "do you note . . ., &c." as a parenthetic question and retain the words of the text as printed by regarding, "do you note, men?" (as Hart does) as addressed to the audience. It is important surely to preserve "men" and thus the word play "men of note—note men", which, probably, was intended.

25. **penny.** Q. and F. read "penne", later Qq. and Ff. "pen". "penny" is Hanmer's, followed by later editors. *Q. & D. W.* would retain the original "penne" (= pen) assuming a "pen—penny" quibble. There may be allusion to the old catch phrase "a pennyworth of wit", embodied (cit. Hart) in

the title of a chapbook *The Chapman of a Peneworth of Wit*
(mentioned in Laneham's letter, 1575) and also a "side-glance"
at Nashe in "pen", as *Q. & D. W.* suggest.

26, 27. **But O, . . . forgot.** Possibly a fragment of a popular
song lamenting the passing of the hobby-horse. It is quoted
again in *Hamlet*, iii. 2. 143. It was evidently so well known that
(as with Moth) the immediate reaction to "but O!" was to continue facetiously "the hobby horse . . .", &c. The hobby-horse
had been an important figure in Morris dances and May games
(see Chambers, *Mediæval Stage*, vol. I, pp. 142, 197, 214, 258–9,
whence the mythologic origin of the hobby-horse appears).
The lapse of the hobby-horse from fashion, though eventually
aided by the Puritans, was not due to them in the first instance.
Change of taste did much no doubt to submerge him, as it did
the mediæval romances. But both lingered on in the seventeenth
century. (See Chambers, op. cit., note (i) 1. 197 and Vines, *Course
of English Classicism*, p. 26.)

28. **callest thou, &c.** Armado is indignant because the term
"hobby-horse" has also an insulting significance when applied
to a woman; cf. "nag" and note thereon in *Antony and Cleopatra*
(this edition), iii. 10. 10, and "hackney" in the present play,
l. 30.

29. **colt,** see note immediately preceding; this also had an
abusive meaning, like the other horse homonyms, when applied
to human creatures. This one was used rather of men than of
women. Cf. *Merchant of Venice*, i. 2. 39, where it is quibbingly
applied to the Neapolitan Prince.

35. **out of heart,** unhappy, depressed; cf. "out of humour".

47. **sympathized,** harmonious, appropriate. Verbs ending
-ize were then recent, Lyly being one of the first to use them.
Hart quotes his *Woman in the Moone* (after 1580): "each one in
course shall signorize awhile" (i. 1. 135, Bond's edition).

message, may be abstract for concrete (= messenger). See
note to this play, ii. 1. 187.

56. **Minimè** (Lat.) = least of all, and so, not at all. Hart
points out that it was proper for pages to know Latin; but if
Moth is "aimed" at Nashe, Nashe, like other University Wits,
was fond of Latin tags. Cf. his *Unfortunate Traveller*, passim.

61. **Thump.** Halliwell (cit. Furness), quoting the "thumped"
of iv. 3. 21, considers this also to refer to the *stroke* of the bullet;
Hart regards it as the imitation of the noise of the gun; which
is more probable in view of the sequence of (1) "thump" followed by (2) "I flee".

62. **juvenal.** Greene in his *Groatsworth of Wit* (1592) refers
to Nashe as "young Juvenall, that biting Satirist", comparing

him allusively to the Roman satirist Juvenal (A.D. 60–140).
Juvenal in the sense of "youth" (see Glossary) was fairly common (*Midsummer-Night's Dream*, iii. 1. 97; *2 Henry IV*, i. 2. 22).
Here we may, if we accept the Nashe theory, suspect a play with
both meanings.

66. **costard,** a head (also an apple). The term is used facetiously; cf. also *Lear*, iv. 6. 248: "'ise try whether your costard
or my ballow be the harder". The joke here is the notion of
" a head with its shin broken ", cf. " the toothache in his heel "
of the nursery rhyme.

67. **l'envoy.** See Glossary, and note to iii. 1. 76 below.

68. **egma . . . l'envoy.** According to several editors Costard
believes Armado's high-sounding words to be a list of proposed
remedies, such as the quack carries about in his " mail " (see
Glossary) or bag. *Q. & D. W.* suggest wittily that, for him
" riddle " stands for " ruddle "; " l'envoy" perhaps for "leni-
tive " and " egma " for something with eggs in it! He prefers
the " home remedy " of a plantain leaf.

72. **spleen:** from this organ excesses of emotion, whether of
mirth or the reverse, were believed to arise; and so the word
came to be used for the emotion itself as in *1 Henry IV*, v. 2, 19,

> a hare-brain'd Hotspur, govern'd by a spleen.

74. **inconsiderate,** here used for " rude, unlearned ".

76. **is not l'envoy a salve?** Despite Hart's note (Arden edn.)
to l. 68 above (66 in his text) I can see no strong evidence of word-
play on salve (ointment) and salvé (salute) before Moth's here;
and even here, while the point of his remark *seems* to be that the
envoy of a ballad is a sort of salute to the person to whom it is
dedicated, he does not seem to take that view when he adds the
l'envoy in l. 84. But perhaps his mention of the goose is a " salvé "
(or allusion) to some person then recognizable, but now forgotten.

77. **it is an epilogue . . . &c.** Armado's definition seems to
amount almost to " dénouement ", one of the senses of " envoy "
given in *N.E.D.*, with a quotation from Massinger, *Bashful
Lover*, v. 1. " long since I look'd for this l'envoy ".

82. **moral,** a maxim (Schmidt): rather, I think, a symbolical
statement. Possibly so called because of the mediæval use of
fables and descriptions (e.g. the Bestiaries) symbolically for
moral purposes. See *N.E.D. Moral*, 3.

84. **fox . . . ape, &c.** Is there any point in this animal rhyme
beyond that of an extremely puerile catch? Armado is caught
by being thus made to illustrate, with nonsense, his pompously
professional definition in ll. 77–8 above; and also to be left
with " goose " at the end—a trick of which modern school life

has its analogues. *Q. & D. W.* suspect some allusion comparable to that in

> the Rat, the Cat, and Lovel the dog,
> Rule all England under the Hog.

95. **sold . . . bargain,** made a fool of him. But the suggestion of Cross and Brooke that Costard believed that " l'envoy " is a goose, and that Armado and Moth have been haggling over " a veritable bird " has its attraction.

97. **fast and loose.** See note to i. 2. 149.

105. **market.** *Q. & D. W.* see here an allusion to the proverb: " three women and a goose make a market ".

116. **I smell . . . in this.** I suspect a trick here. Costard is now convinced that a l'envoy is a trick of some sort, equivalent, perhaps, to the latter-day process of " selling a pup ".

119. **immured,** bound.

121. **purgation,** purgative.

129. **incony.** See Glossary.

Jew, as an apparent term of endearment this occurs also in *A Midsummer-Night's Dream,* iii. 1. 97: " Most brisky Juvenal, and eke most lovely Jew." In both contexts the speaker is a clown of the word-bungling type (in *A Midsummer-Night's Dream* the authors of the entertainment were clowns); it is possible then that their " Jew " is an involuntary " lucus a non lucendo ". On the other hand the popular mind might have seen a false nexus between Jew and jewel, aided perhaps by the proverb of value " worth a Jewes eye " (cf. *Merchant of Venice,* ii. 5. 42).

130. **Remuneration,** another jibe at the pomp of poly-syllables, and possibly also at latinate words; though " remuneration " was no fire-new coinage. *N.E.D.* records it first 1477.

131. **three farthings.** This was a small silver coin: issues were made between 1561 and 1581 (Hart).

132. **inkle.** See Glossary.

133. **it carries it,** " it's a winner ".

135. **out of,** without using.

137. **carnation.** See Glossary.

144. **good my knave:** for the position of " my " in such phrases, see Abbott, § 13; he considers that the possessive adjective is really combined with the noun, as in French *monsieur.*

162. **in print,** precisely, accurately. Cf. *Two Gentlemen of Verona,* ii. 1. 177, " All this I speak in print ", and *As You Like It,* v. 4. 94, where we have it as a parallel to " by the book ".

164. **humorous,** i.e. passionate, amorous: partaking of the humour of love-melancholy.

169. **senior-junior,** so Hanmer and various editors for "Signior Junios" of F. and Q. *Junior* is no doubt correct; but signior surely is preferable, both because it is the reading of Q. and F., and also because it enriches the "conceit" of the line. "Signior" is a title of honour corresponding to "Dan" in the second half of the line. It also suggests "senior"; and Cupid is both junior and (*pace Q. & D. W.*) senior; he is older than man, if we may trust pre-history.

Dan. See Glossary.

170. **folded arms.** See above, note on iii. 1. 17.

174. **'paritors,** "an apparitor, or paritor, is an officer of the bishop's court, who carries out citations" (Johnson). These citations or "summonses" were often made in respect of moral delinquencies arising from imprudent love affairs.

175. **corporal of his field,** his aide-de-camp. *N.E.D.* explains "a superior officer of the army in the 16th and 17th centuries, who acted as an assistant or a kind of aide-de-camp to the sergeant-major" (a sergeant-major might then be the equivalent of a commissioned officer of high rank).

176. **tumbler's hoop,** and so, gaily, decoratively, in the manner of ribbons fastened to the hoop used by the tumbler for juggling with.

178. **German clock.** This is no doubt correct although Q. and F. read "cloake". "Possibly 'cloake' originated from the spelling 'clok'" (*Q. & D. W.*). Several other dramatists imitated this ingenious simile of Shakespeare: Ben Jonson in *The Silent Woman* (iv. 1, vol. I, p. 438, Gifford, see footnote thereto). "She takes herself asunder still when she goes to bed, into some twenty boxes; and about the next day noon is put together again, like a great German clock." Middleton (*A Mad World my Masters*), Webster and Cartwright also use it. German clocks do not seem to have been imported into England much earlier: Hart (Introduction to Arden Ed., p. xxvi) notes the mention of a "faire Germaine clocke" in *The Travels of Sir Jerome Horsey* (Hakluyt Society).

179. **Still,** continually, always.

184. **wightly,** so Cambs. ed., for "whitly", Q. F. But I prefer "whitely", i.e. white-skinned; cf. also Rosaline's "white hand" in l. 158 above. It has been otherwise altered to "witty" (e.g. by Collier and Staunton, misled into thinking Rosaline had a brown skin), "whiteless", &c. But Arrowsmith (*Shakespeare's Editors*) quotes a close parallel from Heywood's *Troja Britannica*, canto 5, st. 74: "That hath a whitely face, and a long nose,

And for them both I wonderous well esteeme her." It also occurs
in North's Plutarch (*Life of Brutus*) and in Cotgrave (" *Blan-
chastre* ").

185. **pitch-balls,** as the folk song says: " she had a black and
rolling eye ".

187 **Argus,** the hundred-eyed herdsman who was set to watch
Io after she had been turned into a cow by the goddess Hera.
He was surnamed " Panoptes " (= the all-seer). Shakespeare
would have found the legends of Argus in Ovid's *Metamorphoses*
(Book I).

eunuch, here used in the sense of custodian.

193. **Joan.** Hart alludes to the proverbial saying, " Joan's as
good as my lady ".

Act IV—Scene 1

4. **mounting mind,** used for the sake of play on the meta-
physical and literal uses of the phrase which was probably not
unfamiliar to the audience. It occurs several times in Elizabethan
literature, in Whetstone's *Remembrance of Gascoigne* (1577),
(cit. Hart) " the mounting minde had rather sterve in need ",
in the *Troublesome Raigne of King John* (1591), and (cit. Dyce)
Peele's *Edward I*.

11. **that** = who.

12. **speak'st,** make mention of.

17. **fair is not,** " fair " was used as a noun, and also as an
adjective. As a noun it is found in *Piers Plowman* (1393): " to
turne the fayre outwarde ". C. x. 85.

21. **saved by merit.** See Introduction.

23. **A giving . . . foul,** a generous person, though *ugly*; cf.
As You Like It, iii. 3. 41: " I thank the gods I am foul."

24–27. **now mercy . . . do't,** this is elliptically expressed.
When mercy (or a merciful person) goes hunting, good shooting,
which hits the animal, is viewed with disfavour; and so I'll
keep my reputation as a markswoman; if I miss, I shall have the
excuse of deliberate missing, for pity's sake; if I hit, &c.

33. **bend.** See Glossary.

36. **curst,** ill-tempered, shrewish.

self-sovereignty, this is variously interpreted. Malone:
sovereignty in oneself (not over oneself). Capell: self-acquired
sovereignty. Furness: " self " = " same ". And " same-sove-
reignty " = " this very sovereignty ", which makes the least im-
peded sense.

41. **commonwealth,** i.e. the King's " Academe ".

42. **God dig-you-den** = God give you good even-(ing). Similar abbreviations were common; cf. " God ye gooden ", *Romeo and Juliet*, i. 2. 58, with variants in the same play, in *Coriolanus, Much Ado*, &c.

55–56. **carve . . . capon,** and 59. **break the neck.** The opening of the letter (and breaking of the seal) is compared to the carving of a chicken. " Poulet " (Cotgrave), "a chicken"; also, " a love-letter or love-message ".

60. **By heaven, &c.** *Q. & D. W.* adduce evidence for supposing that this letter was inserted in 1597 to replace some deleted dialogue; pointing out this inconsistency in the typography of the 1598 quarto, viz. that whereas Armado's letter in i. 1 was printed in italic, this letter has been printed in roman type; the suggestion is that the first had been written in Italian script, the second, some years later at the time of revision in English script (p. 114). As for the style: Halliwell refers to a letter in Wilson's *Arte of Rhetorique*, inserted there, or composed, as an example of the bad " inkhorn " manner that he deplores; it is strongly latinate and reminds us rather of the Limousin student in Rabelais than of Armado, as in this sentence: " now therefore being accersited to such splendente renoume, and dignitie splendidious; I doubte not but you will adiuvate suche poor adnichilate orphanes as whilome ware condisciples with you ". Armado, it is true, uses some latinate words (" indubitable ", " illustrate ", " infallible ", " magnanimous", &c.); but these are established forms, and far less astounding than the neologisms in Wilson's model; moreover, Armado has other tricks as well, the allusions, questions, &c., which have various origins.

62. **More fairer, &c.** Hart cites Sidney, *Arcadia*: " That which made her fairness much the fairer was that it was a fair ambassador of a most fair mind." Both are using the figure *Traductio* or " the Tranlacer " (Puttenham (Arber), p. 213), the turning of words " into . . . sundry shapes ", " fairer, fair, truer, truth ".

64, 66. **The magnanimous . . . Zenelophon.** The antithesis, combined with allusion, is again reminiscent of the style of *Euphues*, but not the pompous double epithets, which partake of the *Bomphologia* or " Pompious speech " of Puttenham (Arber, p. 266). There are numerous double epithets linked with " and " in *Arcadia*, but they are not " pompious "; more so are those in Berners, e.g. Preface to his *Froissart*; and Armado's pomp seems, here at least, to derive something from this stiffer, earlier manner (*c.* 1525).

64. **illustrate,** illustrious: in this sense as early as 1562 and (= illuminated) 1526 (*N.E.D.*).

65, 66. **Cophetua . . . Zenelophon,** see i. 2. 105. Percy has a ballad on this subject in his *Reliques* (q.v.) when the beggar's name is Penelophon. He took this version from Richard Johnson's *Crown Garland of Goulden Roses*, 1612; where it is called *A Song of a Beggar and a King*. This is evidently a more modern version that the one mentioned by Moth, i. 2. 107. There are several references to it in Elizabethan literature, including De- loney's *Gentle Craft* (cit. Hart). Shakespeare refers again to it in *Romeo and Juliet*, ii. 1. 14, " when King Cophetua loved the beggar maid ".

67. **Veni, vidi, vici,** from North's Plutarch, *Life of Julius Cæsar* (1579): " he only wrote three words unto Anicius at Rome; *Veni, Vidi, Vici*: I came, and saw, and overcame." Also used by Puttenham to illustrate *"Parimion,* or the Figure of like letter " (Book III).

    annothanize. Q. and F.; later Ff. " anatomize ". Q. & D. W. point out that " annothomize " occurs in *2 Henry IV*. " Anato- mize " is probably meant.

68. **O base and obscure vulgar:** for double epithets see note to lines 64, 66 above. This exclamatory form of rhetorical ornament is tabulated in Wilson (*Arte of Rhetorique*) as *Exclamatio* (p. 205, Mair, Oxford, 1909).

    vulgar, vulgar tongue. Cf. a close parallel to this condescension on the part of Touchstone, *As You Like It*, v. 1. 52: " Therefore, you clown, abandon—which is in the vulgar, leave . . . &c."

    videlicet. See Glossary.

69. **one . . . two . . . three.** If, as Mair maintains, Shakespeare is satirizing formal rhetoric as expounded by Wilson (see Intro- duction to Wilson op. cit. p. xxxiii) he may here be glancing at Wilson's numbered classifications and analyses as " i. It is honest. ii. It is possible. iii. Easie to be done " (analysing an " Oration demonstrative ", p. 17).

70. **Who came? the king, &c.** The same analysis in Wilson is carried out on pp. 21, 22 by question and answer of this kind; the example used being the account of David's victory over Goliath. Shakespeare may be caricaturing the rather pedantic method of " How did he it? Marie, he put a stone in his sling, . . ., &c.". Hart notes that this was a favourite trick with Gabriel Harvey.

76. **both in one . . . both,** a rhetorical figure or scheme called Regression, and described by Wilson, p. 205.

80. **exchange,** get in exchange.

    rags? robes, this antithesis and alliterative pair is noted by Hart in four different passages of *Euphues' Golden Legacie* (Lodge, 1590). Armado is, on the whole, sparing of " the figure of like letter "—more so than Lyly.

81. **tittles? titles.** Hart: " a quibble of Harvey's ". His citation from Harvey's letter to Spenser, 1579, contains the words: " But to let Titles and Tittles passe, and come to the very point indeede."

tittles. See Glossary.

82. **profane,** because it would be sacrilege to presume to kiss the adored one's feet and so on; profane thy foot with my lips, in fact.

83. **picture,** image, appearance. Cf. *Merchant of Venice* (i. 2. 78): "he is a proper man's picture".

85. **Thus dost thou, &c.** Warburton considered this to be " a quotation from some ridiculous poem of that time "; but it is more probably Shakespeare's, since (1) 'Nemean (not Nem-'ean) is his stressing also in *Hamlet*, i. 4. 83: " As hardy as the Nemean lion's nerve." (2) The allusion and stress came from Golding's *Ovid* (ix. 242), which was a permanent quarry for Shakespeare's classical references. (3) One might almost suspect Shakespeare of caricaturing his own manner; cf. *The Rape of Lucrece*, 421 ff.:

> As the grim lion fawneth o'er his prey,
> Sharp hunger by the conquest satisfied,
> So o'er this sleeping soul doth Tarquin stay,
> His rage of lust by gazing qualified.

Nemean lion. According to the Greek legend this lion, the offspring of Typhon and Echidna, was strangled by Hercules, in the valley of Nemea.

96. **phantasime** (see Glossary) = fantastic fellow. Used also in v. 1. 17 of this play, but apparently nowhere else. Cf. Ital. *fantasima* or *fantasma*.

a Monarcho. An actual character who haunted the court some time before 1580, the date of the publication of Churchyard's Epitaphe on him (in *Churchyard's Chance*, 1580). There we are told, *inter alia*, that he was:

> . . . well disposde, if Prince did pleasure take
> At any mirthe that he poore man could make,

very much like Armado. Nashe (*Have With You to Saffron Walden*, 1596) tells us that he " ware crownes on his shoes ". He was an Italian and, it would seem, a harmless lunatic.

105. **thine another day.** P. A. Daniel (*Athenæum*, 13th Oct., 1883, cit. Furness) explains as " it will be of use to you: you will find the benefit of it hereafter ". He quotes several parallels for this apparently popular phrase, e.g. Ben Jonson (*Tale of a Tub*, ii. 1): " Let 'un mend his manners then, and know his betters . . . and 'twill be his own . . . another day." Shakespeare

does not use the phrase again. The implication of the remark may be: " your experience of what love-letters *may* contain, judging by this one, will no doubt be valuable to you ".

106. **suitor,** then pronounced like " shooter " (which is the reading of Q.; " suitor " being Farmer's emendation). Boyet, possibly referring to the love-letter, means " suitor "; but Rosaline takes him up (l. 107) in the sense of " shooter ". The pun is found elsewhere in Elizabethan literature. Furness cites Lyly, *Euphues and his England*: " There was a Lady in *Spaine*, who after the decease of hir Father hadde three sutors, (and yet never a good Archer)" (p. 70, Bond, Oxford).

107. **continent,** that which contains. Cf. *Antony and Cleopatra*, iv. 14. 40: " Heart, once be stronger than thy Continent, Crack thy frail case."

108. **put off,** and 111. **put on.** Perhaps equivalent to " that was well countered " and " that was well struck ". Hart quotes a passage where they occur in antithesis (Gascoigne's *Hermit's Tale* (Nichols' Progresses, i. 559), 1576): " charged . . . to weare this punishment with patience, which necessyty did putt on, and destyny wold putt off ".

110. **horns,** one of numberless allusions to the superstition that horns, like the song of the cuckoo, denoted inconstancy in love. (See *Antony and Cleopatra* in this edition, note to i. 2. 4.)

112. **deer?** with, of course, the deer-dear quibble, which occurs elsewhere in Shakespeare, e.g. *Merry Wives*, v. 5. 123, *1 Henry VI*, iv. 2. 54, " And they shall find dear deer of us ".

117. **come upon,** tackle, confront suddenly. Cf. *Henry V*, iii. 6. 177, " I hope they will not come upon us now ".

118. **Pepin,** called le Bref, A.D. 714–768, was the first King of the Carlovingian dynasty.

121. **Guinover,** or **Guinevere.** The name, Halliwell notes, was in Shakespeare's time used jocularly or in contempt. This is supported by Florio (*New World of Wordes*, 1611): " Guinedra, a word of mockerie for the Tartares Queene or Empresse, as we say, Queen Guinever." The original Guinevere was the legendary queen of King Arthur.

122. **touching the hit it,** i.e. in regard to the subject of " hitting " as mentioned in the well-known song.

123. **Thou canst not, &c.,** a well-known song (and dance tune) of the time; Furness reprints the music, which appears in Chappell's *Popular Music of the Olden Time*. There are several more or less contemporary references to it, of which Stephen Gosson's (*Quips for Upstart Newfangled Gentlemen*, 1595, cit. Hart) is the nearest: " *Can you hit it* is oft their daunce."

128. **A mark,** the conversation (up to l. 134) becomes heavily charged with the technicalities of archery, with which, as with those of hunting (cf. *Taming of the Shrew*, Induction, beside iv. 2 of this play) Shakespeare was thoroughly familiar.

130. **mark . . prick,** the mark must be taken here to be the equivalent of " target "; though generally a mark was " whatever is shot at ". A prick was the centre of the target (Furness); but it seems also to have been used of a wand or stick set up as a target—a difficult one indeed.

mete. See Glossary = measure, and so, aim at.

131. **Wide o' the bow hand,** in modern parlance, a miss at nine o'clock (to the left of the target). The bow was held in the left hand.

132. **clout.** See Glossary.

133. **hand . . . out,** " out of form, out of practice ".

134. **upshoot,** or upshot, was the best shot at any given moment of the competition. Hart quotes Middleton, *Family of Love*, v. 3: " an arrow that sticks for the upshot against all comers ".

pin, a wooden nail (painted black) that kept in place the white " clout " of the centre mark; the " bull's eye ". Cf. Middleton, *No wit no Help like a Woman's*, ii. 1. (cit. Hart): " I'll cleave the black pin i' the midst of the white."

136. **rubbing,** a term in bowling more frequently used as noun by Shakespeare; encountering obstacles (other bowls) in the course of the moving bowl, which is thus diverted. Cf. " every rub is smoothed on our way ", *Henry V*, ii. 2. 188.

140. **obscenely,** perhaps for " obscurely ". Bottom in *Midsummer Night's Dream*, i. 2. 111, misuses this word, intending, perhaps, "seemly".

141. **Armado, &c. . . . nit.** Dyce and Staunton observe that this passage appears to be out of place and irrelevant. *Q. & D. W.* suggest that this may possibly refer to an episode in the 1593 version, where " Armado and Moth appeared . . . to cut some capers with the Princess and her Ladies ", which was cancelled to give place to the letter in 1597.

o' th' one. Rowe's 2nd emendation: Q.1 reads " ath toothen " and F. " ath to the ".

145. **nit,** properly a louse-egg, but here used for " diminutive creature ". Rather contemptuous; cf. *Taming of the Shrew*, iv. 3. 110:

Thou flea, thou nit, thou winter cricket, thou.

146. **Sola.** It seems to have been a stock feature for certain clowns on the Elizabethan stage to come on and go off shouting; cf. Lancelot Gobbo, *Merchant of Venice*, v. 1. 39, and Launce, *Two Gentlemen of Verona*, iii. 1. 189. Perhaps one or more clown actors made a speciality of comic " bellowing ".

Scene 2

1. **done . . . conscience,** cf. 2 *Corinthians*, i. 12: " for our rejoicing is this, the testimony of our conscience, that in simplicity and godly sincerity . . . we have had our conversation in the world . . ." Nathaniel is making his *apologia* for being present at the worldly sport of hunting.

3. **sanguis, in blood.** Holofernes is showing off his Latin; but *sanguis* is the Latin for " blood " not " *in* blood ". Is Shakespeare deliberately making him an inaccurate, rusty scholar, as a country schoolmaster might have become? *Q. & D. W.* seem to think so.

in blood, in full vigour, in perfect condition. Cf. *Antony and Cleopatra*, iii. 13. 174.

4. **pomewater.** See Glossary.

5. **cælo . . . terra.** Why is the ablative form of *cælum* (Lat. sky) used? is it again a mistake of Holofernes?

10. **buck of the first head.** Steevens quotes from the *Return from Parnassus* (1602), ii. 5: " I caus'd the Keeper to sever the rascall Deere, from the Buckes of the first head: now sir, a Bucke of the first yeare is a Fawne, the second yeare a pricket, the third yeare a Sorell, the fourth yeare a Soare, the fift a Buck of the first head, the sixt yeare a compleat Buck " (ed. Macray, p. 107).

11. **haud credo,** (Latin) " I don't believe it."

12. **pricket,** see note to l. 10.

13. **yet, &c.,** this long qualifying statement seems designed to show Holofernes in his most patronizing and superior mood, attempting to give Dull's " barbarism " the benefit of the doubt, but finally deciding that little benefit is due.

insinuation, a term used by Wilson (*Arte of Rhetorique*), pp. 99, 103 (Mair's Oxford edition), and defined as " a privie twining or close creeping in, to win favour with much circumstaunce, called insinuation ".

14. **in via,** (Latin) in the way.

facere, (Latin) to make.

15. **replication.** (1) a rejoinder; in law, a reply to a reply, e.g. plaintiff's reply to the defence. There seems to be definitely the idea of an informative or explanatory reply. (2) replication (Replicatio (Latin) occurs as a rhetorical term) = repetition; that does not seem to be the meaning here, but the former (1).

ostentare, (Latin) to show; esp. to show off, make a display.

16. **inclination,** note the jingle of the recurrent " -ation ", which is no doubt deliberate for the effect of pedantic pomp. Mason attributed the same fault to Dr. Johnson. (*Epistle to Dr. Shebbeare*, pub. 1777):

O for a thousand tongues! and every tongue
Like Johnson's arm'd with words of six feet long,
In multitudinous vociferation
To panegyricize this glorious nation
Whose liberty results from her taxation.

18. ratherest, obsolete in standard English, but still a " live "
form in sixteenth century. *N.E.D.* cit. Fisher, *Spiritual Consolation*, 1535, " your soule, when you would ratherest have it
stirred ".

unconfirmed, raw, inexperienced (Schmidt). Cf. *Much Ado*,
iii. 3. 123: " That shows thou art unconfirmed." We may suspect
either an anti-climax here, or that Holofernes' way of being
" superior " is to affect a particular horror at rustic " greenness ".
Contrast with his own University *savoir vivre*. Sir Nathaniel
similarly poses as a man of " taste and feeling ", at Dull's expense,
in his next speech.

insert, introduce (into conversation). Cf. *Merchant of
Venice*, i. 3. 94: " Was this inserted to make interest good?"

21. bis coctus, (Latin) twice cooked or twice sodden; an
allusion to the Greek proverb δὶς κράμβη θάνατος (" cabbage
twice is death ") and cf. in Juvenal, Satire VII, l. 154, *occidit
miseros crambe repetita magistros*, " cabbage served up again is
death to the wretched master "; referring to the boredom of
stale repetition. Lyly has it in English (*Euphues and his England*,
vol. ii, p. 154) (Bond): ". . . who left out nothing that before I
put in, which I muste omitte, least I set before you Coleworts
twise sodden." Dull has *repeated* himself.

28. which we of taste . . . are. Q. reads " which we taste,
and feeling, are ". Tyrwhitt supplied the " of " and has been
generally followed.

which we = as to which we (are men of taste and feeling);
the sentence is parenthetic; and the " which " refers to the
barren plants; " with reference to which, we (on the contrary)
are men of taste and feeling, and should be thankful that those
qualities (parts) are developed in us more than in him "; a
pharisaical sentiment. A similar construction is found in *Henry
V*, ii. 2. 159 (see Abbott, § 272):

But God be thanked for prevention;
Which I in sufferance heartily will rejoice.

Nevertheless neither the sense nor the line (which is too long)
runs easily; and the parenthesis may have been added (see
Q. & D. W., p. 154) at the time of revision.

30. patch. See Glossary. The line means: it would be equally
unbecoming for a fool to be put to learning and sent to a school.

31. omne bene, (Latin) all is well.

31. **being . . . mind,** agreeing with the statement of a learned man of ancient times. Hart cites, among several instances, Golding's *Ovid* (vii. 449): " Here men (so auncient fathers said that were as then alive) did breede of deawie Mushroomes."

32. **many . . . wind,** the application of this gnomic sentence may be: " we can put up with fools, though we may not like them ".

35. **Dictynna.** Steevens notes that this uncommon title for Diana (the moon) occurs in Golding's *Ovid (Metamorphoses)*: " Dictynna guarded with her traine, and proud of killing deere."

39. **raught.** See Glossary.

40. **allusion . . . exchange,** " the play of wit (or of ideas—the joke, in fact) holds good with Adam's name, just as with Cain " (so Warburton). It is however possible that with " exchange " there may be some punning reference to the change of the moon, as Brae suggests.

41. **collusion,** " a trick or ambiguity, in words or reasoning " (*N.E.D.*). As *Q. & D. W.* point out Dull's apparent blunders are sometimes quite *apropos*.

44. **pollusion** = pollution. The form on which Dull has stumbled is noted as a variant in *N.E.D.*

50. **Perge,** (Latin) proceed.

51. **abrogate** = do away with, put an end to.

scurrility here seems to mean " impropriety " of any kind. So Puttenham uses it (p. 274, Arber): " Yet will ye see . . . . how pleasant speeches and favoring some skurrility and unshamefastness have now and then a certaine decencie." Wilson (p. 4) finds " scurrilitie, or ale-house jesting ", odious.

52. **affect the letter,** use alliteration; as was freely practised by the pre-Spenserian poets (cf. Turberville). Puttenham, counselling a moderate indulgence, also seems to think that it " argues facility " (p. 262): " . . . such composition makes the meetre runne away smoother, and passeth from the lippes with more facility by iteration of a letter than by alliteration."

argues, indicates.

53. **pricket,** for the technical terms for deer in this doggerel, see above, note to l. 10.

55. **yell . . . L,** by pronunciation of the time a pun.

57. **one more L,** referring to the spelling " sorrell "; the two l's standing in Roman characters for two fifties.

60. **he claws him,** i.e. Nathaniel " scratches the back of " (flatters) Holofernes. The talent (talon) quibble is obvious.

63. **forms, figures, &c.** Holofernes is probably referring to the " elevated style " mentioned by Wilson (169, " the great

or mightie kinde ") and Puttenham (164, " a stile to be lift up and advaunced by choyce of wordes, phrases, sentences and figures, high, lofty, eloquent, and magnifik in proportion "). Both are probably in debt to Quintilian.

65. **ventricle of memory.** In a passage (cit. Furness) from Vicary's *Anatomie of the Bodie of Man* (1548) the brain is said to be divided into three parts or ventricles: " in the thirde Ventrikle . . . is founded . . . the vertue Memorative ". Wilson in his long discussion of memory (op. cit., p. 208–18) is aware of this theory, and stresses the importance of memory to the literary man.

pia mater, the membrane enclosing the brain. (" pia mater " is Rowe's restoration of Q. and F. " primater ".)

66. **mellowing** or ripening (of opportunity).

73. **Mehercle!** a Latin exclamation (literally, an oath " by Hercules ").

ingenuous, probably means "endowed with native wit " (= " ingenious ", a then not infrequent confusion. *v. N.E.D.*).

75. **vir sapit . . . loquitur** (Q. sapis: later edd. sapit); from Lily's Grammar: "*Vir sapit qui pauca loquitur*, that Man is wise that speaketh few things or words."

78. **quasi,** (Latin) as if.

pers-on. Malone refers to a passage in Blackstone's *Commentaries*, where the derivation of " parson " from Latin *persona* is mentioned: " A parson, *persona ecclesiae*, is one that hath full possession of all due rights of a parochial church." Holofernes follows up pedantry with the pun " pierce one "!

82. **piercing a hogshead!** Hart makes it clear that this is very probably a reference to the Harvey-Nashe controversy (see Introduction, p. x); and notes this passage in Gabriel Harvey's *Pierce's Supererogation* (1592–3), a reply to Nashe's *Pierce Peniless* (1592): " She knew what she said, that intituled Pierce, *the hoggeshead* of witt: Penniles, the tosspot of eloquence: & Nashe the very inventor of Asses." From this it appears that hogshead was used (as also perhaps by Costard in l. 81) in the sense of " blockhead ".

83. **turf,** i.e. clod.

88. **Fauste, precor, &c.** (Q. " facile precor gellida, quando pecas omnia sub umbra ruminat "—more bungled Latin: see note to l. 3 above): " Faustus, I beg, while all the cattle ruminate beneath the cool shade." With these words Mantuan's first Eclogue begins. Baptista Spagnuoli (surnamed Mantuanus from his birthplace, Mantua, 1448–1516) was one of the most eminent writers of Latin poetry in the Italian Renaissance. He was also General of the Carmelite order. The eclogues had

become a regular school-book, and it was no sign of deep learning to be able to quote from them—the reverse in fact—as this sarcastic quotation from Harvey (*Foure Letters*, cit. Hart) demonstrates: " He lost his imagination a thousand waies, and I believe searched every corner of his Grammar-Schoole witte (for his margine is as deeplie learned, as *Fauste precor gelida*) to see if he could finde anie meanes to relieve his estate." Nashe refers to the quotation in his reply, *Foure Letters Confuted*. Mantuan was prescribed as a text book at St. Paul's School in the Statute of 1518, and was used at St. Bees in 1585 (Baynes, cit. Furness). The point of the quotation here is that it is part of Holofernes' elaborate make-believe that he is not burning with curiosity about the letter; he glances round at the rustic scenery, which brings pastoral poetry (he would have us know) to mind: he quotes Italian, and hums a tune with studied abstraction like Edmund in *Lear*.

91. **Venetia, &c.** (Q. had this corrupt version: " Vemchie vencha, que non te unde, que non to perreche." The restoration was Theobald's.) This Italian tag is thus translated in Florio's *First Fruites*, 1578: " Venise woo (who) seeth thee not, praiseth thee not " (cit. Furness).

94. **ut, re, &c.** He does not sing up the scale (which would be ut-re-mi-fa-sol-la); neither does Edmund in *Lear*, i. 2. 153: his phrase is fa-sol-la-mi. *Q. & D. W.* express the belief that Holofernes is again blundering by singing up the scale but attaching the wrong syllables to the sounds; but in view of Edmund's phrase one might have some grounds for suspecting that either (*a*) Holofernes was singing a phrase too or (*b*) taking *Q. & D. W.*'s view, both he and Edmund made mistakes or (*c*) Shakespeare made mistakes. (*a*) seems the most easily tenable.

95. **Horace,** the famous Latin poet, Quintus Horatius Flaccus, 65–8 B.C.

98. **a staff, a stanze,** the terms are synonymous = a group of verse lines arranged in a pattern as a unit.

lege, domine, (Latin) read, sir.

99. **If love, &c.** This sonnet was published by Jaggard in *The Passionate Pilgrim*, 1599.

103. **bias,** natural inclination.

113. **apostrophas.** Ben Jonson's *Grammar* (as quoted by several editors) gives this definition: " *Apostrophus* is the rejection of a vowel from the beginning or end of a word;" and Nathaniel is accused of not having rejected a vowel where he should. The vowel in question (in the last line of the sonnet) is difficult to find; but it will be noticed that this line as it stands is not, as the others, an Alexandrine, but an eleven-syllabled one. *Q. & D. W.* following Gollancz, conclude that Holofernes blun-

deringly used " apostrophas " for diæresis; a diæresis in "sings " would restore the scansion:

>   That sing-ës heaven's praise with such an earthly tongue.

But syllabic 3rd sing. -es was not a normal Elizabethan form; as *plural* or *genitive singular*, -es, " though surely an archaism in Shakespeare's time, is still occasionally met with in his verses " (Vietor, p. 111). " The ' sing-es ' conclusion, though attractive, seems sufficiently conjectural to warrant a search for an alternative. Now if Nathaniel had missed the iambic stress of the line (" miss the accent ") by reading out eleven syllables: " That sings | heavens | praise with | such an | earthly | tongue." Holofernes might have taken this for a *ten*-syllabled line spoilt by pronouncing "heaven" as two syllables instead of one with aphæresis (apostrophus) (Shakespeare uses both forms, Vietor, 114–15). "That sings | heav'ns praise | , &c." The sonnet is slightly altered in *The Passionate Pilgrim*, but the shortening of the last line remains:

>   . . . O do not love that wrong
>   To sing heaven's praise with such an earthly tongue.

If this is a surreptitious version of the sonnet taken down at the play, the pirate, like the rest of the audience, would presumably have seen the joke about " sings—sing-es ", and had it impressed on his memory that "sings", which can be made dissyllabic, was the key-word. But so little was this the case that he actually substituted an unchangeably monosyllabic form of the verb. The joke was not over "sings " but over "heaven".

114. **supervise the canzonet,** read the poem.

canzonet. See Glossary.

115. **numbers ratified,** mere words in metrical form; verse-rhythms arranged in correct order (but only after the apostrophus is found as Charlton points out). According to Puttenham " numerositie " is " rithmus ", " a certaine flowing utterance by slipper words and sillables " (p. 91).

facility, ease.

116. **cadence.** Puttenham, p. 93: " this cadence is the fal of a verse in every last word with a certain tunable sound "; he seems to mean the last strong stress in a line—the one which may be used for rhyme.

caret, (Latin) it is wanting.

Ovidius Naso. Publius Ovidius Naso (43 B.C.–A.D. 18), the Latin poet, author of *Fasti*, *Metamorphoses*, *Tristia*, &c., banished by Augustus to Tomi. The exquisite and decorative character of his poetry had inspired the later middle ages and early renaissance; and, largely through Golding's translation, it now inspired Shakespeare and his contemporaries.

118. **jerks,** strokes; especially such as schoolmasters use for educational ends. Not used elsewhere by Shakespeare.

Imitari, (Latin) to imitate (Q. and F. imitarie); possibly " picked up " from Cicero, *de Oratore.*

124. **superscript,** address.

snow-white. See above, note to line iii. 1. 184.

126. **intellect,** meaning, purport.

130. **sequent,** follower (rare in this sense).

132. **Trip and go.** Furness quotes Chappell: "it was one of the favourite Morris-dances of the sixteenth and seventeenth centuries, and frequently alluded to by writers of those times." Charlton gives the words from Nashe (*Summer's Last Will and Testament,* 1600), of which two lines will illustrate the rhythm:

> Trip and goe, heave and hoe,
> Up and downe, to and fro.

136. **Have with thee,** off with you.

138. **father,** the reference is here, more probably than in line above, to one of the early fathers of the church. Hence Holofernes' Protestant fear of "colourable colours" in some Popish writer.

139. **colourable colours,** plausible pretexts (as Furness) or perhaps casuistry, such as a good Protestant might suspect in Popish works!

142. **pen,** penmanship. Hart and others quote Lodge's *Rosalynde* (1590): " How like you this sonnet?" quoth Rosader. " Marry," quoth Ganymede, " for the pen well, for the passion ill."

144. **before repast** (" before " Q., " being " F.). The Q. reading gives a simple and satisfactory meaning.

147. **ben venuto,** (Rowe: Q. bien venuto); welcome (Ital.).

150. **the text.** Which text? probably one in Sir Nathaniel's imagination, and an early variant of a literary quip still popular; cf. E. Wallace, *The India Rubber Men,* Chap. I: " The Good Book says, ' As a bird is known by his note, so is a man by the company he keeps '."

152. **certes.** See Glossary.

154. **pauca verba,** (Latin) " few words ", " not a word ".

Scene 3

2. **pitched . . . toil . . . toil . . . pitch,** an example of " Regression " (Wilson, 205).

pitched a toil, set a trap or snare.

pitch, referring to Rosaline's black eyes.

4. **the fool.** Costard, who said it in i. 1. 297.

6. **Ajax.** Son of Telamon, one of the Greek chieftains who besieged Troy. Mortified by the advice of Athena that Achilles' arms should be awarded to Odysseus and not to him, he madly slaughtered the sheep of the Greek army, believing that he was killing his enemies; finally he stabbed himself.

10. **lie in my throat,** tell the most complete and heart-felt lie. Hart quotes Sidney, *Arcadia*: " ' Thou liest in thy throat,' said Zelmane."

17. **in,** in love, in the same predicament as I am.

21. **thumped,** hit; not the same meaning as " thump " in iii. 1. 61.

bird-bolt, a blunt-headed arrow for killing birds, knocking them over but not wounding them. Cf. *Much Ado*, i. 1. 36: " And my uncle's fool . . . subscribed for Cupid, and challenged him at the bird-bolt."

left pap. Cf. *Midsummer-Night's Dream*, v. 1. 305: ". . . that left pap, Where heart doth hop."

49. **triumviry** (Rowe ed. 2 for Q. triumpherie) or triumvirate.

corner-cap of society, a three-cornered cap (as well as four-cornered) was worn, at Universities, by divines and also (*Q. & D. W.* point out) by judges—the black cap, to which those editors suspect an allusion. Women were aping this form of hat when Stubbes wrote (*Anatomie of Abuses*, 1583, N.S.S., p. 69) that they wore " Lattice cappes with three hornes, three corners I should saie, like the forked cappes of Popishe Priests, with their perriwincles, chitterlynges, and the like apishe toyes of infinite varietie."

of society, either " of our ' academe ' ", or " of our association as lovers and as perjurers ".

50. **Tyburn,** and so, gallows. Tyburn on the N, side of Hyde Park was for centuries a place of public execution. There seems to have been a triangular gallows there; *Q. & D. W.* draw attention to this passage in Lyly's *Pappe with a Hatchett,* 1589 (Bond, Vol. II, 401): " There's one with a lame wit, which will not weare a foure cornerd cap, then let him put on Tiburne that hath but three corners."

simplicity, folly.

54. **guards,** trimmings, ornamentation. Farmer believes this to refer to the tawdry finery then worn by Cupid on the stage.

55. **slop** (Theobald; Q. and F. " shop "), loose trousers.

56. **Did not, &c.,** in the *Passionate Pilgrim*, with several verbal alterations; " could not " for " cannot " line 2. " My vow was " for " Vows are but " in line 9; " doth " for " dost "

line 10; " Exhale " for " Exhalest " line 11; " To breake " for " To lose " in the last line; and a few changes in punctuation.

66. **in thee it is,** probably " it becomes thy property, part of thee ". He is shelving the responsibility.

67. **then,** when that has once happened (but *Passionate Pilgrim* alters this sense by placing a comma before " then ").

69. **to lose,** so as to lose; omission of " as " after " so " is fairly frequent in Shakespeare; cf. " so fond to come abroad ", *Merchant of Venice*, iii. 3. 10.

70. **liver-vein,** passionate vein; the liver was believed to be the organ where fervid passions originated. Guenevora's " liver boyles " in Hughes' *The Misfortunes of Arthur* (1587, Cunliffe, *E.E. Classic Tragedies*, p. 230) and Pistol's is " burning hot " (*Merry Wives*, ii. 1. 118).

71. **green goose,** young girl; cf. above, note to i. 1. 97.

72. **we are . . . way,** we have " erred and strayed ".

74. **All hid.** Cotgrave gives " *Cline-mucette*: The game called Hodman-blinde; Harry-racket; or, are you all-hid?" (cit. Hart).

77. **More sacks to the mill,** i.e. " they all come rolling in ". Cf. Nashe, *Pasquil's Apologie* (1590) (cit. Hart): " To the next, to the next, more sacks to the Myll ". Furnivall sees an allusion to a boys' game (in introduction to Q. facsimile of this play).

78. **woodcocks,** fools, dupes, who are easily caught. Cf. *Twelfth Night*, ii. 5. 93, Fabian, speaking of Malvolio: " Now is the woodcock near the gin ".

80. **coxcomb,** conceited fool; " a proud woodcocke ", as Cotgrave has it.

82. **she is not, corporal** (so Q. F.). Biron is calling Dumaine a corporal (see note above to iii. 1. 175); a corporal of love's field, as he had formerly described himself. So Capell; but Theobald, reading, " but corporal " (for " not c."), maintains that corporal = " corporeal " and refers to the lady; the sense would then be " she's no wonder—but mere flesh and blood ". Neither explanation is very satisfactory. Why should Dumaine be called corporal and not Longaville? Or why (taking the other interpretation) should the lady be called " corporal " by way of retort to Dumain's praise, since he does not call her incorporeal? It is not a very pointed retort.

83. **hath,** probably 3rd plur. as in *Merchant of Venice*, iii. 2. 270: " Hath all his ventures failed?"

quoted, (Capell and other for *coted* of Q. F.) set down, and so demonstrated; her hair has shown amber itself to be ugly.

84. **raven,** a black *fowl* (pun with foul).

85. **Stoop;** this may be an adjectival use, as Schmidt hints.

93. **incision,** cutting for the purpose of letting blood.

94. **saucers,** or bowls, used for catching the blood. Barber-surgeons would exhibit them as an advertisement of their trade. (So Halliwell, cit. Furness.)

97. **On a day, &c.** This poem appears in *The Passionate Pilgrim* with " gan " for " can " l. 6; " wisht " for " wish " l. 8; " alas " for " alack " l. 11; ll. 15–16 " do not . . . thee " are omitted in *P.P.*; and the pointing of *P.P.* is different in many respects. The poem was also included in *England's Helicon*, 1600, with further slight alterations, the chief being " shepherd " for " love " in the 7th line.

103. **That,** so that. " So " before " that " is frequently omitted; cf. Abbott, § 283 and v. 2. 9 of this play.

104. **Wish,** subjunctive. Abbott, § 368, finds no other instance in Shakespeare of " (so) that " plus subjunctive. He seems however a little doubtful of the reading even so, and suggests that *-ed* or *-es* may have dropped out. F.2 has " wished "; but Q. reads " wish ".

115. **for Jove,** to be Jove; he would renounce his divinity.

118. **fasting,** longing, hungry (so Johnson).

120, 121. **Ill . . . note;** " one evil deed (i.e. perjury) making a precedent for another would thus acquit me of perjury." It would not, of course; but Biron is perversely arguing that " two wrongs make a right ", as may be seen from the last line of his speech.

example, as a verb, is fairly common in Shakespeare; cf. i. 2. 112 of this play.

123. **far from . . . society,** i.e. your love makes you selfish; since " misery loves company " merely for its own consolation.

131. **wreathed,** folded; see note above to iii. 1. 17.

136. **reek,** steam, as though the sighs were a visible vapour.

142. **so infringed.** (Q. infringed); the " so " suggested by Walker, amongst other conjectures to amend the metre.

144. **leap and laugh,** as in Sonnet 98: " That heavy Saturn laugh'd and leap'd with him " (cit. Hart).

146. **by me,** about, concerning me (Abbott, § 148). Cf. " How say by the French lord?", *Merchant of Venice*, i. 2. 60.

151. **coaches,** (Rowe ed. 2, for "couches" of Q. F.) see the 9th line of the King's poem (l. 31 of this scene).

154. **like of,** " of " was used after a verb that was not always transitive, as " hope " or " like ", especially in the case of verbs once used transitively (Abbott, § 177). Cf. *Much Ado*, v. 4. 59: " I am a husband if you like of me."

156. **o'ershot,** off the target; to have shot wide of the mark, gone astray. Cf. *Julius Cæsar*, iii. 2. 156: " I have o'ershot myself to tell you of it."

157. **mote,** (and *beam* in next line) referring to the passage on the mote and beam in N.T. (Matthew, vii. 3–5). Q. and F. read " moth " for " mote " (Rowe's spelling); but the word is the same.

160. **teen.** See Glossary.

162. **gnat,** a poor, contemptible insect.

162–166. **To see . . . toys.** A parallel, with the satiric conception of great " worthies " doing trivial things, occurs in Rabelais. See Introduction, p. xx.

163. **Hercules.** He was, like Hector, a favourite with Shakespeare, among the heroes of Greek legend.

gig, a top.

164. **to tune,** i.e. play the music for.

165. **Nestor.** The oldest and most dignified of the Greek chieftains who besieged Troy. In *Troilus and Cressida*, i. 3. 61, Ulysses calls him " thou most reverend for thy stretch'd out life ".

push-pin, or put-pin, " a child's game in which each player pushes or fillips his pin with the object of crossing that of another player ".

166. **Timon.** Timon the Misanthrope was an Athenian, and friend of Alcibiades. Shakespeare probably obtained most of his information about him from passages in Plutarch's *Lives* of Antony and of Alcibiades. In the former we are told that they called Timon " a viper and malicious man unto mankind " (North's translation). Cf. also Shakespeare's *Timon of Athens*.

laugh, i.e. with appreciation; not in derision.

170. **a caudle** (so Q.; *candle* Ff. Q.2): a drink for invalids, especially for women giving birth, made of sweet gruel, wine, &c. Biron is sarcastically prescribing " slops " for the love-sickness of his friends.

176. **With . . . inconstancy.** This line, which appears to be incomplete, has been variously emended; e.g. later Ff. " men, like men of strange inconstancy ", " men like you, men of inconstancy " (Walker, Dyce, &c.), " vane-like men of strange inconstancy " (Warburton), " men like women of inconstancy " (Collier), " moonlike men, men of inconstancy " (Kinnear *Cruc. Shakesp.*), which last is followed by *Q. & D. W.* Why not " men like—men, men of inconstancy!"? i.e. with men who are like nothing but ordinary men, i.e. " deceivers ever ". Johnson and Heath accept this sense (but not this wording). It is not impossible that the printer may inadvertently have reduced three " men " to two.

178. **love,** so Q., the Duke of Devonshire's copy, of which Griggs' facsimile is easily available. This reading is followed by numerous editors, early and late. Other copies have " Ione " (= " Joan ", *v.* Biron's speech, the final couplet to Act iii above). " Ione " was probably the correct reading, printed in the earlier copies of the edition until (as *Q. & D. W.* explain, p. 102) " something went wrong with the type ", which perhaps was misplaced; the word was then wrongly reset as " Love "; and so, copies printed after the mishap contained this error. Such practices, I regret to note, are not entirely unknown in modern printing presses!

179. **pruning me,** tidying myself. Cf. " a bird preening its feathers ". " Prune " and " preen " appear to be related.

181. **state,** the act of standing, " in the present instance . . . opposed to gait (i.e. motion) " (Steevens). " The graceful pose of standing " is perhaps even nearer the mark for this context.

a brow, a face, as often in Shakespeare. Cf. *Midsummer-Night's Dream,* v. i. 11, " a brow of Egypt ".

183. **A true man,** an honest man. Cf. *1 Henry IV,* ii. 2. 102, where the term is again contrasted with " thieves ", " the thieves have bound the true men ". (And see l. 211 of this scene, below.)

185. **present.** As Hart points out (probably following White), this is a rare use, in the singular, of the word with the special sense it bears in the legal term " by these presents ", i.e. by these writings here presented.

186. **makes.** The King intends " makes " in the neutral sense of " does ", " is doing "; but afterwards quibbles with it as used in the phrase " make or mar ", where the two are opposed —probably because Costard emphasizes " makes " (" it makes nothing, sir ") in a comical manner.

190. **misdoubts,** mistrusts. Cf. *3 Henry VI,* v. 6. 14, " the bird misdoubteth every bush ".

198. **passion,** emotion.

200. **loggerhead,** blockhead.

203. **mess,** a party of four. Hart quotes Lyly, *Mother Bombie,* ii. 1: " Foure makes a *messe,* and we have a *messe* of masters that must be coozened." Biron, like the goose in the l'envoy, has " stayed the odds by adding four " (iii. 1. 93 above). May not this be a detail of design on Shakespeare's part? Cf. Dumain's " now the number is even ".

204. **He . . . liege.** There seems to be one " you " too many for a " mess ", unless both " and you's " refer (doubled for emphasis) to the King.

208. **turtles,** turtle-doves, lovers, i.e. Jaquenetta and Costard.

214. **cross,** run counter to, oppose.

215. **of all hands,** " from all sides ", " to whichever side one looks ", hence, " in any case " (Abbott, § 165).

218–221. **that like . . . breast?** Indian sunworship is referred to by Sir John Davies, in a " revision " stanza of his *Orchestra* (No. 131) first published 1596:

> As when the Indians, neighbours of the Morning,
> In honour of the cheerful rising Sun,
> With pearl and painted plumes themselves adorning,
> A solemn stately measure have begun;
> The god well pleased with that fair honour done,
> Sheds forth his beams and doth their faces kiss
> With that immortal glorious face of his.

Furnivall (in Griggs' Quarto) quotes Spedding's note to the effect that this is probably one of the passages added when the play was " newly corrected and augmented ".

220. **strooken.** See Glossary.

222. **peremptory,** unawed, audacious.

eagle-sighted. It was believed from ancient times that the eagle alone was capable of gazing unharmed at the sun. Pliny refers to it; but it is found in English literature before the Elizabethan " craze " for Pliny, in Chaucer, *The Parlement of Foules*, 330–1:

> Ther mighte men the royal egle finde,
> That with his sharpe look perceth the sonne.

227. **attending star,** alluding, perhaps, to the belief that the moon constantly had a star in close proximity. Hart refers to Lodge's mention of the star, " Lunisequa ", in *Euphues' Golden Legacy*, 1590.

231. **as at a fair,** possibly as different types meet at a fair. The simile appears to be dragged in for the sake of the pun.

232. **worthies,** worthiness, supreme qualities of beauty. Cf. *Two Gentlemen of Verona*, ii. 4. 166, " to her whose worth makes other worthies nothing ".

233. **that . . . seek.** As punctuated here " that " may be relative, with the sense " which Want (personified as the most efficient Searcher) her very self could seek out ". In Q., however, there is a comma after " wants "; and " that " may = " so that " (see Abbott, § 283), " so that Want herself has no further work to do ". " That " after a comma, clearly meaning " so that ", occurs in v. 2. 9.

235. **painted rhetoric,** perhaps " an artificial aid to beauty ". Cf. *As You Like It*, ii. 1. 2, 3:

> Hath not old custom made this life more sweet
> Than that of painted pomp?

237. **too short . . . blot.** Two ideas seem to be condensed here: (*a*) praise falls short of the truth; (*b*) praise itself is but a calumny or stain (blot) on her beauty.

244. **wood divine,** " wood " is Theobald's reading (also in Rowe's 1st edition) for " word " of Q.

248. **If . . . look,** i.e. if Beauty in person does not learn to look with her (Rosaline's) expression or aspect—that of a dark-haired girl, in fact.

251. **the suit of night,** " suit " is one of the numerous conjectures (which include " scowl ", " shade ", " soil ", " stole " " shroud ", " cloak ") for the " schoole " of Q. But Acheson believes that " schoole of Night " (see Introduction, p. x) is the genuine reading, and an allusion to a contemporary clique. This view has the support of *Q. & D. W.*

252. **beauty's . . . well,** i.e. the true badge of beauty is one that matches the sunlit sky—lightness, in fact. In view of Biron's retort about the spirits of light, this interpretation appears to be supportable.

255. **painting and usurping hair;** " and " was wanting in Q., " painting " may amount to " artificial " (see note to line 235 above), or " dyed ". The whole phrase means no doubt a blonde or red wig.

257. **fair,** with a quibble on " beautiful—light ".

259. **native . . . now.** Natural light hair is now regarded as merely artificial and so not true beauty, since the fashion for genuine (natural) beauty has been set by Rosaline's dark head. The meaning of the passage, quoted by Hart, in Lyly's *Campaspe* (Vol. II, p. 346, Bond) is not quite parallel: " but such a common thing it is amongst you to commend, that oftentimes for fashion sake you call them beautifull, whom you know black ". " black " here still stands for " not beautiful "; Shakespeare's point is that Rosaline has made black to be accepted as beautiful.

261. **brow,** presumably, in the removed sense of " coiffure ".

264. **crack.** See Glossary.

271. **devil,** because the (black) devils appear in Doomsday.

282. **quillets.** See Glossary. Possibly the earliest instance of this quite Shakespearian word; cf. *1 Henry VI*, ii. 4. 17:

> these nice sharp quillets of the law.

294. **ground,** basis.

297. **They are . . . fire.** Cf. with l. 345 sqq. in this speech. The repetition is explained by *Q. & D. W.* (pp. 105-8). The contention there is to the effect that a good deal more than these few lines is really repeated—in fact, Biron sets out his main argument twice, beginning the second time with l. 312 (" O,

we have made a vow ", &c., which cf. with l. 290, " And where that you ", &c.); but in his second version he expands, varies and beautifies until we find that at the end of his speech he has put his case more excellently than in version 1, i.e. l. 296–317. Version 1 is believed to have been an earlier draft which Shakespeare wished to have cancelled, substituting version 2 (317–end). But the printer, mistaking his MS. sign of deletion, omitted to do so.

298. **Promethean.** Hart notes the use of this epithet by Chapman in *The Shadow of Night* (*Hymnus in Noctem*):

> Therefore Promethean poets with the coals
> Of their most genial, more than human souls,
> In living verse, created men like these . . .

299. **poisons.** So Q. and F.; Theobald preferred " prisons ", which, however, spoils the parallel with " tires " in l. 301. A drug dulls the spirits as travelling dulls the muscles.

300. **arteries.** It was then believed that the arteries conveyed, not blood, but spirits. Dr. Ellis (*A History of Fire and Flame*, p. 118) quotes Bartholomew Anglicus (*Wks.*), thirteenth century: " And then it is called of physicians the vital spirit; because that from the heart, by the wosen (i.e. arteries) and veins . . . it spreadeth itself into all the limbs of the body . . ."

316. **numbers,** verses; see note to iv. 3. 115, above.

318. **keep,** occupy, inhabit, be or remain in (Schmidt).

323. **all elements,** i.e. throughout the whole body which was composed of four elements.

330. **head of theft is stopp'd,** (when the) keen ears of a thief have reached their limit, and can perceive nothing further. Hart quotes *3 Henry VI*, v. 6. 11–12: " Suspicion always haunts the guilty mind; The thief doth fear each bush an officer." Yet some commentators, including Theobald (who would read " thrift " for " theft "), have attempted variations of this quite comprehensible phrase.

331. **sensible,** sensitive.

332. **cockled,** furnished with a shell; *N.E.D.*, which cites this passage only. (Fr. *coquille* = shell.)

333. **dainty Bacchus.** As god of wine he might also be imagined as god of connoisseurs of wine; or to have had the finest taste of all wine-drinkers.

335. **Hesperides.** The eleventh labour of Hercules was to fetch the golden apples of the Hesperides, the musical daughters of Hesperus (or Erebus) who kept a dragon to guard their orchard. According to one legend, he held the heavens up for Atlas, while the latter obtained the apples; according to another (evidently

followed by Shakespeare) he obtained them himself. Ovid, *Met.*, ix. 190 does not mention Atlas in this connexion.

336. **Sphinx.** According to some Greek legends she was the monstrous daughter of Orthus and Chimæra, speaker of mysterious oracles, and propounder of riddles. On her visit to Thebes she put the well-known riddle which Oedipus answered.

337. **Apollo's lute.** Apollo was the god of light identified with Helios, the Sun; his " hair " would thus be rays of light. He was also god of music. In Homer *Iliad*, 1. 603, he charms the gods by playing to them on the lyre during dinner. Shakespeare may have had some echo of this story in his mind when he wrote the two following lines.

338, 339. **And when . . . harmony.** " When love speaks, the responsive harmony of the voice of all the gods makes heaven drowsy " (Knight, cit. Furness). See note above.

340, 341. **Never durst . . . sighs.** Acheson (as *Q. & D. W.* remind us) quotes as a parallel two lines from Chapman's *Shadow of Night* (see Introduction):

> No pen can anything eternal write
> That is not steeped in humour of the Night.

343. **humility.** " Humilitie is a gentleness of the mynde, or a gentle patience withoute all angre or wrathe." Huloet's *Abecedarium*, 1552 (cit. Furness).

352. **loves,** appraises, sets a value on (*Q. & D. W.*); or perhaps " love which imparts value to men ". (See *N.E.D.*, love v², 2.)

358. **charity.** Romans, xiii. 10 (Greek, πλήρωμα οὖν νόμου ἡ ἀγάπη), A.V. " . . . love is the fulfilling of the law ".

363. **get the sun of,** get advantage of. " In the days of archery, it was of consequence to have the sun at the back of the bowmen, and in face of the enemy." (Malone cit. Furness.)

364. **glozes,** pretences. " favourite word with Green, not used again by Shakespeare " (Hart).

369. **homeward,** on the way home.

377. **allons!** (Q. and F. read " alone ", which was " a common perversion of the time " (*Q. & D. W.*, p. 164).)

cockle, used loosely for weeds growing in corn, and alluding to the parable of the tares, Matt. xiii. 25; where, in Wyclif's version " cockel " is actually used, as Hart points out.

Sow'd cockle . . . corn may imply (as Halliwell) " as a man soweth, that shall he reap ". The remainder of Biron's speech (see note below) shows the application.

378. **whirls,** " comes full circle ", like the wheel of fortune. Shakespeare seems to be thinking of a wheel rather than of a balance. (So *N.E.D.* and Schmidt.)

380. **If so . . . treasure.** The implication is: we are not the genuine gold of men who keep their oath; but the copper, gold's counterfeit, since we have been false to the oath. And false men must not be astonished if their lady-loves turn out to be false as well; it is poetic justice.

Act V—Scene 1

1. **Satis quod sufficit,** (properly *satis est quod sufficit*) " enough is enough ". " Quod " is Rowe's emendation for " quid " of Q., F. But see above, note to Act iv, 2. 3.

2. **your reasons, &c.** Dr. Johnson admires the style of this speech, calling it " a finished representation of colloquial excellence ". Hart demonstrates that the sequence of clauses in apposition is favoured by Gabriel Harvey.

3. **sententious,** aphoristic. Wilson (118) recommends the gathering of " sentences " (proverbs) in amplification, which " commends much the matter ". Puttenham deals with the " Figures sententious " in Book III, Chap. xix. It will be seen that most of them make for the quasi-epigrammatic nature of the proverb.

4. **affection.** (So Q. and F.1; " affectation ", F.2, &c.) See Glossary.

5. **strange,** original, new.

6. **quondam,** (Latin) former, which has passed.

7. **intituled, nominated, or called,** an empty and pompous use of the triplet—an ornament of old and honourable standing in English rhetoric. When Latimer (*Sermons*, 1535–52, passim) uses it he adds emotional force or new ideas in doing so. Contrast with this.

9. **Novi hominem, &c.** (Latin) " I know the man as well as (I know) you." This tag comes from Lily's *Grammar* (1549), appearing under the head of *quasi*. (So Cruickshank, *Noctes Shakespearianae*, repeated by modern editors.)

12. **thrasonical,** bragging, conceited; coined from the proper name of Thraso, a " vaine glorious " character, as Sidney (Apologie) calls him in the *Eunuchus*, a comedy by the Latin playwright Terence (194–159 B.C.). The word seems to have been favoured by the writers of the " University wit " period, e.g. Nashe, Harvey and Greene, as noted by Hart.

picked, neat, finicky. Hart quotes Nashe, *Foure Letters Confuted*: " Shrouded a *picked* effeminate Carpet Knight under the fictitionate person of Hermaphroditus."

13. **peregrinate,** foreign, outlandish. This seems to be a word of Shakespeare's coinage, deliberately in the " inkhorn " manner.

16. **staple,** thread, fibre, material.

17. **phantasimes.** See Glossary.

insociable, incompatible, intolerable. Shakespeare does not use the word again in this sense.

point-devise, extremely neat or exact. (< M.E. *at point devis,* prob. = O.F. *a point devis* (*N.E.D.*).) Chaucer has the form " at point devys " in *Cant. Tales, Milleres Tale* (l. 502 from l. 1 of M.'s Prologue).

18. **rackers,** those who strain. There follows an interesting description of the pedantic straining of contemporary spelling and pronunciation by renaissance enthusiasts for latinization and others.

18, 19. **dout . . . doubt, det . . . debt.** Emerson (*History of the English Language,* § 191): " The older forms of *debt, doubt* are *dette, doute. . . .* Under the influence of the renaissance, French words were made to conform in spelling during the sixteenth century to Latin words from which they were derived. Hence the useless *b* in *debt, doubt,* because of their original connexion with Latin *debitum, dubitare.*" Holofernes, of course, prefers the latinate spelling, with full pronunciation of the intruded consonant.

20, 21. **calf, half, neighbour,** loss of -l- before consonants had begun in the fifteenth century (Wyld, *History of Colloq. Eng.,* p. 297); fricative " gh " or " h " was then also becoming mute in certain positions (*ibid.,* p. 70). *N.E.D.* records the spelling " nye-bore " as early as 1388. Puttenham (Arber, p. 129) would not " stick to say thus (delite) for (delight), (hye) for (high) ", a pronunciation which usage was imposing: but Holofernes adheres doggedly to the principle that if letters are there they should be pronounced. Vietor (p. 101) considered that the " gh " in " neigh-bour " was mute in the pronunciation of Shakespeare.

22. **abhominable.** False analogy derived " abominable " from *ab homine* (Latin)—" what is alien from humanity "; whereas the true derivation is *ab omine.* Holofernes, who was no great scholar, accepts the wrong form and insists on an " h " where none should be. The form " abhominable " was widely used by the Elizabethans. In Shakespeare's *Rape of Lucrece,* as Vietor (p. 102) points out, in Q.1 of 1594, it occurs twice (704, 921) " abhomination ".

23. **insinuateth me of insanie,** " suggests insanity to me " (Hart, who notes that " insinuate " occurs several times in Puttenham).

of. As may be seen from Abbott, § 174, 177, many verbs were then followed by an " of " which is lost in more modern English. Cf. *Cymbeline,* iii. 6. 92: " We'll mannerly demand thee of thy story " (which, however, is not strictly parallel).

23. **insanie.** (Q. and F. *infamie*; Theobald, *insanie*.) This word is noted first in *N.E.D.* (following Steevens) as occurring, 1572, in Holme's *The Fall and evil Successe of Rebellion from Time to Time*:

> After a little insanie they fled tag and rag.

anne intelligis, domine? (Latin) do you understand, sir?; but *nonne* (as Johnson suggested) may be intended by " ne ".

25. **Laus . . . intelligo,** (Latin) Praise (be) to God, I understand well. Theobald read " bone " (which is false Latin) for " bene " of Q. F., which the note below may justify.

26. **Bon, &c.,** (nearly follows Camb. ed. for " Bome boon for boon prescian " of Q. F.) " Good! very good! Priscian (i.e. correct Latin grammar) a little damaged!" There would be more point in this remark if Nathaniel had said " bone " for " bene "; and the " bome " of Q. F. may stand for a surprised repetition of this " howler ": " Bone! bon, fort bon'," &c. Holofernes has aired his Italian and Latin, he airs a few French words here, and in l. 137 (*allons!*).

Priscian, a Roman grammarian, and author of *De Arte Grammatica*, who was teaching at Constantinople about A.D. 525, was long the accepted authority on this subject; so that to speak false Latin was known, almost proverbially, as " breaking Priscian's head ". Holofernes is polite enough to hint that Nathiel has scratched, rather than broken, Priscian.

28. **videsne quis venit?** (Latin); he means: Do you see who comes? The construction looks like an indirect question with indicative, which normally would be rejected as false Latin; but as Mr. H. Box points out, dependent interrogations with indicative are found in Plautus and Terence, and very occasionally in later poets; so we can give Holofernes the benefit of the doubt, if we wish.

29. **video, et gaudeo,** " I see and rejoice." Furness quotes Baynes, *Shakespeare Studies* (p. 181): " These scraps of Latin dialogue exemplify the technical Latin intercourse between masters and pupils in the school work, as well as the formal colloquies the latter were required to prepare as exercises." He quotes examples from a manual, including " quis obviam venit?" and " diminuit Prisciani caput " (he breaks Priscian's head).

30. **Chirrah;** Armado's affected pronunciation of " sirrah ".

31. **Quare,** (Latin) " why?".

36. **alms-basket.** Halliwell (cit. Furness): " the refuse of the table was collected by the attendants . . . and put into a large basket, which was called the alms-basket, the contents of which were reserved for the poor ".

38. **honorificabilitudinitatibus.** Although by this time the word was humorously recognized and quoted as " the longest word known ", Furness adduces evidence by Herman that it may have been used more seriously by some writers in the middle ages, in which period it probably originated.   It appears in Elizabethan works of later date than *L.L.L.*; e.g. Nashe's *Lenten Stuffe* (1599) and Marston's *Dutch Courtezan* (1604) (noted by Steevens).   " It means something like the state of being capable of honors (*sic.*) " (Cross and Brooke).

39. **flap-dragon,** perhaps similar to the Christmas " snap-dragon " of raisins and burning brandy; something edible, or potable; in any case, it is to be swallowed whole. According to Nares it was sometimes a small burning object afloat on a cup of liquor. Shakespeare (*Winter's Tale*, iii. 3. 100) uses the verb " flap-dragon " for " to swallow whole ".

41. **peal,** as of bells, so the outpouring of words, perhaps with satiric reference to a prospective debate among the assembled " high-brows ". But in fact Moth's own " note " is heard shrilly and often.

43. **horn-book,** " a leaf of paper containing the alphabet (often with the addition of the ten digits, some elements of spelling and the Lord's Prayer) protected by a thin plate of translucent horn, and mounted on a tablet of wood with a pro-jecting piece for a handle ". *N.E.D.*

44. **a, b, . . . head.** *Q. & D. W.*, p. 204, note that in the horn-book, after the consonants, came " the vowels, each surmounted by a horizontal stroke or horn, and, after these, simple com-binations of vowels and consonants, such as *ab, eb, ib, ba, be, bi,* &c. . . ."

45. **pueritia,** (Latin) childhood, youth.

48. **Quis,** i.e. " who are you calling a sheep?"

consonant, perhaps a mere voiceless sign without even the sound that a vowel has.

49. **The third.** Theobald's emendation of " the last " (Q. F.). This may be right; the game would be to make Holofernes say " I ", to add " the sheep ", and continue " Oh, you (are the sheep) ". Modern children play similar " catch " games.

53. **Mediterraneum.** Hart notes that this form occurs in Greene's *Menaphon.* One may also note the extravagant praise awarded by Armado to this very puerile " venue of wit "; Shake-speare seems to be satirizing the low level of it, which might be compared with that of the clownish spelling episode of " Ignor-ance " in *Wit and Science* (*Lost Tudor Plays*, Farmer, pp. 153–5). Cf. also the Fable of the (Christ Church) College play (? 1581) *Bellum Grammaticale*, where the pronouns and prepositions

march in military guise on the stage. Grammatical and ortho-
graphical fun were well-known features of academic drama;
Shakespeare may well have been laughing at this now rather
elderly fashion.

54. **touch,** either, quality or sort of wit; or metaphorically
from the musical use; a sweet touch on the instrument of Wit.
Used literally in *Merchant of Venice,* v. 1. 67; with

> With sweetest touches pierce your mistress' ear.

venue, so Dyce. Q. and F. " vene we "; a thrust or stroke in
fencing (Q. & D. W.). Here, of course, metaphorical.

56. **wit-old,** a quibble on " wit old ", and " witold "—a
variety of cuckold (one whose wife is faithless).

57. **figure.** The Figures of Rhetoric, Speech, and Thought,
had loomed largely in the doctrine of classical rhetoricians such
as Cicero and Quintilian, who influenced renaissance teachers on
the subject, from Wilson to the mere pedant. Puttenham gives
a formidable list of them. Wilson (170) defines a figure as " a
certaine kinde, either of sentence, Oration, or worde, used after
some newe or straunge wise, much unlike to that which men
commonly use to speake ".
Holofernes inquires, " which rhetorical figure are you using?"
Moth, according to Q. & D. W., purposely takes figure to mean
" logical figure " and replies " horns " (the horns of a dilemma)
with obvious *double entendre* (see note, above, to l. 56).

61. **circum circa,** (Latin) " round and round ". So Theobald,
for " unum cita " of Q. F., which makes no sense.

gig. See note above to iv. 3. 163.

65. **halfpenny purse.** See Q. & D. W., p. xxii. Is this another
allusion to Nashe, " Pierce (-purse) Penilesse "? The halfpenny
purse was actually used for " the little silver halfpence of the
time " (Hart). Cf. *Merry Wives,* iii. 5. 152: " he cannot creep
into a halfpenny purse, nor into a pepperbox ".

68. **ad dunghill.** Cruickshank (*Noctes Shakespearianae,* cit.
Furness) suggests that this may have been a schoolboy's perversion of the phrase "ad unguem" (lit. " to the finger-nail ")
which occurs at the end of Lily's Grammar.

71. **Arts-man, preambulate.** Teacher of the arts (i.e. the
Humanities) go on in front. " Preambulate " is a crabbed inkhorn term. (Latin *praeambulo,* walk before, is post-classical.)

singuled, singled (out).

72. **charge-house,** presumably, a boarding school (*v. N.E.D.*).
Not found elsewhere. Theobald suggested " church-house ".

73. **mountain.** What is the point of the question and the
repeated allusion to the mountain, *mons,* &c.?

Robertson (*Shakespeare and Chapman*) suggests that the Hill was Hitchin Hill, where Chapman was a schoolmaster. A. R. Bayley (N.Q., 1925, cxlviii, 399, 417) believes that Harrow school is meant. He refers to mention, at a Manor court held May, 1475, of " le Church House . . . beside the churchyard of the Parish Church of Harrowhyll ". In a deed of 1596 " the now school or Church House " is mentioned. The master of Harrow school at the time seems to have been Anthony Rate (*d*. 1611). But Bayley is not convincing.

82. **liable,** appropriate, fit. Cf. *King John*, iv. 2. 226, " apt, liable to be employed in danger ". Holofernes' praise is not mere politeness. " Posteriors " is a " figure " which would naturally appeal to a schoolmaster.

measurable, proportionate, and so, suitable.

83. **chose,** past participles resembling preterite forms were common with Shakespeare and the Elizabethans; cf. " took " (= taken), *Julius Cæsar*, ii. 1. 50; " wrote " (= written), *Lear*, i. 2. 93, &c., &c.

86. **inward,** confidential.

87. **remember thy courtesy.** Shakespeare had not forgotten this joke by the time he came to *Hamlet*, v. 2. 109 (to Osric unbonneted), " I beseech you, remember—". In an age very conscious of etiquette, these absurd little incidents would certainly amuse the audience. Cf. also another, though different in detail, from *Antony and Cleopatra*, ii. 2. 28, &c.

93. **excrement,** " that which grows forth ", hair, moustache.

94. **let that pass;** like " this gear ", it was evidently a popular colloquial phrase of the time. Cf. *Merry Wives*, i. 4. 15, Dekker, *Shoemaker's Holiday*, &c.

99. **chuck** = chick; used endearingly.

100. **ostentation,** here, merely " show ".

101. **antique,** " grotesque pageant " (Hart).

105. **Nine Worthies.** Hector, Alexander, Julius Caesar (Gentiles); Joshua, David, Judas Maccabaeus (Jews); Arthur, Charlemagne, Godfrey of Bouillon (Christian). This list seems to have been varied; Hart notes the inclusion of Scipio (by Greene) and Gideon (by Nashe). Here Pompey and Hercules appear among them.

109. **illustrate,** illustrious.

113. **Joshua, &c.** Q. reads " Joshua, your selfe, my selfe, and this gallant Gentleman *Judas* . . . &c.". Whichever way we take it, it looks as though one of the characters is to be presented unnecessarily by two actors. The problem is discussed by *Q. & D. W.* (p. 168). The vital point as regards the text as printed, is that probably something came to be omitted after " myself "—the name of a Worthy, no doubt.

115. **pass,** accomplish, execute, enact (*Q. & D. W.* who refer to *Taming of the Shrew*, iv. 4. 59): " We'll pass the business privately."

121. **strangling a snake.** The jealous goddess Hera sent two serpents, but he strangled them (Pindar, *Nem. Odes*, i. 54 ff.).

132. **fadge.** See Glossary.

134. **Via,** go on! Florio (cit. Hart) *New World of Wordes*, " an adverbe of encouragement, much used by commenders . . ."

139. **tabor,** a small drum, used generally to accompany a pipe or trumpet.

hay. See Glossary.

Scene 2

The length of this scene is probably due _n part to later additions. It is this scene which makes Act V by far the longest in the play, as Spedding (see Quarto facsimile introduction) points out. He illustrates this theme with ll. 825–858, which he believes to be expanded from an " original speech of six lines ". Next he shows some reason for believing that some lines of the older version, intended to be cancelled in favour of the new, were allowed by mistake to stand.

From an artistic point of view one is rather oppressed, if anything, by the crowding in of incidents at the end to fill up and work out the fable; the end of *Antony and Cleopatra* may give a similar impression and, to a lesser extent, the fifth act of *The Comedy of Errors*.

2. **fairings,** " presents given or bought at a fair; and hence, a complimentary gift of any kind " (*N.E.D.*).

10. **wax,** grow; with a pun on the wax of the seal.

12. **shrewd unhappy gallows,** accursed bad-luck-bringing gallows bird.

14. **He made her melancholy, &c.** *Q. & D. W.* (p. 129) mention that Lefranc traces this story to an incident in the *Mémoires* of Marguerite de Valois.

18. **light,** a cluster of puns on " light " follows; Hart lists them as: 18, merry; 19, casual or unimportant; 20, frivolous or wanton; 21, information; 22, a candle; (25, wanton); 26, light in weight.

22. **taking . . . snuff,** expressing resentment or annoyance. *N.E.D.*: " the original reference was no doubt to the unpleasant smell proceeding from the smoking snuff of a candle, i.e. with a ' snuff ' or ' sniff ' of contempt; but there may also have been association with ' snuff sb²'."

26. **I weigh not you.** I am not your weight. But Katharine takes it up in another sense. "Oh! I carry little weight with you, then?"

28. **past cure . . . care.** (Thirlby, Theobald, for " care . . . cure " of Q. F.) The amended order is supported by *Macbeth*, iii. 2. 11: " Things without all remedy Should be without regard," and also, I think, by the context, which fully permits Rosaline to apply this proverb thus insultingly: " you are such a ' hopeless case ' that you're past caring for ".

In *Sonnet cxlvii* Shakespeare is giving the proverb a special twist not applicable here: " past cure I am, now reason is past care ".

29. **Well bandied,** " a good rally "; " set " is, of course, also a tennis term.

33. **My favour,** pun on love-gift—face or appearance.

35. **numbers,** verses, followed by quibble of " numbering " in its literal sense.

37. **fairs,** fair women.

42. **a text B,** a B in text-hand, " one of the more elaborate and formal of the various Elizabethan scripts " (*Q. & D. W.*) requiring more (black) ink than other letters.

43. **'Ware pencils.** Beware of pencils, i.e. paint-brushes. There may also be a pun on " pensils ", the pennon on a lance; for Rosaline and Katharine are using " portrait-painting " as weapons against each other, in a duel of malicious description.

let me . . . debtor, don't let me die without paying you back, blow for blow.

44. **red . . . letter.** The red letters in almanacs, used to mark the Sundays. " Golden " may be used loosely as a synonym of red, especially if Katharine's hair was a metallic red.

45. **full of O's,** pock-marks or spots.

46. **A pox of,** " a plague on ".

I beshrew, I curse, condemn.

52. **profound simplicity;** as a comment on hypocrisy, this might be rendered " a deep and treacherous appearance of sincerity ".

61. **in by the week,** caught, imprisoned. A fairly common expression in literature of the time, but not exactly explained. Some commentators note it in *Ralph Roister Doister*, i. 2: " He is in by the week; we shall have sport anon."

67. **perttaunt-like.** So Q. For this puzzling word " perttaunt " many emendations are suggested; pedant (Theobald), portent (Hanmer) pensaunt (Grant White), pageant (Capell), pendant(Hart), planet (Orger, and *Q. & D. W.*). If the word,

whatever it is, should be amplified by l. 68, none of these is quite satisfactory, since neither a planet nor a pendant (e.g.) can be properly said to keep a fool. Some word suggesting " tyrant " or " patron " would fulfil these conditions. A *prelate* (Wolsey) kept a fool.

state, condition.

68. **fate,** i.e. the power ruling his destiny.

80. **stabb'd,** i.e. with a stitch in the side.

82. **encounters,** abstract for concrete, encounterers ", warriors. Cf. *Antony and Cleopatra*, ii. 2. 51: " some true reports (= reporters) That drew their swords with you."

mounted, here = prepared.

84. **arguments,** probably references to the masque, and so " themes or subjects of the dramatic entertainments ".

88. **charge,** load, like a gun.

92. **addrest,** bent, directed.

97. **knavish,** boyish.

102. **presence,** i.e. the Princess's.

109. **rubb'd his elbow,** an itching elbow was supposed to betoken delight. Cf. Nashe, *Lenten Stuffe* (cit. Hart), " Their elbows itch for joy ".

fleer'd. See Glossary.

111. **finger and . . . thumb,** which, presumably, he snapped.

117, 118. **That in . . . tears.** With the exception of spelling and a comma after folly, this follows Q. and may be paraphrased: " that in this excess of mirth, tears were shed like those of a serious emotion such as might check their folly." " Appears " is one of the many s-plurals in Shakespeare.

121. **Muscovites or Russians.** See Introduction.

guess. There is no rhyme to this. It has been suggested by by Walker that the previous line is missing.

122. **parle.** (Q. parlee) = to converse.

123. **love-feat . . . advance,** (Walker suggests " love-suit "); will prosecute the activities of courting.

135. **removes,** exchanges of the " favours ".

144. **display'd,** i.e. with masks off.

146. **to the death,** they will be immobile even if they die for it; cf. " faithful unto death ".

147. **penn'd,** written out (and learnt, not too perfectly, by Moth).

155. **intended game,** *their* intended game.

Stage Directions. **Blackamoors.** These play no other part in the drama as it stands, and are perhaps a remnant of the earlier version of the play. (See *Q. & D. W.*, p. 172.)

159. **taffeta,** because wearing taffeta masks.

172. **You were best.** The remnant of the old impersonal construction in which " you " was really a dative; but it came in time to be regarded as the subject of the verb (Abbott, § 352).

daughter-beamed. The " son-sun " pun was evidently considered a good one in its day; and Shakespeare uses it several times.

173. **brings,** puts.

185. **measured,** in loose sense of " paced ", walked.

186. **measure,** a dance.

190. **measured,** measured mathematically, accurately. Such art required for its appreciation a younger and more exuberant savour of difference in word-meaning than is ours to-day.

201. **accompt,** account, reckoning, counting. The point is that their inexhaustible store of dutiful love enables them continually (" still ") to perform acts of devotion without keeping account of them in a grudging manner.

203. **like savages.** See above, note to iv. 3. 218-221.

204. **clouded,** by her mask. (So Hart.)

205. **such clouds,** masks, that touch women's faces.

209. **moonshine in the water,** a proverbial expression for an illusion, a mere appearance. Hart notes among instances of it, one in *The Proverbs of John Heywood*, 1546.

210. **change,** there may be some quibble here, with reference (*a*) to the moon; (*b*) to " change " = " a round in dancing " (*N.E.D.*) or to " change " as a musical term (*Q. & D. W.*), " modulation ".

211. **not strange,** not incomprehensible to you (though the language of Muscovites may be!).

216. **Yet still, &c.** In Q. this single line is given to the King, and the next two, " the music . . . vouchsafe it " to Rosaline. The text seems to be muddled here; and a line ending with a rhyme to " man ", which has no rhyme, may have dropped out, as Malone believed. The restoration, giving the King the line " The music . . . to it ", as in this edition, follows Theobald.

218. **Our ears vouchsafe it.** Rosaline, wilfully misunderstanding " motion ", replies, " our ears grant that the music has motion ".

220. **nice,** squeamish, fastidious.

223. **More measure of this measure.** The next "item" in the formality of the dance, after the hand-taking and curtsey, is the kiss. Several editors quote from the song in *The Tempest*, i. 2, beginning:

> Come unto these yellow sands,
> And then take hands:
> Curtsied when you have, and kissed . . .

The King demands a fuller *measure* (amount or allowance) of the procedure of the dancing (measure) so as to include the kiss.

225. **Prize.** (Q. prise; Rowe, price). So F4. If this is correct, the word is evidently used with a meaning similar to "price": "set a value on".

228. **Twice to your visor.** The point of this is obscure. Q. & D. W. suspect a lost topical allusion; Hart believes it to be a hint by Rosaline that, in saluting the mask only, she knows that it is not her own lover behind it.

229. **deny,** refuse; as quite frequently in Shakespeare. Cf. *Lear*, ii. 4. 84: "Deny to speak with me?", &c.

233. **two treys,** two threes; trey, a "three" at dice.

nice. See above, note to l. 220. It may be used here almost in the sense of "clever".

234. **Metheglin,** a Welsh drink fermented from honey and herbs; Sir Hugh Evans (*Merry Wives*, v. 5. 171) includes it in his list of dissipations.

wort, sweet unfermented beer. (*Q. & D. W.*)

malmsey, a strong sweet wine of Greece (Monemvasia); more anciently called "malvezie" (*malvoisie*, Fr.).

236. **cog,** to practise certain tricks at throwing dice (*N.E.D.*); to cheat. *N.E.D.* points out that "to cog" does not mean "to load the dice".

238. **gall,** i.e. the part of me whence bitter feelings rise, the part susceptible to taunts.

239. **change,** exchange.

243. **without a tongue.** *Q. & D. W.* quote from Mr. W. J. Lawrence's letter in *T.L.S.* of 7/6/23, which explains this *double entendre*: "the vizard . . . was kept in place by a tongue, or interior projection, grasped in the mouth".

247. **would,** might, could if you would.

248. **Veal, quoth the Dutchman;** "veal", apparently then pronounced like *veil* (and so punning on the mask) would sound like a Dutchman's pronunciation of "well". There is another pun, taking the "long" ending of Katharine's previous speech, with "veal"—"long-veal—Longaville", by which she inti-

mates that she has " spotted " him (so *Q. & D. W.*). So, with
" veal ", she affords his " speechless vizor half " a word.

250. **part,** divide, like a keepsake.

No . . . half. " Calf " if divided might be imagined to split
up into ca/alf. She replies that ca(tharine) won't be his better
'alf. (See *Q. & D. W.*, p. 174.) Cf. *Julius Cæsar*, ii. 1. 274:
" That you unfold to me, yourself, your half . . ."

251. **ox,** i.e. a dull stupid creature; probably with some reference to " horns ". Cf. the jokes about " ox " and " ass " in
Merry Wives, v. 5. 126, and *Troilus and Cressida*, v. 1. 65.

262. **arrows, bullets.** This line as it stands is abnormally
long. Several editors refer to Capell's comment on " bullets ";
" probably a prior word of the poet's, changed for ' arrows ',
left with it in his copy, and so printed together."

264. **dry-beaten,** beaten without drawing blood; soundly
beaten. Twice in *Romeo and Juliet*, iii. 1. 82 and iv. 5. 126 (" dry-
beat you with an iron wit ").

265. **simple.** The word was possibly used here with intentional ambiguity; as " straight-forward, innocent ", it can convey
both a compliment and a sarcasm; while at the same time it
may be taken as " slow, blunt, insignificant ".

269. **Well-liking,** fat. Tapers were made of fat.

270. **kingly-poor.** *Q. & D. W.* point out that this is a " reversed " pun on " well-ly-king "—" king-ly-poor "!

flout, jest, mock.

275. **weeping-ripe,** ready to cry. Furness quotes Sidney's
Arcadia (C.U.P. repr., 1590 ed., p. 107): " But Lalus (even
weeping-ripe) went among the rest."

for a good word. For want of . . ., &c.

276. **out of all suit,** quite beyond what was suitable.

277. **service.** Hart suggests a quibbling reference in this
and the preceding line to an old law-term, " suit and service ".
The two words recur together in ll. 827–8; the meaning of the
phrase is well seen in the passage (cit. Hart) from Yonge's translation of Montemayor's *Diana* (1598): " he should never have
got any other guerdon of his suites and services, but onely to see
and to be seene . . ."

278. **No point,** not at all. See note to ii. 1. 189 above. Here
is also a quibble on " sword-point ".

280. **Qualm.** With " qu " pronounced as " c ", a pun would
be possible with " calm ", as occurs in *2 Henry IV*, ii. 4. 39,
" an they be once in a calm, they are sick ". Longaville may be
supposed, when " conversing apart ", to accuse Katharine of
being " calm " or cold.

282. **statute-caps.** Hart's very informative note refers to enactments of 1582, that London prentices should wear " a woollen cap, without any silk in or about the same ". So, " statute-caps " here stands for prentice-heads, which may contain better wits, as Rosaline says, than the noble heads in question.

286. **sure** = fast, close (presumably in view of the simile).

290. **digest,** i.e. accept without retaliation.

297. **damask,** flesh-coloured, pink (the Damascus rose). The word is chosen, no doubt, for the pun's sake.

298. **vailing,** lowering—letting down the clouds that hide them; so unmasking or unveiling. Again, a quibble.

304. **shapeless gear,** clumsy or roughly cut clothing.

307. **carriage,** bearing, behaviour. See note to i. 1. 272.

310. **Whip,** hurry, dash.

run o'er land. So F.3 (Q.1 " runs ore land ").

land. Perhaps, as Walker believes, " land " is " here the same as *laund* . . . otherwise *lawn* " (cit. Furness). Cf. *3 Henry VI*, iii. 1. 2: " For through this laund anon the deer will come."

316. **pecks up.** Q. (" picks ", Ff.).

319. **wakes.** See Glossary.

wassails. See Glossary.

320. **gross,** wholesale.

322. **pins the wenches,** perhaps favours, ribbons, &c., given by the wenches.

324. **carve,** " speak affectedly " (*Q. & D. W.*). But taking into consideration the context of the word as used by Falstaff in *Merry Wives*, i. 3. 45 ff., it is quite possible that more than this was implied; perhaps " speak or gesticulate in an affected manner suggesting admiration "; " to perform a gesture of flirtation ".

326. **ape of form,** follower of fashions in etiquette.

327. **tables,** backgammon.

328. **in honourable terms,** in the politest language.

329. **mean,** a middle part, alto or tenor, in music (so Grove).

333. **whale's bone.** (= whal-es, two syllables.) Editors note that this simile appears in mediæval literature, e.g. in the Romance of Sir Eglamore, ante 1400 (cit. Hart). The fact that this cliché had so old an origin may account for the fact that the *-es* of " whales " remained syllabic; as it does also in Spenser, *F. Q.*, iii. 1, stanza 15. The " whale's bone " was probably walrus tusk.

339. **madman.** (So Q.) This word interferes with the metre, and " man " (Theobald) is no doubt right. The printer's eye,

as *Q. & D. W.* explain, would be caught by the " mad " of " madam ", just below in the next line; and so the error would occur.

341. **Fair . . . foul,** i.e. " fair weather " when it is hailing is but foul weather. Beaumont and Fletcher (*Two Noble Kinsmen* and *The Faithful Friends*) and Dekker (*Old Fortunatus*) repeat this pun. (See Furness, p. 264.)

349. **virtue,** presumably influence, power.   Johnson believes that the King meant " goodness " as well; anyhow, the Princess (l. 350) takes up the word in that sense.

350. **nickname,** wrongly name.

362. **mess.** See above, note to iv. 3. 202.

366. **to . . . days,** in (according to) the manner (fashion) of these days.

370. **talk'd apace,** chattered, talked away.   Hart refers to Tibet Talkapace in *Ralph Roister Doister* (q.v.).

371. **happy,** felicitous, well devised; cf. *1 Henry IV*, v. 4. 162:
        I'll gild it with the happiest terms I have.

377. **lose light,** are dazzled (by the sun, " heaven's fiery eye "). Cf. above, i. 1. 77 ff.

your capacity . . . store, your mental capacity is such that compared with your vast wealth of wit and wisdom . . .

381. **fool . . . full,** a pun.

396. **face of brass.** *N.E.D.* quotes this passage as the first example of this actual phrase; though *brazen-faced* is recorded, 1571.

398. **flout,** a mock. See above, note to l. 270.

401. **wish,** request.

402. **wait,** attend, serve; as frequently in Shakespeare. Cf. *Antony and Cleopatra*, v. 2. 53, &c.

405. **my friend,** my beloved.

406. **a blind harper's song,** and so, like a popular ballad sung by street or tavern musicians. Cf. Puttenham (cit. Hart, Arber, p. 97): " Blind harpers or such like taverne minstrels that give a fit of mirth for a groat."

407. **Taffeta . . . silken,** in antithesis to *russet . . . kersey* (for which see note below) of line 414.

408. **Three-piled,** used of the richest velvet (with the thickest pile). Perhaps there is also word-play on " pile = heap up ".

spruce, affected. Cf. also v. i. 12 above.

affectation. (So Rowe and others for *affection* of Q.)   The rhyme word of l. 410 (" ostentation ") and the alternative rhyme scheme, demand this change.

409. **Figures pedantical,** i.e. those pedantic Figures of rhetoric (such as Puttenham enumerates, see note to l. v. 2. 57).

410. **blown.** Cf. " fly-blown ".

414. **russet . . . kersey.** See Glossary. These coarse, peasant fabrics are contrasted with the taffeta and silk of l. 407.

415. **la!** (" *law* " Q. F.) See Glossary.

416. **sans.** Hart writes, " sans is a ' spruce affection ' (affectation) ", and notes that it is common in Lyly; cf. *Mother Bombie*, ii. 2. 26 (Bond, Vol. III, p. 188): " The boy hath wit sance measure, more than needs."

417. **Sans " sans ",** without any more " sans ".

trick, a touch (Schmidt).

418. **rage,** madness, distemper.

420. **" Lord have mercy on us '',** " the warning inscription on the door of a plague-stricken house," also pinned on a corpse being taken to burial (so *Q. & D. W.*). " Unknown earlier than the 1592–3 visitation " (of the plague); so Hart.

424. **Lord's tokens,** word play on (1) " Lord's tokens ", as the plague-spots were called; (2) the tokens or presents given to the ladies by the lords.

425. **free,** (1) free from infection; (2) heart-free (a quibble).

426. **states,** (1) health; (2) estates (*Q. & D. W.*).

undo us, remit our forfeiture or indebtedness.

427–428. **how . . . sue?** " How can these be liable to forfeiture who begin the process? The jest lies in the ambiguity of ' sue ' which signifies to prosecute by law, or to offer a petition " (Johnson, cit. Furness).

429. **to do with you.** " I won't have any sort of dealings with you whatever." Perhaps the phrase " those that sue " has prompted him to this repudiation.

435. **well advised,** in your right mind (so *Q. & D. W.*, who refer to *Comedy of Errors*, ii. 2. 217: " Sleeping or waking, mad or well-advised?").

441. **force not,** think nothing (of forswearing). Cf. *Rape of Lucrece*, 1021: " For me, I force not argument a straw."

460. **Neither of either.** Malone tells us that it was a common expression of the time. It is noted in *The London Prodigal* (1605), *A Yorkshire Tragedy* (1608).

461. **consent,** here, " a conspiracy ".

463. **dash,** spoil, upset.

like a Christmas comedy. See Chambers' *Mediæval Stage*, 1. 226, 408 ff. A considerable amount of " ragging " seems to have attended the Christmas performances, where the tradition of licence evidently survived. One performance (at St. John's College, Oxford, 1607) was " a messe of absurdities ", *dashed* with " two or three cold plaudites ". No doubt the rustic performances in remoter parts were more uproariously dashed. The writer of this note has witnessed the Christmas play of St. George at Heading-ton, as late as 1910.

464. **please-man,** " pick-thank or parasite " (Hart).

zany, " a stage buffoon who imitated the tricks of the principal clown or fool " (*Q. & D. W.*).

465. **mumble-news,** gossip, tattler.

trencher-knight, who is only valiant at the dinner-table. Cf. " carpet-knight ".

Dick, a contemptuous term like " jack " (as in *Richard III*, i. 3. 72); a " fellow " (cf. *Pickwick Papers*, Chap. xv).

466. **smiles . . . in years,** puckers his face, through laughing, into wrinkles—the sign of advancing years.

467. **disposed,** i.e. disposed to laugh.

470. **of she,** of the woman.

472. **in will and error,** i.e. first through our own choice, and now through a mistake.

473. **Much upon this,** very much in this way.

475. **know . . . foot,** this apparently meant, at that time, " be in her favour ", be her intimate friend. A quotation (noted by Hart) from Lyly's *Euphues and his England*, suggests the same meaning (p. 68, Bond): " but you shall not know the length of my foote, untill by your cunning you get commendation ".

by the squier. (So Q.: Rowe, square.) " Squier " is an old form of " square " = carpenter's rule. So, " accurately, exactly " (cf. Latin, *ad amussim*).

476. **laugh . . . eye,** " jest very intimately with her " (*Q. & D. W.*).

478. **Holding a trencher,** presumably as a trencher-knight; polite function. Cf. the " handing round " of cups, &c., by gentlemen at a " Victorian " afternoon tea.

479. **allow'd,** admitted, " passed ", licensed. Cf. i. 2. 124 above, and *Twelfth Night*, i. 5. 101, " an allowed fool " (cit. Hart).

480. **smock,** a woman's *camisole*. From the context, Biron seems to mean, not so much " you live and die a mere effeminate creature ", but " you live and die completely under female domination ".

482. **like a leaden sword,** i.e. like a (comparatively) harmless stage-sword.

483. **manage** (Theobald's alteration; Q. nuage, F. manager), a riding-school term for " a short gallop at full speed " (*N.E.D.*).

483. **career,** a charge on horseback, in the tiltyard. Cf. *Much Ado*, v. 1. 138: " I shall meet your wit in the career, an you charge it against me."

484. **straight,** (charging or tilting) with the spear levelled straight at the adversary; and so " honourably "; because it was considered shameful to break the spear across the body of the opponent. *v. All's Well,* ii. 1. 68, and Schmidt " across ".

488. **vara . . . pursents.** Costard's pronunciation, elsewhere in this play, seems to be as correct as that of the other characters; but this looks like an attempt to indicate regional dialect. " vara " is noted (*N.E.D.* and Wright) as a northern form of " very "; but metathesis of *r* (present-pursent) is chiefly S.W. See also " whereuntil " (below l. 494), and Costard's refusal to fight with a pole like a northern man. The fact that he knew anything about the very local long poles of the north might be a " bull point " for his northern origin; he is *pretending* to regard pole-fighting as low.

491. **You cannot beg us,** periphrastic for . . . " you cannot beg us for fools " (Hart). To beg someone for a fool was to apply for guardianship over a person legally proved to be an idiot, (so Nares); and simple addition formed one of the tests for the person examined by the Court as to the state of his wits (for more modern literary accounts of such examination see Galt, *The Entail*, Surtees, *Handley Cross*).

494. **whereuntil,** whereunto. " till " meaning " to " (local) was distinctively northern (as to-day). See *N.E.D.* and Wright's *Dial. Dict.*

502. **parfect.** (The Q. reading, which probably represented the right pronunciation for Costard; cf. " gardon ".) He means, perhaps, " perform ".

503. **Pompion,** he means Pompey. The name would suggest a pompion (pumpkin) to his rustic mind.

506. **degree,** rank, title.

512. **company,** i.e. " company's ".

516, 517. **contents . . . presents.** (So Q. Several commentators have attempted to alter the passage; e.g. " contents Dies . . . that it doth present ", Hanmer: ". . . of them which it presents ", Malone, Craig). When zeal (without skill) tries to please, pleasure is fully absorbed in the intense zeal of the actors in their production—a production in fact entirely dependent on zeal; i.e. we sympathize pleasurably with the keenness of the actors and so forget their lack of skill.

Dr. Johnson, alluding to the parallel passage in *A Midsummer-Night's Dream*, v. 1. 85 ff., notes that " this sentiment of the Princess is very natural, but less generous than that of the Amazonian Queen " (q.v.).

"contents" is followed by a verb with the not infrequent s-plural ("dies"). The meaning of "dies" is certainly rather strained if "contents" stands for "content" a "pleasure"; *Q. & D. W.* take it as "subject-matter of the play"; which "dies" (i.e. loses interest) in comparison with the keenness of the actor who presents it ("it" being of "presents"); it is good will, and not a good play, that attracts.

518. **Their form . . . mirth,** she continues, less sympathetically, their failure in proficiency makes for an excellent joke. There is a play on two meanings of "form": (*a*) method, order; (*b*) a "good" shape, or development.

528. **too, too,** an intensive repetition; "excessively" vain. Cf. *Hamlet*, i. 2. 129, "this too, too solid flesh".

529. **put . . . guerra,** try it by the fortune of war. (Italian phrase.) The point of this remark is not obvious; but if Armado is still concerned with the Princess's last speech, he may mean that competition will decide whether he or the school-master is the more fantastical.

couplement, couple.

535. **four Worthies . . . other five.** There seems to be something wrong here; as the text stands there are five worthies, and the King's adherence to four is strangely forced. But if this list of worthies is a later substitution for a cancelled list in rhyme (as *Q. & D. W.* suggest) it may well be that the cancelled passage would have given a more satisfactory clue to the dispute over the number of worthies in ll. 543–4.

541. **Abate . . . novum.** (So Q. Malone and several commentators read "*a* throw"): "barring or accepting a throw in the dice-game called 'novum'". The true name of this game was "novum (*novem*) quinque", from the two principal throws—nine and five.

543. **amain.** See Glossary.

545. **libbard's head,** leopard's head. Theobald saw here a reference to old-fashioned garments: "upon the knees and elbows of which, it was frequent to have, by way of ornament, a leopard's or a lion's head". The joke may amount to this "in the old conventional costume, of course".

550. **targe.** See Glossary.

557. **My hat to a halfpenny,** a current "bet" of the time; occurs also in Lodge, *Wits Miserie* (cit. Hart, Furness), 1596: '. . . and it is his hat to a halfe penny but hee will be drunke for companie".

561. **scutcheon.** See Glossary.

562, 563. **stands too right,** and **smells "no".** Referring to two personal details recorded about Alexander in North's *Plu-*

tarch: (a) ". . . . Alexander's manner of holding his neck, somewhat hanging down towards the left side "; and (b) ". . . I read also in the commentaries of Aristoxenus, that his skin had a marvellous good savour, and that his breath was very sweet . . .", &c. The implication here is that Sir Nathaniel had not a marvellous good savour; Boyet's nose discovers the fact, as Biron (and *Q. & D. W.*) notice.

571. **scraped . . . cloth.** Oil-paintings on canvas were used as wall-hangings. Nares quotes a passage from Rastell, showing that Sir Thomas More had this form of decoration; and another showing that the Worthies were so pictured (Whitlock, *Zootomia*, 1654, p.171): " That Alexander was a souldier, painted cloths will confess; the painter dareth not leave him out of the nine worthies."

572. **your lion, &c.,** the heraldic ages not merely translated the classic heroes into knights of romance but gave them coats of arms. Several editors and Parker's *Glossary of Heraldry* quote, with variations,[1] Gerard Legh, *Accedens of Armourye* (1563 and 1591), where Alexander is given this coat-of-arms: " Gueules " (gules) " a Lion or, seiante " (sitting) " in a charger, holding a battle ax argent ".

579. **o'erparted,** i.e. the *part* or character allotted to him is too heavy. (So Malone.)

581. **sort,** manner; as frequently in Shakespeare. Cf. " in a more fairer sort ", *2 Henry IV*, iv. 5. 201.

584. **canis,** (Q. canus) Latin, a dog. Cerberus was the three-headed dog who guarded the entrance to the underworld of classic myth.

586. **manus.** Latin, hand.

587. **Quoniam . . . ergo.** Latin, since . . therefore.

589. **state,** dignity.

594. **clipt,** cut short, with a pun on "(y)cleped "

600. **you are my elder,** " a proverbial bit of chaff " (Hart). Cf. *Comedy of Errors*, v. 1. 423:

> Not I, sir; you are my elder.

601. **Judas . . . elder,** an old tradition. Dyce quotes " Sir John Maundeville " (1364) (Pollard, 1905, p. 62) " and fast by is yet the tree of elder that Judas hanged himself upon, for despair that he had, when he sold and betrayed our Lord ".

605. **cittern-head.** A cittern (or citten) was a stringed musical instrument like a guitar, but all the strings were of metal. It had " usually a head grotesquely carved at the extremity of the neck and finger-board " (Nares). Some forms had two necks.

---

[1] I regret that I have not had time to check the *variae lectiones*.

606. **bodkin,** a large hairpin with an ornamental carved or jewelled knob; Hart quotes a passage from Nichols' *Progresses* (1586-7), in which one is modelled like a fly, and one like a spider.

607. **Death's . . . ring,** i.e. a skull engraved on a signet ring as a " memento mori ".

609. **Cæsar's falchion.** Cæsar's sword. Mediæval legend attributed to Cæsar an enchanted sword named *Crocea Mors* (yellow death).

610. **flask,** possibly an ornate powder-flask = " a soldier's flask " (*Romeo and Juliet*, iii. 3. 131). So Halliwell.

611. **half-cheek,** side-face.

613. **the cap . . . tooth-drawer.** Several editors quote Taylor, *Wit and Mirth*, 1630: " In Queen Elizabeth's dayes, there was a fellow wore a brooch in his hat like a tooth drawer, with a Rose and Crown and two letters." The correspondence on this ref. in *T.L.S.*, Feb., 1926, is interesting but not closely documented.

618, 619. **lion . . . ass,** referring to Æsop's fable of the ass in the lion's skin.

623. **humble,** here = " kind " (*v.* Schmidt).

624. **it grows dark.** Possibly hinting that Judas has held the stage too long—so long in fact, that twilight is setting in—as it often did during winter afternoon performances at an Elizabethan theatre. Collier declared that torches were of old called Judases (cit. Furness).

626. **Achilles.** As the *Iliad* recounts, Achilles, the Greek chieftain, was the main opponent, and eventually the slayer, of Hector. The joke here is the pretence that Armado's Hector is too terrifying even for Achilles.

628. **Though . . . merry.** This remark has the air of having been transposed hither from some more appropriate context; it is not a rejoinder to Biron's joke, whereas the King's quibble on " Trojan " takes up Biron's drift. Quite tentatively, I suggest that it would have had more connexion with the matter had it occurred before Armado's entry and nearer to Holofernes' " This is not generous ", &c. Dumain might then well have replied: " I know I am a cruel mocker and that my taunts may come home to roost; the critic may be justly criticized: but I don't care,—' for to-night we'll merry be!'."

630. **a Troyan,** (1) a Trojan or native of Troy; (2) (as a cant term) a dissolute fellow, a common sort of associate, as in *Henry V*, v. 1. 32: " Base Trojan, thou shalt die."

632. **clean-timbered,** " well-built "; but here probably used with the ulterior meaning " as thin as a wooden post ". Hart quotes Jonson *Every Man out of his Humour*, Induction, " a well-timbered fellow, he would have made a good post ".

634. **calf,** with allusion to " calf " the animal, which like " ox " could mean " fool ".

635. **small,** i.e. of the leg; the thin part. Armado was evidently spindle-shanked.

638. **armipotent,** powerful in arms: " a conventional epithet of Mars " (*Q. & D. W.*). Cf. Chaucer, *Knight's Tale*, 2441, " Mars the stierne god armypotente ".

640. **A gilt nutmeg.** (Q. gift nutmegg.) A nutmeg was a useful present for those who took their morning ale spiced; and the gilding of them was a common practice. Hart quotes several allusions including Jonson, *The Gipsies Metamorphosed*, 1621: " I have lost an enchanted nutmeg, all gilded over . . . to put in my sweetheart's ale a mornings."

641. **A lemon.** A lemon stuck with cloves was also used to smell " during the time of pestilence " (Halliwell, cit. Bradwell, *Physicke for . . . the Plague*, 1636).

647. **breathed,** with such good wind, in such fighting fettle.

653. **Hector,** said to be one of the names given to dogs.

666. **infamonize;** this word is possibly coined as a skit on " infamize " (i.e. " defame ") which, Hart believes, was the creation of Nashe.

673. **Greater than . . . huge.** Stewart (*Text. Diff.*, p. 67) introduces a certain " ascending order " of " greatness " into this badinage, by punctuating as follows: " Greater than great. Great great great Pompey. Pompey the huge:" ascending from " great " to " huge ".

676. **More Ates.** Ate was the classic goddess of Strife.

680. **sup,** nourish. Transitive use; cf. *Taming of the Shrew*, Induction, 1. 28: " But sup them well, and look unto them all."

682. **northern man.** See above, note to l. 488. Hart quotes a passage from Harrison's *Description of England* (1577–87), in which the Borderers' " excessive staves " are described. Costard's contemptuous reference to " fighting with a pole " gives him away, one might argue.

688. **take . . . lower,** (1) help you to strip for the fight, and (2) " take you down a peg " (so *Q. & D. W.*).

695. **bloods,** gallant men. Cf. " as many and as well-born bloods ", *King John*, ii. 1. 278.

697. **go woolward,** wear wool next the skin. Nares has several quotations showing that this torture was enjoined for penance, including one from Staveley's *Romish Horseleech*: " to go wulward, vii yere. *Item*, to fasten (fast on) bred and water the Fryday vii yere." Armado thus disguises the truth that he cannot take off his shirt as he has not another.

704. **Mercade.** See Introduction.

712. **day of wrong . . . little hole.** Hart points out that Armado is here adapting a proverb found in Heywood's *Proverbs* (1546), " I see day at this little hole ". The speech is, as Hart reminds us, to Armado's credit.

day of wrong, i.e. the truth that I have done wrong.

discretion, probably " the ability to discern what is right ".

721. **liberal opposition,** over free or even " wanton " show of resistance.

723. **converse of breath,** conversation. Breath = " sound, voice "; cf. *M.N.D.*, ii. 1. 151: " dulcet and harmonious breath."

725. **nimble.** So Theobald and others for ' humble ' of Q. F.

728, 729. **The extreme . . . speed.** *Q. & D. W.* pronounce this passage to be corrupt. The intention of the poet was probably to state that the urgency of the " eleventh hour " accelerates the resolution of problems about which, hitherto, there has been hesitation.

730. **loose,** the act of discharging the arrow (term in archery): " the critical moment " (Schmidt).

732. **progeny,** i.e. the bereaved daughter, the Princess.

735. **argument,** theme, subject.

740. **double** (so Q. Capell, *deaf.* Collier and others, *dull*), extremely strong; cf. *Othello*, i. 2. 14:

> a voice . . . .
> As double as the Duke's.

742. **badges** (*Q. & D. W.* " bodges "); if " badges " is the correct reading, does it not refer to honest plain words? He wishes to interpret the King's obscurity in plain terms, which are the true badges (signs) of serious love. The King, he hints, is quite serious in intention, if involved in style.

747. **And what . . . make.** Here is something of the rambling periodic construction of Elizabethan prose (cf. Sidney's *Apology*) put into metre. The skeleton of the structure (as punctuated) is " And what . . . hath seemed ridiculous (for love is full of absurdities), what is nothing but a motley—all this your eyes have tempted us to assume." The punctuation of the speech (in Q.) is dubious; and it is possible that the clause " and what . . . glance " may be governed by " fashioning " (l. 745).

748. **strains,** tendencies, motions of the mind. Cf. *Cymbeline*, iii. 4. 94, " no act of common passage, but A strain of rareness ".

751. **strange,** for Q. F. " straying ", which several editors believe to be a misprint for " strange " (such as occurs in Lyly's *Euphues*, Bond, 1. 252). *Q. & D. W.* suggest that if Shakespeare's own

spelling had been " straing " or " strayng " the misprint might
easily have followed. On the other hand, despite the protest of
these editors, this poetic conceit of " shapes appearing to stray "
(move, pass away) " as the eye doth roll " is quite acceptable.
We daily accept wilder things in poetry.

752, 753. **subjects . . . object,** a somewhat similar antithesis
occurs in Lyly's *Campaspe*, i. 1. 75 (Bond, II, p. 319): " You
shal not be as abiectes of warre, but as subiectes to *Alexander*."

754. **loose love,** the context suggests " careless, frivolous
love ". Schmidt renders " too unrestrained, lax ".

758. **Suggested,** tempted; cf. *All's Well*, iv. 5. 47: " I
give thee not this to suggest thee from thy master."

769. **bombast and . . . lining.** Bombast was a padding
material of wool; the Princess is not characteristically feminine
in using dress-making similes to express the " tricking-out " or
ornamentation of dull time. Biron's speech, v. 2. 407 ff. betrays
an equal familiarity with the terms of a trade then as urgently
appealing to men as to women of fashion.

770. **devout,** serious.

this in our respects. (Q. *this our respectes*. Hanmer, *this
in our . . .*) **respects,** regards, feelings (for you).

777. **world-without-end.** Cf. Sonnet LVII:

　　　Nor dare I chide the world-without-end hour.

Borrowed probably from our liturgy (Malone).

779. **dear,** grievous, extreme. The Princess doubtless uses the
word deliberately, to hint, with a quibble, at the state of her
heart.

785. **twelve celestial signs,** a readily understandable peri-
phrasis (Wilson, p. 175) for " year "; cf. Spenser, *F. Q.*, Bk. ii,
2. 44: " Now hath faire *Phoebe* with her silver face Thrise seene
the shadowes of the neather world," for " three months ".

789. **weeds,** clothes. *They* are not going woolward for penance.
Hart suggests reference to a vegetarian diet.

793. **challenge me, challenge me,** the rhetorical " scheme "
which Wilson (p. 200) calls " Doublettes " or " Geminatio ver-
borum ".

795. **instant,** reading of F.: " instance ", Q.

800. **intitled** (reading of F: " intiled ", Q.), having a claim or
legal title.

801, 802. **If . . . rest,** if I should refuse this, or more—merely
in order to lull my energies into sloth by pampering them.

804. Hence ever then (so F.: "hence herrite then" Q.). *Q. & D. W.* following Pollard, propose the reading "hermit" as a correction of the mis-print "herrite". See their edn., p. 183, and 190.

805–10. And what . . . sick. Many editors bracket these lines as redundant, in view of Rosaline's speech lines, 829–57. Once more, we may suspect that this passage, of earlier date, should have been cancelled in favour of the later new version (Rosaline's lines, 829–57), but by mistake it became "fossilized" in the text. (See *Q. & D. W.*, pp. 108–9.)

806. rack'd; as the line stands, this word must be "racked" into meaning "extended to the top of their bent" (Malone)— a vile phrase. *Q. & D. W.* suggest that "too" = "to", a substitution for "till" ("till your sins are expiated by the rack), which would ease the situation.

807. attaint. See Glossary.

812. A wife? (so earlier Cambs. edrs., and Dyce). Q. gives these words to Katharine.

822. friend, lover.

824. the liker . . . young. *Long*-aville evidently has the misfortune to be tall.

827. suit . . . service. See l. 2 of this scene above.

833. all estates, "all sorts and conditions of men".

839. still. See Glossary.

841. fierce, ardent; furiously active.

847, 848. begot of . . . fools, i.e. fostered or encouraged to spring from the wanton genius of jesting (loose grace), when shallow-minded hearers praisingly attribute such a genius to those who are merely fools. She means that he is encouraged in his folly by flatterers.

852. dear, grievous, heartfelt. See above note to l. 779, and cf. *Hamlet*, i. 2. 182, "my dearest foe" (cit. Craig).

861. bring you, accompany you.

863. Jack hath not Jill. An old proverb occurring, Furness notes, in Heywood's *Epigrammes* upon Proverbs, 1567, "All shal be well, *Jacke shall have Gill* . . .". And cf. *Midsummer-Night's Dream*, iii. 2 461: " Jack shall have Jill; Nought shall go ill "

873. dialogue, i.e. antiphonal song. But no doubt Shakespeare may have had in mind the mediæval debate-poems, such as *The Owl and the Nightingale* (thirteenth century), where the two birds take sides in an argument. Cross and Brooke mention an early debate between winter and spring called *Conflictus Hiemis et Veris*, ascribed to Alcuin (A.D. 735–804).

879. **maintained,** supported, backed (Hart). See preceding note. The Cuckoo and the Owl support, respectively, the dubious pleasures of Spring and Winter.

881. **lady-smocks,** the cuckoo flower.

882. **cuckoo-buds,** buttercup, marsh-marigold, and cowslip have been suggested as equivalents for this name.

899. **blows his nail.** *Q. & D. W.* concur that this means *not* " warms his hands " but " waits patiently with nothing to do "; i.e. is out of a job or " plays ", in modern parlance. Hart quotes *3 Henry VI*, ii. 5. 3: " What time the shepherd, blowing of his nails," i.e. at leisure.

906. **keel**. See Glossary.

908. **saw**. See Glossary.

911. **crabs,** crab-apples, put into hot spiced ale. Stage Dir. *Armado*: F. gives this speech to Armado. Q. prints it without any allocation at all, and in bigger type than the rest of the text. In Q. the play ends at " Apollo ". F. adds: " You that way, we this way."

Q. & D. W. remark, anent " the words . . . Apollo ", that the sentence may conceivably have been a comment on the play by someone to whom Shakespeare had lent it for perusal. If so, what does he refer to? Possibly the plain-spoken rustic song (the words of Mercury) after the earlier sonnets with their elegant conceits (Songs of Apollo). The Roman god Mercurius was, compared with Apollo, rather " low "; he was the god of commerce and sharp practice. Cf. Ovid, *Fasti, v.* 680–93, and *Winter's Tale,* iv. 2. 23 ff.

ESSAY ON METRE

§ 1. **Metre as an Indication of Date.**

(a) Rhyme and Blank Verse.

Blank verse is rightly regarded as the staple metric form used by Shakespeare for his plays; but there are a few of these in which other metric forms (as in *A Midsummer-Night's Dream*) or prose (as in *Twelfth Night*) abound. Generally speaking in the earlier plays the proportion of rhyme to blank verse is higher than in the later. In *Love's Labour's Lost* there is substantially more rhyme, as well as more prose, than blank verse, the proportions being approximately: rhyme, 10·6; prose, 10·9; blank verse, 5·7.[1] There are over 1000 rhymed lines in *Love's Labour's Lost*, far more than in any other play by Shakespeare. *A Midsummer-Night's Dream* (probably composed a few years later) comes second with some 730 lines, and blank verse at 878 (Fleay's figure). The late plays contain blank verse lines in thousands (highest over 2500) and rhymed lines seldom over 100; the proportion is reversed.

Variety of metre and rhyme is of more importance in *Love's Labour's Lost* than elsewhere in Shakespeare's dramas: it is largely on this kind of ornament that the play depends for its peculiarly lyrical and musical quality. This special consideration must not be lost sight of if and when we decide that this rhymed work in our play is early work, as it is (see Introduction). But rhyme is not made a main organic feature of the later plays, where, as Mr. A. D. Innes writes: " It is only to be found occasionally at the close of a scene or a speech to round it off— probably a concession to stage tradition analogous to the similar use of ' gnomæ ' in Greek plays, and of a ' sentiment ' in modern melodrama."

Of the varieties of rhymed measure to be decided later, one at least suggests that Shakespeare when using it, had not yet abandoned the kind of verse-form found in the drama of a phase

---

[1] After Fleay.

that was by that time passing: this is the loose jingling verse used in the dialogue of ii. 1, iv. 1 (see Introduction, pp. xiv–xvi). With the exception of *The Comedy of Errors*, there is very little of this doggerel in Shakespeare's plays; the tragedies and the later comedies are free from it.

(b) Blank Verse.

Such blank verse as there is in this play is of a comparatively regular, " early " type. Mr. Innes has told us that " English blank verse did not come into use till the sixteenth century; and at the commencement of its career, the rules which regulated its employment were strict. It was only when the instrument was becoming familiar that experiments could be ventured upon, and variations and modifications freely introduced. The changes in the structure of blank verse between the time when Shakespeare commenced writing and the time of his retirement are great; and the variations in this respect are among the most important indications of the date of any given play. That is to say, broadly speaking, the less strictly regular the metre, the later the play."

In *Love's Labour's Lost* the regular type ending on a single syllable predominates; two-syllable or double endings are much more frequent in later dramas. By way of example, Fleay notes only nine double endings in this play, as compared with 726 in the much later drama of *Cymbeline*.

§ 2. Rhymed Verse.

There are two main uses of rhymed verse in Shakespeare's plays: (a) for incidental songs, &c; (b) for dialogue.

(a) The incidental lyrics, with their great variety of metre (i.e. of rhyme-patterns, line-patterns, syllable- and stress-patterns) form one of the more notable decorations of Elizabethan drama as a whole. In *Love's Labour's Lost* there are both incidental songs sung to music, and sonnets read aloud. The Debate of *Ver* and *Hiems* at the end of the play was no doubt a musical item comparable with the dialogue-song in a pageant (1591) mentioned by Hart (Arden edition, p. 180, q.v.); the form of the stanzas, especially the arrangement of the bird-call refrains, would probably be determined in part by musical considerations.

Of the sonnets only one (Longaville's, iv. 3. 56) has the normal scheme of 14 ten-syllable lines, arranged as is usual in Shakespear'e sonnets, viz. in 4 alternate rhyming quatrains, with a final couplet added; the rhyme-scheme being a b a b | c d c d | e f e f | g g . The King's " sonnet " has 16 ten-syllable lines, the last four of which rhyme couplet-wise: Dumaine's is a lyric piece in octo-syllabic couplets; Biron's (iv. 2. 99) has the normal Shakespearean sonnet form except that the lines have twelve syllables. But the term " sonnet " was not in the Elizabethan age applied exclusively to the 14-line form: *Thomas Watson*, for example, uses an 18-line form for his *Hecatompathia*. But any short poem, preferably a love-poem, might then be called a sonnet.

The 6-line stanza of *Venus and Adonis*, rhymed a b a b c c , occurs in the burlesque verse by Armado (iv. 1. 85) and sometimes in the dialogue. Like the sonnet, it is a metre of the more refined order; Spenser uses it in his December Eclogue (*Shep. Kal.*) which is included in the more " aristocratic " group; whereas the measure of " The Playful Princess pierc'd and prick'd " belongs to the rude rustical tradition of the ballad. It is a " fourteener " with double-ending rhyme, i.e. its type is that 14-syllable line which, chopped into two at the eighth syllable, makes the first half of a " ballad measure " stanza.

(*b*) In the dialogue of this play there are two chief kinds of rhymed verse: (i) the smooth running ten-syllable lines as used in i. 1. 70 ff., and elsewhere (ii) the various sorts of more jerking and jingling lines of which Boyet's speech (ii. 1. 233) affords one example.

In (i) Shakespeare varies the simple couplet with stanzaic forms, such as the a b a b c c sixtain already mentioned, and with alternate rhyming, as in iv. 3. "Alexander" uses, appropriately, a stanza with the Alexandrine in v. 2. 559. In no other play does Shakespeare arrange the rhyme so elaborately; there is, however, for example, limited rhyme variation in the dialogue of *Two Gentlemen of Verona* (cf. end of i. 3). Stanzaic dialogue with a ten-syllable line basis had been fairly common in the Interludes on which that in the Clowns' play of *A Midsummer-Night's Dream* seems to be modelled (v. 1). For the real thing, *v.* opening speech of *Thersytes*, or dialogue in *The Four Elements*, where the more sober speeches retain this type of metre, while for the more uproarious, jingle is used. Shakespeare seems to follow this practice in *Love's Labour's Lost* to the extent that the *most* uproarious dialogue is in jingle (but also in prose, as in v. 1).

(ii) The jingling metres are of different kinds: one with a " three time " movement is used extensively:

Me | 'thought all his | 'senses were | 'locked in his | eye (ii. 1. 241);

but it is often looser and more irregular:

'One o' these | maids' 'girdles | for your 'waist | should be 'fit (iv. 1. 50).

Triple-time lines of half this length are used, appropriately for the " snip-snap " dialogue in ii. 1:

> *Biron.* What's her 'name | in the 'cap | ?
> *Boyet.* Rosa'line, | by good 'hap |.

Note also the use, for a similar purpose, of short " iambic " lines, i.e. based on the two syllable unit, but only three units in length:

Ros. The 'hour | that 'fools | should 'ask.
Biron. Now 'fair | be'fall | your 'mask! (ii. 1. 122–3)

Less frequently lines approximating to the Fourteener appear, with a double-time movement:

To 'see | him 'walk | be'fore | a 'lad | y 'and | to 'bear | her 'fan (iv. 1. 142).

Note also the Fourteeners in the dialogue of the Worthies, v. 2. 549. There is little of such jingle or doggerel elsewhere in Shakespeare's work, except in *The Comedy of Errors.*

§ 3. Blank Verse and "Iambic" Verse.

Apart from the "three time" jingle referred to above, Shakespeare's poetic lines, of which the most used variety is the ten-syllable "blank verse" line have, at least in the earlier stage of his poetic development, a basic pattern or unit of two syllables, of which the first is unstressed and the second stressed: this unit being called, not very correctly, an "iambus" or "iambic foot" by some theorists.

Form of the ten-syllable line in blank verse and rhyme.[1]

Our study of versification is commonly restricted to that of Latin and Greek. When we examine English verse-structure, a distinction at once appears. In the classical verse the governing element is quantity; in English it is *stress*. And inasmuch as stress is much less definite than quantity, the rules of English verse cannot be given with the same precision as those of Latin and Greek. But we may begin with certain explanations as to what stress is *not*. A "stressed" syllable is not the same as a long syllable; nor is stress the same as *sense*-emphasis. Any strong or prolonged dwelling of the voice on a syllable, for whatever reason, is stress. So, while a syllable must either be long or short, there are many shades of gradation between the unstressed and the strongly stressed. And as in Greek tragic verse a long syllable may, in certain positions, take the place of a short one, so a moderately stressed syllable may often in English take the place of an unstressed one.

To start with, then—to get at the basis of our metre—we will take no account of weak stress, but treat of all syllables as if they must either have no stress or a strong stress; and throughout, the word stress, when used without a qualifying adjective, will mean strong stress. The acute accent (´) will be used to mark a stress, the grave (`) to mark a weak stress, the ⌣ to mark a syllable sounded but not stressed.

The primary form of the Shakespearian line is—five feet each of two syllables; each foot carrying one stress, on the second syllable; with a sense pause at the end of the line, and generally

---

[1] Adapted, with full acknowledgment, from the essay in *Antony and Cleopatra* in this edition.

a slight pause, marked by a comma perhaps, after the 2nd or 3rd foot. This is called a cæsura.

> To whom he sends, and what's his embassy (ii. 1. 3).

Normal Variations.

If there were no variations on this, the effect would be monotonous and mechanical after a very few lines.

(i) The first variation therefore is brought about by the stress in one or two of the feet being thrown on the first instead of the second syllable, which is known as " inverted " stress. The stress is thrown back much more commonly in the first foot of the line than elsewhere; and in the other cases the stressed syllable often follows a pause.

> 1st foot. 'Beauty | is 'bought | by 'judg | ment 'of | the eye (ii. 1. 15).
> 2nd foot. Pell 'mell, | 'down with | them ! 'but | be 'first | advis'd (iv. 3. 362).
> 3rd foot. As | wit | turn'd 'fool: | 'folly | in 'wis | dom' hatch'd (v.2.70).
> 4th foot. And 'win | them 'too: | there'fore | 'let us | de'vise (iv. 3. 366).
> 5th foot. I 'hear | your 'grace | hath 'sworn | out 'house | 'keeping (ii. 1. 103).

(This last is not a perfect example of what is really a late blank-verse development.)

(ii) Secondly, variety is introduced by the insertion of an extra unstressed syllable which is not extra-metrical, analogous to the use of an anapæst instead of an iambus.

As a general rule, however, such extra syllables are very slightly pronounced; not altogether omitted but slurred, as very often happens when two vowels come next each other, or are separated only by a liquid (see § 6).

There are few such variants in the regular-type verse of *Love's Labour's Lost*, but cf.:

> 'Seemeth | their 'con | ference; | 'their | con'ceits | have 'wings (v. 2. 261),

though " conference " was probably pronounced " conf'rence ", i.e. as two syllables. Other irregular rhymed lines, even though they occur in patches of regular ten-syllabled lines, may be regarded as lapses into jingle, cf. the passage beginning:

> This is the liver-vein, which makes flesh a deity (iv. 3. 70–7).

But possibly l. 90 in the same passage may contain true extra-syllabic variations from the norm:

> A'men, | so 'I | had 'mine: | is not 'that | a good 'word?

(iii) The converse of this is the (very rare) omission of an unstressed syllable. This is only found where the stress is very strong, or when the omission is really made up for by a pause.

> Suggest | ed us | to make. | (-) There | fore ladies (v. 2. 758).

(iv) Extra-metrical unstressed syllables are added before a pause, sometimes after the second foot, rarely after the third.

> 2nd foot. O vain | petit | ion(er)! beg | a great | er matter (v. 2. 208).

Possibly the presence of an extra syllable after the third foot may explain in part the irregularity of (v. 2. 339)

Till this | madman | show'd thee? | (and) what art | thou now?

since there happen here to be no other " jingle " lines in support of this isolated instance. But the influence of jingle on regular lines constitutes a particular problem in *Love's Labour's Lost*.

Extra-metrical syllables are not uncommon at the end of a line; but in the present play the use of numerous dissyllabic rhymes accounts largely for this; double endings to blank verse being comparatively rare at this early stage. Nevertheless they are to be found:

'Nothing | but 'peace | and 'gent | le 'vis | it'ation (v. 2. 180).

The increasing frequency of extra-metrical syllables is a useful approximate guide to the date of a play. But they are never so frequent in Shakespeare as in some of the younger dramatists.

(v) The variation which perhaps most of all characterizes the later plays is the disappearance of the sense-pause at the end of the line. At first, a clause running over from one line to the next is very rare; in the last plays, it is extremely common. (The presence of a sense-pause is not necessarily marked by a stop; it is sufficient for the purpose that the last word should be dwelt on; the pause may be merely rhetorical, not grammatical.) The proportion of run-on lines in this play is especially low; Furnivall's figure is, for *Love's Labour's Lost*, one in 18·14; in *The Comedy of Errors*, another early play, it is one in 10·7.

§ 4. Weak Stresses.

The basis of scansion being thus settled, we may observe how the rules are modified by weak or intermediate stresses, which are in fact the chief protection against monotony.

(i) Lines in which there are not five strong stresses are quite common; e.g.:

The 'pay | ment 'of | a 'hun | dred 'thou | sand 'crowns (ii. 1. 129).

In the fifth foot particularly, the stress is sometimes extremely slight; but such " light " or " weak " endings are more characteristic of the later plays.

(ii) On the other hand, lines in which there are two stressed syllables in one foot may be found:

'Other | 'slow 'arts | en'tire | ly 'keep | the 'brain (iv. 3. 318).

A foot with a double stress is not infrequently preceded by a pause, or by a foot with a very weak stress only:

'Study | to 'break | it and | 'not 'break | my 'troth (i. 1. 66).

In the third foot there is scarcely a perceptible stress; possibly, " and " (through length and fuller pronunciation, see (iii) below) has it.

(iii) It will be observed that there are never fewer than three strong stresses, and that almost always any foot in which there is no strong stress at any rate has one syllable with a weak stress, and that very often such a foot has two weak stresses, preventing the feeling that the line is altogether too light. Thus a syllable which is quite unemphatic acquires a certain stress merely by length, as in some of the above cases. And, speaking broadly, a very strong stress in one foot compensates for a weak stress in the neighbouring foot. The line last quoted (i. 1. 66) might be taken as an exception to these general rules. But even so, we must remember that Elizabethan " and " was more strongly pronounced than very weak modern " and ".

§ 5. Irregularities.

(i) Occasionally lines occur with an extra foot; i.e. an additional stress after the normal ten syllables.

A 'hun | dred 'thou | sand 'more; | in 'sure | ty 'of | the 'which, | (ii. 1. 135).
　1　　　　2　　　　　3　　　　4　　　5　　　6

This belongs to an exclusively " blank verse " passage, and is not a " jingle " line, though irregular; but in *Love's Labour's Lost* abnormally long lines of the " jingle " type are sometimes (see above) inserted into speeches otherwise consisting of the ten-syllable line.

(ii) Short incomplete lines of various lengths are also found, especially in broken, hurried, or excited dialogue, and at the beginning or end of a speech. Sometimes the gap may be filled up by appropriate action, or a dramatic pause. Such lines are less frequent here in unrhymed verse dialogue than in rhymed, but cf.:

> *Ros.* Did I not dance with you in Brabant once?
> *Biron.* I know | you did. (2 feet.)
> *Ros.* How needless was it then to ask the question?
> *Biron.* You must | not be | so quick. (3 feet.)

(iii) Interjections and proper names (especially vocatives), are in this play occasionally extra-metrical.

But ('Katharine) 'what | was 'sent | to 'you | from 'fair | Du'maine? (v. 2. 47).

In nearly every instance observe that an unusual stress or an irregularity comes either at a pause, whether at the beginning of a line or in the middle; or at the end of a line in which there is a break.

§ 6. Apparent Irregularities.

(i) Difficulties occasionally arise from the fact that words in Shakespeare's day were sometimes accented in a different way

from that of the present day, and sometimes even bear a different
accent in different places in Shakespeare's own writing. Thus:
we say " re'venue ", Shakespeare " reven'ue ". On the other
hand, we say " complete' ", Shakespeare has sometimes " complete' " sometimes " com'plete ". In effect we must often be
guided by the verse in deciding on which syllable of a word the
accent should fall, because custom had not yet finally decided
in favour of a particular syllable. Speaking broadly, the tendency
of the modern pronunciation is to throw the accent far
back.

(ii) Similarly, when two vowels come together (as in words
ending with -ion, -ius, -ious, and the like) we are in the habit
of slurring the first, and sometimes of blending it with the preceding consonant; so that we pronounce " ambit-i-on " " am-
bishon ". In Shakespeare the vowel in such cases is sometimes
slurred and sometimes not, in the same word in different places;
usually the former in the middle of a line, often the latter at
the end. In such cases we must be guided simply by ear in deciding
whether the vowel is slurred or sounded distinctly. And we have
to decide in exactly the same way when we are to sound or not
to sound the terminal -ed of the past particle.

(iii) So again in particular words, a vowel seems to be sometimes mute, and sometimes sounded. Thus we have " ign'rant "
in ii. 1. 100, but " ignorance " in ii. 1. 101.

(iv) In a large number of words where a liquid (l, m, n and
especially r) comes next to another consonant an indefinite
vowel sound is sometimes introduced between the two letters
(just as now in some places one may hear the word " helm "
pronounced " hellum "), which may be treated as forming a
syllable, and sometimes the vowel is actually inserted, as in
thorough = " through ".

(v) Conversely, a light vowel sound coming next a liquid is
often sounded lightly and in effect dropped.

(vi) th and v between two vowels are often almost or entirely
dropped and the two syllables run into one; as in the words
" whether ", " whither ", " other ", " either ", " ever ", " never "
" even ", " over ". " Heaven " generally, " evil", " devil "
sometimes, are treated as monosyllables.

Vowels separated by a w or an h are habitually slurred and
pronounced practically as one syllable.

(vii) " Fire " and similar words which in common pronunciation are dissyllables (" fi-er ", &c.) are commonly but not always
scanned as monosyllables, as in i. 1. 176.

(viii) Other ordinary contractions, such as " we'll " for " we
will ", " th' " for " the " before a vowel, &c., though not shown
in the spelling, are frequent.

§ 7. General Hints.

(i) Often there are many possible ways of scanning a particular line, and the one adopted must depend on the individual taste of the reader. Thus he can frequently choose between § 3 (ii) and § 6.

(ii) Irregularities are most common:

    (*a*) In passages of emotional excitement.
    (*b*) Before or after pauses.
    (*c*) Where proper names are introduced.

GLOSSARY

affection (v. 1. 4), assuming, affecting: affectation (an obsolete form).

amain (v. 2. 543) (*a+main* <O.E. *mægn*, force), swiftly (i.e. with full power).

attaint (v. 2. 807) (originally p. part. of attain (O.F. *ateindre*) subsequently (=attainted) or *attaint*, associated wrongly with *taint*, Lat. *tinctus*, " dyed "), convict, prove guilty.

bate (i. 1. 6), beat back, or blunt the edge of. Abbrev. of " abate " (O.F. *abatre*, beat down).

bend (iv. 1. 33), direct, point, like a weapon. Frequent in this sense in sixteenth century. The meaning is arrived at by transferring the " bending " of a bow to other strictly unbendable weapons (e.g. guns); and then, as here, to metaphorical uses.

brawl (iii. 1. 8), a kind of French dance resembling a cotillon (*N.E.D.*) (poss. related to Fr. *branler*, move from side to side).

canzonet (iv. 2. 114) (< Ital. *canzonetta*, little song), a short song or verse.

carnation (iii. 1. 137) (ultimately Lat. *carnem*, flesh): flesh-coloured, bright pink; but sometimes used for a deeper red, e.g. " resembling raw flesh " (cit. *N.E.D.*).

certes (iv. 2. 152) (<O.F. *certes* or *a certes*), certainly, assuredly.

chapmen (ii. 1. 16) (<O.E. *ceap*, barter+*mann*), trader, salesman.

clout (iv. 1. 132) (<O.E. *clut*, cloth, patch), a mark or target shot at.

complements (i. 1. 166 and iv. 2. 134) (Lat. *complementum*, that which fills up or completes), i. 1. 166; accomplishments in etiquette, elegance; iv. 2. 134, observance of ceremony.

concolinel (iii. 1. 3). " Not satisfactorily explained "(Cross and Brooke), who give two of the more likely looking possibilities of origin: (1) a corruption of " can cailin gheal " (Irish)=" sing, maiden fair ", (2) a corruption of the first words of a French song, " Quand Colinelle . . ."

condign (i. 2. 25), worthily deserved (<Med. F. *condigne* <Eccles. Lat. *condignus*).

crack (iv. 3. 264), boast (*obs.* or *dial.* in this sense, *N.E.D.* <O.E. *cracian*, break with a sharp sound).

dan (iii. 1. 169) (O.F. *dan*, Lat. *dominus*, lord), Master.

day (-woman) (i. 2. 125) (or *dey*: O.E. *dæge*, O.N. *deigja*. maid), a dairy woman. Cf.

169

Chaucer, *C. T. Nunne's Pr. T.* 26, " a maner deye ".

deuce-ace (i. 2. 45) (Fr. *deux* (O.F. *deus*), two+Fr. *as* <Lat. *as*, unity), a throw of dice with two and one (the ace) uppermost.

fadge (v. 1. 132), fit, suit, be suitable. (Etymology unknown: first found in 16 cent. *N.E.D.*)

fleer'd (v. 2. 109) (? of Scand. origin; cf. Dan. dial. *flire*, grin), to grin, grimace (obs.).

hay (v. i. 139) (origin uncertain). A country dance having a winding or serpentine movement, or being of the nature of a reel (*N.E.D.*).

hight (i. 1. 246), is called (<O.E. *hatan*, call. In M.E. " hoten ", " hight " were used in both active and passive sense; the form " hight ", with passive sense, survived longest).

imp (i. 2. 5, v. 2. 583) (O.E. *impa*: Gk. ἔμφυτος, engrafted), a young shoot; and so young person; or playfully " young urchin ", " young devil ".

incony (iii. 1. 129, iv. 1. 139), rare, pretty, nice. (A cant word, of unascertained origin, prevalent, *c.* 1600, *N.E.D.* ? connected with *uncanny* or F. *inconnu*.)

inkle (iii. 1. 132) (deriv. uncertain. ? connected with Dutch *enckel*, " single "), a kind of linen tape.

keel (v. 2. 906), to cool, by stirring, skimming, &c. (obs. form of "cool". O.E. *cœlan, celan*.)

kersey (v. 2. 414), a sort of coarse, narrow cloth; and so here, " rough ", " homespun ".

la! (v. 2. 415), a variant of the interjection " law " later confused with " lor " (=Lord, see *N.E.D.*).

l'envoy (iii. 1. 67) (l'envoy, envoy: O.F. *envoiier*, to send). The last or parting words of an author; a dedication or postscript; also, a catastrophe, dénouement (*N.E.D.*2).

meed (i. 1. 255) (<O.E. *mēd*), reward.

mere (i. 1. 146), entire, downright, sheer. (Lat. *merus*, undiluted.)

merriness (i. 1. 197), " the quality or condition of being merry " (*N.E.D.*). Now rare: first noted *Cursor Mundi*, 1300: app. a normal word in Shakespeare's time though only once used by Shakespeare.

mete (iv. 1. 130) (<O.E. *metan*), to measure; and so to aim at (i.e. measure the distance to the target).

passado (i. 2. 168), a forward thrust with the sword, in fencing, one foot being advanced at the same time (altered from Fr. *passade* or Sp. *pasada*).

patch (iv. 2. 30) (? from the patched motley clothing, or from Ital. *pazzo*, a fool). A fool. *N.E.D.* notes that " Patch " was said to have been the nickname of Cardinal Wolsey's fool.

phantasime (iv. 1. 96, and v. 1. 17) (Ital. *fantasima* or *fantasma*), fantastic fellow. Not found elsewhere.

pomewater (iv. 2. 4), the old (obs.) name of "a large juicy kind of apple". (*N.E.D.*) (<*pome* (<late Lat. *poma*)+ water.)

preposterous (i. 1. 234) (Lat. *præposterus*, in reversed order), wrong way round, and so, out of place, improper.

quillets (iv. 3. 282), quibbles, subtle distinctions. (? Abbrev. of *quillity*, perhaps altered from quiddity, med. Lat. *quidditas*. Dowden (*Hamlet*, v. 1. 108, Arden Ed.) derives from Lat. *quod libet.*)

raught (iv. 2. 39) (now archaic, preterite of "reach", <O.E. (northern) *rahte*), reached.

russet (iv. 2. 414), a coarse red-brown homespun woollen cloth. Here adj. metaph. = "rough", "unsophisticated". (< O.F. *rousset*, red).

saw (v. 2. 908), saying, discourse, sermon. (O.E. *sagu*.)

scutcheon (v. 2. 561), shield, with coat-of-arms painted on it. (apheic form of *escutcheon* < O.F. *escusson* < Lat. *scutum* = shield.)

sneaping (i. 1. 100) (= snape<O.N. *sneypa*, to outrage, disgrace) nipping, biting, checking growth.

still (v. 2. 839), perpetually, continually. This use of "still" is not uncommon in literature up to the nineteenth century. Frequent in Shakespeare, as "Still quiring to the young-eyed cherubins". *Merchant of Venice*, v. 1. 62.

strooken (iv. 3. 220), an obsolete form of p. part. of vb. "strike".

targe (v. 2. 550) (<O.E. *targe, targa* prob. <O.N. *targa*), a small round shield or buckler.

teen (iv. 3. 160) (<O.E. *teona*, hurt), grief, vexation.

tharborough (i.1.182) (corrupt form of *thridborough*, itself prob. corrupted from *fridborgh*,<O.E. *friðborg*, peace pledge (Skeat)). Petty constable of a township or manor (*N.E.D.*).

tittle (iv. 1. 81) (M.E. *titel*, orig.="title"), a small stroke or point in writing; and so, something minute; a trifle.

vassal (i. 1. 244), servant, subject (<O.F. *vassal* from Celtic origin. Celtic type *wassos*, servant) (Skeat).

videlicet (iv. 1. 68) (Lat., contracted from *videre licet*, it is possible, and so, clear, to see). Came to mean, as a mere explanatory particle, "namely".

wake (v. 2. 319) (=vigil; as cf. O.E. *nihtwaca*, night watch; a festival-vigil; and so), a festival.

wassail (v. 2. 319) (cf. O.E. *wes hal*, "be in good health"), a salutation used when offering a cup of wine to a guest; and so, more generally, a feast, revel.

welkin (i. 1. 214) (<O.E. *wolcen*, cloud), the sky.

wot (i. 1. 91) (O.E. *wat*, inf. *witan*), know.

SHAKESPEARE'S STAGE IN ITS
BEARING UPON HIS DRAMA.

§ 1. The structure and arrangements of the Elizabethan theatre are still under discussion, and many points of detail remain unsettled. The last twenty years have produced a very extensive and highly technical literature on the subject, chiefly in England, America, and Germany. It is based especially on the new evidence derived from (1) the original stage directions, (2) contemporary illustrations and descriptions. The following summary gives the conclusions which at present appear most reasonable, neglecting much speculative matter of great interest.

§ 2. When Shakespeare arrived in London, soon after 1585, theatrical exhibitions were given there in (1) public theatres, (2) private theatres, (3) the halls of the royal palaces, and of the Inns of Court.

Of the 'public' theatres there were at least three: The Theater, the Curtain, both in Shoreditch, and Newington Butts on the Bankside or Southwark shore. About 1587, the Rose, also on the Bankside, was added. All these were occasionally used by Shakespeare's company before 1599, when their headquarters became the newly built Globe, likewise on the Bankside. Of the 'private' theatres the principal, and the oldest, was the Blackfriar, on the site of the present *Times* office. It was also the property of the company in which Shakespeare acquired a share, but being let out during practically his whole career, does not count in the present connexion. At court, on the other hand, his company played repeatedly. But his plays were written for the 'public' theatre, and this alone had any influence in his stage-craft.

§ 3. The 'public' theatre differed from the other two types chiefly in being (1) dependent on daylight, (2) open overhead, and (3) partially seatless; and from the court-stages also, in (4) not using painted scenes. While they, again, had the rectangular form, the typical 'public' theatre was a round or octagonal edifice, modelled partly on the inn-yards where companies of players had been accustomed to perform, prior to the inhibition of 1574, on movable stages; partly on the arenas used for bear-baiting and cock-fighting;—sports still carried on in the 'theatres', and in part dictating their arrangements.

The circular inner area, known thence as the 'cock-pit', or 'pit', had accordingly no seats; admission to it cost one penny (6d. in modern money), and the throng of standing spectators were known as the 'groundlings'. More expensive places (up to 2s. 6d.) with seats, were provided in tiers of galleries which ran round the area, one above the other, as in modern theatres; the uppermost being covered with a thatched roof.

§ 4. **The Stage** (using the term to describe the entire scenic apparatus of the theatre) included (1) the *outer stage*, a rectangular platform (as much as 42 feet wide in the largest examples) projecting into the circular area, from the back wall, and thus surrounded by 'groundlings' on three sides. Above it were a thatched roof and hangings but no side or front curtains. In the floor was a trap-door by which ghosts and others ascended or descended. At the back were (2) two projecting wings, each with a door opening obliquely on to the stage, the *recess* between them, of uncertain shape and extent, forming a kind of inner stage. Above this was (3) an upper room or rooms, which included the actors' 'tiring house', with a window or windows opening on to (4) a *balcony* or gallery from which was hung (5) a *curtain*, by means of which the inner recess could be concealed or disclosed.

§ 5. The most important divergence of this type of structure from that of our theatres is in the relation between the outer stage and the auditorium. In the modern theatre the play is treated as a picture, framed in the proscenium arch, seen by the audience like any other picture from the front only, and shut off from their view at any desired moment by letting fall the curtain. An immediate consequence of this was that a scene (or act) could terminate only in one of two ways. Either the persons concerned in it walked, or were carried, off the stage; or a change of place and circumstances was *supposed* without their leaving it. Both these methods were used. The first was necessary only at the close of the play. For this reason an Elizabethan play rarely ends on a *climax* such as the close of Ibsen's *Ghosts*; the overpowering effect of which would be gravely diminished if, instead of the curtain falling upon Osvald's helpless cry for "the sun", he and his mother had to walk off the stage. Marlowe's *Faustus* ends with a real climax, because the catastrophe *ipso facto* leaves the stage clear. But the close of even the most overwhelming final scenes of Shakespeare is relatively quiet, or even, as in *Macbeth*, a little tame. The concluding lines often provide a motive for the (compulsory) clearing of the stage.

In the *Tragedies*, the dead body of the hero has usually to be borne ceremoniously away, followed by the rest; so Aufidius in *Coriolanus*: "Help, three o' the chiefest soldiers: I'll be one". Similarly in *Hamlet* and *King Lear*. In *Othello*, Desdemona's bed was apparently in the curtained recess, and at the close the curtains were drawn upon the two bodies, instead of their being as usual borne away.

The close of the *Histories* often resembles the dispersing of an informal council after a declaration of policy by the principal person ; thus *Richard II.* closes with Bolingbroke's announcement of the penance he proposes to pay for Richard's death; *Henry IV.* with his orders for the campaign against Northumberland and Glendower; *King John* with Falconbridge's great assertion of English patriotism.

In the *Comedies*, the leading persons will often withdraw to explain to one another at leisure what the audience already knows (*Winter's Tale, Tempest, Merchant of Venice*), or to carry out the wedding rites (*As You Like It, Midsummer-Night's Dream*); or they strike up a measure and thus (as in *Much Ado*) naturally dance off the stage. Sometimes the chief persons have withdrawn before the close, leaving some minor character—Puck (*Midsummer-Night's Dream*) or the Clown (*Twelfth Night*) —to wind up the whole with a snatch of song, and then retire himself.

§ 6. But the most important result of the exposed stage was that it placed strict limit upon dramatic illusion, and thus compelled the resort, for most purposes, to conventions resting on symbolism, suggestion, or make-believe. It was only in dress that anything like simulation could be attempted; and here the Elizabethan companies, as is well known, were lavish in the extreme. Painted scenes, on the other hand, even had they been available, would have been idle or worse, when perhaps a third of the audience would see, behind the actors, not the scenes but the people in the opposite gallery, or the gallants seated on the stage. Especially where complex and crowded actions were introduced, the most beggarly symbolic suggestion was cheerfully accepted. Jonson, in the spirit of classical realism, would have tabooed all such intractable matter; and he scoffed, in his famous Prologue, at the "three rusty swords" whose clashing had to do duty for "York and Lancaster's long jars". Shakespeare's realism was never of this literal kind, but in bringing Agincourt upon the stage of the newly built Globe in the following year (1599) he showed himself so far sensitive to criticisms of this type that he expressly appealed to the audience's imagination—"eke out our imperfections with your thoughts"—consenting, moreover, to assist them by the splendid descriptive passages interposed between the Acts.

It is probable that the Elizabethan popular audience did not need any such appeal. It had no experience of elaborate 'realism' on the stage; the rude movable stages on which the earliest dramas had been played compelled an ideal treatment of *space* and a symbolic treatment of *properties*; and this tradition, though slowly giving way, was still paramount throughout Shakespeare's career. Thus every audience accepted as a matter of course (1) the representation of *distant* things or places simultaneously on the stage. Sidney, in 1580, had ridiculed the Romantic plays of his time with "Asia of one side and Africa of the other", indicated by labels. But Shakespeare in 1593-4 could still represent the tents of Richard III. and Richmond within a few yards of one another, and the Ghosts speaking alternately to each. Every audience accepted (2) the presence on the stage, in full view of the audience, of accessories irrelevant to the scene in course of performance. A property requisite for one set of scenes, but out of place in another, could be simply ignored while the latter were in progress; just as the modern audience sees, but never reckons into the scenery, the footlights and the prompter's box. Large, movable objects, such as beds or chairs, were no doubt often brought in when needed; but no one was disturbed if they remained during an intervening scene in which they were out of place. And "properties either difficult to move, like a well, or so small as to be unobtrusive, were habitually left on the stage as long as they were wanted, whatever scenes intervened" (Reynolds).

Thus in Jonson's *The Case is Altered* (an early play, not yet reflecting his characteristic technique), Jaques, in III. 2, hides his gold in the earth and covers it with a heap of dung to avoid suspicion. In IV. 4, he removes the dung to assure himself that the gold is still there. The intervening scenes represent rooms in Ferneze's palace, and Juniper's shop; but the heap of dung doubtless remained on the stage all the time. Similarly in Peele's *David and Bethsabe*, the spring in which Bethsabe bathes; and in his *Old Wives' Tale*, 'a study' and a 'cross', which belong to unconnected parts of the action.

It follows from this that the *supposed locality of a scene could be changed* without any change in the properties on the stage, or even of the persons. What happened was merely that some properties which previously had no dramatic relevance, suddenly acquired it, and *vice versa*; that a tree, for instance, hitherto only a stage property out of use, became a *tree* and signified probably, a wood. The change of scene may take place without any break in the dialogue, and be only marked by the occurrence of allusions to a different tenor.

Thus in *Doctor Faustus*, at v. 1106 f., Faustus is in "a fair and pleasant green", on his way from the Emperor's Court at Wittenberg; at v. 1143 f., he is back in his house there. In *Romeo and Juliet*, I. 4. 5, Romeo and his friends are at first in the street; at I. 4, 114, according to the Folio, "they march about the stage and serving-men come forth with their napkins"; in other words, we are now in Capulet's hall, and Capulet presently enters meeting his guests. This is conventionalized in modern editions.

§7. The Inner Stage.

An audience for which the limitations of the actual stage meant so little, might be expected to dispense readily with the concessions to realism implied in providing an actual inner chamber for scenes performed 'within', and an actual gallery for those performed 'aloft'. And the importance and number of the former class of scenes has, in fact, been greatly exaggerated.

Applying modern usages to the semi-mediæval Elizabethan stage, Brandl (*Einleitung* to his revised edition of Schlegel's translation) and Brodmeier (Dissertation on the stage conditions of the Elizabethan drama), put forward the theory of the 'alternative' scene; according to which the inner and the outer stage were used 'alternately', a recurring scene, with elaborate properties, being arranged in the former, and merely curtained off while intervening scenes were played on the outer, or main stage. But while this theory is plausible, as applied to some of Shakespeare's plays (e.g. the intricate transitions between rooms at Belmont and piazzas at Venice, in the *Merchant*), it breaks down in others (e.g. *Cymbeline*, II. 2, 3; *Richard II.*, I. 3, 4), and especially in many plays by other dramatists.

It is probable that the use of the 'inner stage' was in general restricted to two classes of scene : (1) where persons 'within' formed an integral though subordinate part of a scene of which the main issue was decided on the outer stage; as with the play-scene in *Hamlet*, or where Ferdinand and Miranda are discovered playing chess in *The Tempest*; (2) where a scene, though engaging the whole interest, is supposed to occur in an inner chamber. Thus Desdemona's chamber, Prospero's cell, Timon's cave, Lear's hovel, the Capulet's tomb.

§8. The Balcony.

There is less doubt about the use of the balcony or gallery. This was in fact an extremely favourite resource, and its existence in part explains the abundance of serenade, rope-ladder, and other upper-story scenes in Elizabethan drama.

From the balcony, or the window above it, Juliet discoursed with Romeo, and Sylvia with Proteus (*Two Gentlemen of Verona*, IV. 2); Richard III. addressed the London citizens, and the citizen of Angers the rival Kings. From the window the Pedant in *Taming of the Shrew*, V. 1, hails Petruchio and Grumio below; and Squire Tub, in Jonson's *Tale of a Tub*, I. 1, puts out his head in answer to the summons of Parson Hugh. But whole scenes were also, it is probable, occasionally enacted in this upper room. This is the most natural interpretation of the scenes in Juliet's chamber (IV. 3, 5). On the other hand, though the Senators in *Titus Andronicus*, I. 1, "go up into the 'Senate House'", it is probable that the debate later in the scene, on the main stage, is intended to be in the Senate-house by the convention described in § 6.

For further reference the following among others may be mentioned:—

G. F. Reynolds, *Some Principles of Elizabethan Staging* (*Modern Philology*, II. III.); A. Brandl, *Introduction* to his edition of Schlegel's translation of Shakespeare; V. E. Albright, *The Shakesperian Stage* (New York); W. Archer, *The Elizabethan Stage* (*Quarterly Review*, 1908); W. J. Lawrence, *The Elizabethan Playhouse and other Studies* (1st and 2nd series); D. Figgis, *Shakespeare, a study*.

From one or other of these, many of the above examples have been taken.

C. H. H.